IMMORTALITY

STARTLING EVIDENCE for HUMAN SURVIVAL of PHYSICAL DEATH

IMMORTALITY

STARTLING EVIDENCE
for HUMAN SURVIVAL
of PHYSICAL DEATH

Jess Stearn

THE
DONNING COMPANY
PUBLISHERS
NORFOLK / VIRGINIA BEACH

The Donning Company/Publishers
5659 Virginia Beach Boulevard
Norfolk, Virginia 23502

Library of Congress Cataloging in Publication Data

Stearn, Jess
  A matter of immortality

  1. Moreno, Maria. 2. Spiritualism. I. Title.
BF283.M587573 1976   133.9'1'0924 [B]   76—11543
ISBN 0-89865-755-5
Printed in the United States of America

This book is dedicated to everyone searching for a more meaningful purpose in life—and death.

For tho' from out our bourne of time and place
  The flood may bear me far,
I hope to see my Pilot face to face
  When I have crossed the bar.

TENNYSON

Contents

1

Enter the Spirits

IT WAS LIKE any other day for medium Maria Moreno. She sat on her favorite bench, near the grave of actor Tyrone Power, and meditated deeply, free of the discordant vibrations of the living—and the dead. For, as she well knew, the spirits didn't long cling to the bodies which had been so ceremoniously interred under the bright green sod. There was only moldering flesh and bone under the gray stones that stretched out for as far as the eye could see. Whatever spirits there were had long since departed for the boundless universe of timeless energy and space.

Her eyes closed, she fell into a trancelike half-sleep, in which she was still dimly aware of her surroundings. Misty images of her special angels and saints floated by, as in this state of euphoric relaxation she replenished the energies lost in culling the spirits for those wishing to pierce the great unknown. She nodded peacefully, refreshed to the core, feeling the energy course through her body from her solar plexus to her pineal gland or third eye. And then as she prepared to doze off, a hand appeared to reach out and touch her shoulder. She shook it off, thinking it a dream. But then a voice rang out, clear and cold.

"I want you to convey a message for me."

At sixty, Maria Moreno had been the instrument for thousands of messages from the other side, but this was the first time one had arrived in a cemetery or when she was not fully in trance.

She stood up, and the voice continued.

"My name is Lydia, and you are sitting by the foot of my grave."

The medium looked down, and saw the simple slab over the raised earth, with the name Lydia on it, and the legend, 1931 to 1972.

Where she had heard only a voice, Maria now saw the apparition of a sweet-faced woman, with long, dark hair and soft, blue eyes. Her face held a secret sorrow.

"In a few minutes," she said, "three people will arrive to visit my grave. They come every day at four-thirty, with flowers, and they weep until my heart aches for them. Tell them not to come any more, that I am not dead, but alive, and that they should go on with their lives, and stop grieving."

"And who are these people?" asked Maria.

"They are my mother and father and sister. They loved me, and will not let me go."

"But why should they listen to me?" said Maria. "They have not consulted me."

"True," said the vision, "but I will give you the information that will convince them that you are speaking for me."

"I do not think so," said Maria. "They enjoy their sorrow."

"Oh, no, it is only that they have little else, and do

not understand that life is everlasting. Nothing lies in that coffin but the flesh. There are no ghosts living in graveyards."

They communed together for a few moments in Lydia's Turkish tongue, which Maria understood at the moment, though she had never consciously heard it spoken, and the apparition that was Lydia gave the medium the information necessary to impress the family.

Maria listened dutifully, then gave a slight shrug. "They are too old," she said, "to change their ways."

"Tell them what I told you, and we will see."

Maria looked at her wristwatch. The two hands were just reaching 4:30 P.M., as a car pulled up to the roadside near Lydia's grave. A dark woman in her forties and an aging couple, moving with difficulty, climbed out of the automobile and slowly walked toward Maria. They held a wreath of beautiful flowers. With only a scanty look at the short, swarthy stranger with the high cheekbones, they tenderly dropped the flowers and kneeled by the sacred mound, weeping.

As they stood up, finally, Maria addressed them boldly, yet gently.

"Do not weep any longer," she said.

They looked at her, startled, and drew back the least bit.

Maria dramatically pointed to the grave.

"Lydia gave me a message for you."

The three looked astounded at the name. Their eyes darted around uncertainly. But there was no help in sight. Maria gave them no respite.

"You," to the younger woman, "are Tara, is that not right?"

The dark woman nodded, blinking a little. "How did

5

you know that?"

Maria pointed now to the heavens. "She, Lydia, told me. She wants you to take care of the mother and father." She motioned to the elderly couple, who were regarding her by now as if she were a madwoman.

"Lydia says your mother should watch her diabetes, and she is concerned about your father's arthritis. He should not be coming here at all, particularly not in this weather."

Their eyes widened.

Tara spoke for the three. "How do you know all this?"

"Lydia told me."

Tara shook her head incredulously.

"And for her daughter, she is worried about the cast on her leg. But the bones will soon mend if she is careful. Tell her that her mother loves her.

"And," she paused, "give her love to Sandor, and tell him that she is sorry they couldn't make that last trip together."

"Sandor!" exclaimed Tara. "How do you know that name?"

"She tells me that is her husband."

They looked at her as if she were the apparition, and began to edge carefully toward their car. Maria Moreno inched right along with them.

"Lydia wants you to know she is sorry that she dieted the way she did. The drugs the doctor gave her affected the kidneys, and so she died prematurely."

Lydia, indeed, had struggled to slim down for the European trip planned with her husband. Her collapse and death had followed, just as Maria had heard it from Lydia.

She had one last message for Lydia's loved ones. "Come

if you like once in a while, but not every day. It does not help."

They looked at her mutely, not knowing what to say in their bewilderment.

"She tells me to tell you: 'I am not dead, I live. Death is the beginning, life the unreality. Grieve for me no longer.'"

As she thought about it later in her Hollywood home, Maria was not surprised at the visitation. "Nothing was in the grave. She came to me from space, because I was a medium. She wanted her family to know that she was happy now, and didn't like seeing them unhappy." Maria had never seen the family before, nor heard their name. They didn't know what to make of it. They had been living one way all their lives, thinking of death as the end, and it was hard to change.

"I still see them there," said Maria.

Some time after this incident, Maria took me to her favorite meditating ground. There was a lone figure, a dark, middle-aged woman, bending over Lydia's grave.

"Are you Lydia's sister?" I asked.

She nodded, and looked past me to Maria, smiling for a moment, then went back to her task of tenderly banking the flowers on the grave.

"What of the message that your sister still lives?" I asked.

She shrugged, "I only know what the medium says."

"Where else could the information have come from?"

She stepped back and looked at the grave with dewy eyes. And without a word sidled past us to her car.

Maria regarded her sympathetically.

"Please believe that she still lives," she said softly. "She told me."

The door of the car closed, and Tara drove off, her eyes rigidly fixed on the road.

It did not seem to me that anybody had been helped.

But Maria did not agree. "The mother and father were not there today. Maybe they listened."

Maria Moreno's spirits did not move in casually, but seemed to respond to some urgent human need. They usually identified themselves by name, family, profession, startling the sitters with their disclosures. The listeners sat spellbound as the dead correctly foretold disastrous earthquakes, a new asteroid which might one day collide with the earth, sundry revolutions and holocausts in scattered parts of the globe, even Jesus's second coming at the end of the century.

Maria also appeared to possess a rare healing power, which was not hers alone. Her spirit doctors transcended time and space to heal the ailing, myself and others I knew, with inexplicable metaphysical injections, manipulations, and surgery, all incredibly painless. Still other spirits from the misty past guided her self-induced trances to aid those troubled with emotional and financial problems. It was all remarkable, but what intrigued me most was the apparent source of the endless information. For if the little lady with the twinkling eyes was correct, then she and her spirits had truly shown that death is but the beginning. Maria's dead seldom touched on trivialities. From the sex symbol of one generation, Marilyn Monroe, to the silent screen star, Rudolph Valentino, they not only discussed the most personal of problems, but presented a provocative picture of what their afterworld was like.

Maria was aware that the material Western world looked upon spirits as so much nonsense, conjured up by those frightened of death, or life. She well understood the problem. In a practical reference, it was difficult to comprehend how spirits could walk, talk, think, dress, and manifest themselves to a select few. There were so many questions there seemed no answers for. If human beings indeed survived in spirit, what happened in this twilight of endless space and time to prepare the soul for its eventual return? What determined this reappearance? And why, if due back anyway, did they intercede, even briefly, in human affairs?

Maria's own faith came out of her experiences. The revelations described by the people she sat for were enough to exclude clairvoyance in her own mind, and establish the sending point. Her sources came through clearly, naming themselves and the people they wished to reach. And they had messages of immediate import. This usefulness, with its accurate pinpointing of situations, had impressed the noted Los Angeles parapsychologist and physician, Dr. Eugene Jussek. "Once they bridge the great gulf," said Jussek, "spirits should have more to say than just hello. How many times does a white crow have to appear to establish that all crows are not black?"

There was a wide range of literature on survival, but even vouched for by scientists, it smacked of wishful thinking. In another generation, the physicist Sir Oliver Lodge was convinced that he had established contact, spiritually, with his son Raymond, killed in battle. Sir Arthur Conan Doyle, creator of Sherlock Holmes, also satisfied himself, through mediums, that life was continuous. But the evidence was trivial in content, subjective in nature, and did not exclude the alternatives of clairvoyance or telepathy. The scientists, it seemed to me, were not very scientific. "I would have been more impressed," agreed Dr. Jussek, "if they had not so conveniently found what they were looking for."

Maria Moreno was a different kind of medium. More often than not, the people she sat for were interested only in the average run of worldly affairs. They neither thought of communing with another world, nor conceived of such a place. "All I wanted to know," said one young lady, "was whether I was going to marry Michael. Instead, my dead grandmother, grandfather, uncle, and brother all came through by name, to warn against another brother's suicide attempt." Forewarned, she was able to abort the attempt. As for Michael, he was already married, and wasn't good for her anyway. They were right on all counts.

Spirits? She wasn't sure. But who else but they were privy to the darkest family secrets, which even she had not been aware of?

Jussek had established his own criteria for spirit communication. "The messages should have special meaning for both sender and receiver, relating to intimate information not generally known, and should, preferably, apply to events the sitter had no prior knowledge of, yet verifiable with time and effort."

In this way, wishful thinking would be excluded, and the investigation substantially objective, rooted in the nature of the material. In her trancelike state, not knowing what she was saying, Maria herself appeared to be objectively oriented, accepting her mission as a clear channel of God. It was something she couldn't sell, but cheerfully gave away, taking only enough in the way of donations to keep body and soul together. She often refused larger sums, not wanting her powers to become confused by money. She carefully kept a ministerial detachment. Even as a child, when she first discovered her gift, she guarded against the thought vibrations of the living. She had never progressed beyond the sixth grade, yet was able to communicate in automatic writing in Arabic, Japanese, Turkish, and even more esoteric languages no longer spoken. But the spirits were not always benevolent. At seventeen, she had an unforgettable experience, which told her much. She was slim and lovely then, and much sought after by the swain of her native Tampico, Mexico. She had been able to handle the most ardent, except for one who trailed after her, stormily proposing marriage.

"Become mine," he cried, "or I will kill myself."

She only laughed, thinking him melodramatic. But he shot himself to death. Shortly thereafter, she was abruptly awakened in the night, and saw a face close to hers. It was her dead suitor's. She felt herself pinned down in bed and screamed as his lips crushed hers. With that, a sharp pain shot through her, and she cried aloud, "The kiss, the kiss."

In the morning, babbling deliriously, she was rushed off to the hospital. Her illness was diagnosed as spinal meningitis, the "kissing disease."

Had it not been for her father, who was spirit oriented, she might not have recovered. He said she would have to forgive her suitor, so his spirit would not remain earthbound. She forgave, releasing the spirit presence, and within forty-eight hours, she was fully recovered.

I took the story with a reasonable grain of salt, asking: "Did this spirit ever return?"

Her broad face broke into a grin. "He has no reason to haunt me any more. I am an old lady."

My first meeting with Maria Moreno was one I would

never forget. I had made an appointment, shortly after I moved to California, without mentioning even my name. "Don't tell me who you are," she had said over the phone, "just be here at three o'clock."

I had been shocked recently by the death of a friend, Diane Ralphs, in Mexico. She was the proverbial girl with everything: youth, beauty, health, intelligence and money. I wondered if Maria could tell me how it had happened. I hoped for nothing more.

I arrived on the hour to see a short, stocky woman with a dark, reddish complexion, sitting behind a narrow table which wobbled uncertainly on flimsy legs. She gave me a penetrating glance from behind her steel-rimmed glasses, and motioned me into a stiff-backed chair.

"Have you ever been to a medium before?" she asked.

"A few times, but they seldom go in trance."

"Then they are not mediums, because the guides come to us in the trance state—Clarita the Gypsy, Dr. Jallikete, Pepe the Hunchback, and the rest. In deep meditation sometimes I have a clear channel, and the guides are not necessary, but it is easier with the guides."

Her operation was certainly dramatic. She no sooner closed her eyes and took a deep breath, than she began to flail the air with her arms, puffing a little in the process.

Her voice, heavily accented until then, suddenly became lighter, sweeter in tone, with a decided lilt. Her face, too, had become more expressive and wore a smile. She seemed to be a different person. "I am the gypsy Clarita," she announced. "I come to reveal the mysteries of the other side, and to help with the problems of this world. Trust in the spirits and you will find help, with faith in God. For only in that faith will you be free."

Maria's Clarita knew I was a writer, just arrived from

the East, divorced, and lonely. My health was good but I had to watch my diet, and to exercise. There was certainly nothing wrong with all this. But I had not been told anything I didn't know, and she had not touched on the reason for my visit. I had always felt that any good psychic should know intuitively why a person was there, and accurately answer his unspoken questions. And so I waited.

Maria's voice suddenly became grave. She seemed deep in concentration. I watched her fascinated, feeling she was on the verge of something. And I was not disappointed. "A girl is in the room," she said, peering beyond my shoulder. "She is glad you are here. She has been thinking of you. She is blonde and blue-eyed, and she has been crying. Her name is . . . ." She frowned a moment, her lips moving as if repeating the name, and not quite accepting it. "It is a strange name for a girl," she said finally. She spelled it out, "R-A-L-P-H-S. Ralphs. Is that not a man's name?"

The butterflies fluttered in my stomach. "No, that is a girl's name."

"You knew her?"

"Yes."

"Well, she wants you to know she is sorry for what she did. It happened in Mexico, and she acted in a moment of depression. She thought she would find peace. It does no good to take your own life, she says. You solve nothing, here or on the other side."

Maria paused for what seemed an eternity. "She took an overdose of drugs. She says that these drugs, like marijuana, LSD, and the rest, are bad, since they confuse the mind and lower the resistance. Do you follow?"

I nodded, too stunned to speak.

"She is concerned about somebody in her family. It is her brother, Billy, she says." Her head came up for a moment. "You know somebody like that?"

"She had a brother named Billy, younger than she."

"She was only twenty-five or six?"

"About that."

Maria peppered her discourse with questions, but they were mainly rhetorical, as if she were encouraging purely routine confirmation.

"She was a rich girl, not right?"

"She was of the Ralphs grocery family here in California."

"But she was lonely and missed love while she was growing up. She says she desperately wanted to be loved."

"Her parents were divorced, and she was sent off three thousand miles to boarding school. That always seemed to bother her."

"She says she felt closest to Billy."

I remembered Billy's handsome, smiling face and quick, magnetic charm.

"Why is she concerned about him?"

"She doesn't want him making the same mistakes she did, getting into bad company in college."

Even as I listened, and occasionally made a comment, I couldn't quite grasp the enormity of what I was witnessing—the presence, presumably in spirit, of a girl very much on my mind. Had the medium picked her out of my consciousness, and dramatized the rest? If this were so, she would have surely gotten my name. Additionally, she had provided information previously unknown to me.

One thing preyed on my mind.

"Why did she take her life?"

"The drugs broke down her emotional reserve, like

she said. She was bitterly unhappy, tormented that she couldn't find the love she wanted all her life."

In this search, this lovely young girl had married three times by the time she was twenty-five.

"Will she find peace?" I asked.

Clarita's voice came through clearly. "You must pray for her. That is what she says. She is interested in the metaphysical, and says you must continue your work. It could help people."

I sighed almost without realizing it, and said under my breath, "It didn't help her."

"Pray for her, and remember her, and she will be with you from time to time."

Maria Moreno now drew a deep breath and opened her eyes. She seemed bursting with energy.

"Was it a good reading?" she asked.

I felt strangely depleted, as though somebody had taken all my energy.

"It was more than I had expected."

She looked at me curiously. "Do you live in California?"

"I just moved out here."

"Good, you have a strong vibration."

I had no idea what that meant.

"You are a channel yourself for the metaphysical."

I wondered whether she had gotten this from the reading.

"I don't remember anything from trance," said she. She again regarded me curiously. "What is your name?"

I told her and her face immediately broke into a gratified smile.

"You will write a book on me one day. It came in meditation after I read *The Sleeping Prophet*."

15

This was a book I had done on the American mystic, Edgar Cayce.

Over the years, we became friends. I visited her many times. And one day, as Diane Ralphs again came through, warning American youth on the insidious evils of marijuana, it dawned on me that Maria Moreno could very well be a vehicle with which to explore the area of survival.

I was intrigued by her spirits. Pepe the Hunchback, specializing in financial matters, had profitably advised me to buy and sell a certain property. Dr. Jallikete, the dean of her medical corps, had prescribed a boiled mixture of cream of tartar, grapefruit peelings, the grapefruit juice and water for a painful bursitis. It cleared up in a few days.

Jallikete was only a voice, with a Japanese intonation, but Pepe the Hunchback was a marvel to behold. Before my eyes, Maria's head drew into her shoulders at an angle, the neck disappearing, as a disfiguring bump formed on her upper back. Her face took on a crafty, guarded look (I suppose the financial adviser), and her voice became husky, like a man's.

With all this, I found it difficult to accept what I couldn't see, smell, taste, hear or touch. It might very well be Clarita, or Jallikete, or Pepe speaking through Maria, but how could I be sure? I had no feeling of an added presence in the room. With Diane Ralphs, I had been startled speechless, but I had not felt her nearness, not even when Maria described her so well and mentioned her passing in a way I later learned was correct. It made one think, to be sure, but still was not totally convincing. If not clairvoyance, which it didn't appear to be, it could still be x, the unknown, illustrative of some natural principle man had not yet stumbled across.

Paradoxically, others experienced the presences I didn't without any clue as to their identity. Thirty-nine-year-old Cam Atkinson, a Hollywood real estate agent, had vividly felt an unseen presence around him, disturbing only because he couldn't account for it. It was almost like an energy force. And though not to be seen, it had definite impact. He had lived with it for four years, accepting it as he would any visitor. "I would be getting ready to say something, and this force would distract me. I could sense it entering the room, drawing close to me, and even listening." It had been mostly a benevolent force, interrupting when he was about to lose his temper or make a bad decision.

He had no idea what it could be. A girlfriend, with whom he had lived, stormily, had taken her life six years before, and a grandfather, to whom he was devoted, had died a year thereafter. But the energy force appeared to have no personality. "It seemed to be telling me something, but what I didn't know." Florida-born Cam Atkinson had been in the New York financial world for years. He was tall, spare, plain-spoken, with few illusions. "I realized people might think I was imagining things, to say the least, but that didn't bother me. What did bother me was the force itself. I got to anticipating it, but it didn't turn up in response to my thoughts. It seemed to come and go as it wished, every third or fourth day. But it was definitely helping me. I would be getting ready to quote a seller's price on a certain property, when I would become acutely conscious of this force. It would distract me for a few moments, and the next thing I knew the purchaser was making an offer considerably larger than what I had intended to say."

He had not equated the force with spirit, since he did not believe in spirits even though he had a vague feeling when Sally died that their lives together were unfinished. At times, it was a comforting thought. Other times, he was distressed that he had not done more for her. "We loved, but like so many people in love, we so often seemed at cross purposes."

He discussed his experience, trying to understand it in the telling, and eventually he found somebody who did not smile skeptically.

This woman recommended Maria Moreno. "She cleared up my business problems, and she might be able to explain this energy force, whether"—she hesitated—"it's something tangible or only in your mind."

The appointment was made. Atkinson was careful not to mention the energy force. "She didn't want to know anything, and I told her nothing."

Nevertheless, he began to look around the cluttered little room curiously. As sure as he was sitting there, the presence was manifesting itself, by the door, the window, behind and to the side of him. He pinched himself and kept his counsel.

Atkinson waited, wondering. But then Maria—Clarita —began to speak, and there was no longer anything to wonder about except what was transpiring. Quickly, he was introduced to the medium's remarkable insight into his personal affairs. Maria mentioned a friend of Atkinson's by name, living in San Diego, beset with an abdominal problem. The real estate agent agreed in astonishment. And then, suddenly, as he was marveling about this, she electrified him with one word.

"Sally," she said, and spelled it out. "You know this Sally?"

"Yes," he said, leaning forward eagerly.

"She is in torment." She, too, had not found tranquility in suicide.

"I had hoped she would find some peace," he said.

"She is sorry for what happened between you and has been trying to establish contact. Have you felt this?"

"I'm not sure."

"She says she has tried to contact you numerous times, but had not the energy force to make a direct message. But she is trying to keep you from making mistakes due to acting in haste. That was her trouble, she often did things without thinking them out first."

That seemed true of them both, as he looked back.

"Have you felt her presence?" Maria asked. "It was she that made you look up several times when you were about to speak hastily."

Atkinson was so moved the tears came to his eyes. "Thank her, and tell her I think of her all the time. I still treasure her love."

"That is good," said Maria. "She is glad for that. She does not want to be forgotten."

Thinking of his intuitive feeling, Atkinson asked, "Is there any chance we may be together one day?"

"That does not depend on her. But it could happen, if it is the karma."

Atkinson was not sure he believed in reincarnation, and karma's credit-and-debit ledger which presumably carried from one life experience to the next, depending on the challenges and the choices.

But for the first time in four years, he breathed easy, now that the distracting presence had been happily identified. There was no doubt in his mind that it was Sally, and he rejoiced that she would try to help him.

He felt a growing peace. Then one night, he dreamed of Sally and himself together in her New York apartment, in a situation similar to that before her death. He mentioned the dream to an associate.

"Why torment yourself?" the man said. "Let the past go."

"I am not tormenting myself," said Atkinson. "For the first time in years, I am not alone."

For the multitudes consulting the medium, her universal message appeared to transcend even the most vexing personal problems. Her work had surfaced at a time when disenchantment swept the Western world. Younger people turned to Eastern philosophies and meditation. The older, once protected by a reassuring Catholicism, or the practical Protestant ethic, were strained to retain their faith through a shattering period of depressed morality. Graham Greene, the convert to Catholicism, whose books turned on hope eternal, seemed to symbolize the current disillusionment of the intellectuals. "With the approach of death," said the aging author of *The Heart of the Matter*, "I care less and less about religious truth."

Eloquently, he quoted:

> "*We are most hopeless who had once most hope,*
> *And most beliefless that had most believed.*"

Just as this brilliant observer dramatized the intellectual's negativism in the face of a rampant tyranny sweeping out from the East, so Maria Moreno, the simple peasant from Mexico, hopefully proffered a pipeline to a benevolent, challenging eternity.

"Listening to her," said Jussek, "you have to believe in God."

2

Spirits or ESP

D R. EUGENE JUSSEK was no ordinary physician. He was a hypnotist extraordinary, an acupuncturist, a parapsychologist with an unusually scientific background. He had specialized in internal medicine at the University of Frankfurt and was trained in psychosomatic medicine in the Jung tradition. He did postgraduate work at New York University and also studied in the Orient, France and Austria, and had practiced successfully in California and Europe for twenty years. But it was his pragmatic interest in the metaphysical, frequently considered in his therapy, that set him apart from the plodding practitioner.

Having a sitting with Maria Moreno, in the interest of psychic research, he had been fascinated by her spirit doctors. "This," said he, with a glint in his blue eyes, "must surely be the answer to the malpractice problem."

He marveled as Dr. Jallikete performed a blood transfusion high in the atmosphere, and Dr. Dermetz did a tracheotomy, while Dr. Karnacke reduced a critical hypertension with an invisible injection. It was wild, crazy, incomprehensible, but it seemed to work.

The doctor, ordinarily immune to illness, had been

cautioned by Maria's doctors that he might become sick if he continued to overwork, and sure enough, overworking, he had been bedded with a bad shoulder and then a bad back. He was advised of a serious legal problem, and this also turned out as forecast by Clarita, with the ubiquitous Pepe the Hunchback stepping in at the last moment to retrieve the situation. "I wouldn't have believed it," said the marveling doctor, "if it all hadn't happened as Maria Moreno said."

He went back to the medium, trying to gain some insight into the source of her wonderful gift. Were these doctors indeed products of the spirit world or of her dramatic subconscious, clairvoyantly conceived and then dramatized in keeping with her belief in her supernatural guides?

His own parents were alive in Frankfurt, Germany, and few intimates had crossed over. He had very little in the way of spirits to identify with. But Maria, unaccountably, began talking about Vera. "Vera is calling you," said she. "She needs to talk about her will. She has been sending out impulses all week, and wants you to know that she loves you and your family."

The only Vera Jussek knew was the elderly physician, Vera de Fernando. She was living in Boulder City, Nevada, the last he heard. He remembered her well. She had been a patient treated by him in Europe with cell therapy for general well-being. She had responded beautifully. He had no reason to believe she was dead, but he had been out of touch for five or six years.

"Who is this Vera?" he asked.

"She is somebody you helped in the past, who is extremely grateful to you. She regards you as her only friend. She wants desperately to contact you about the final provisions of her will. You healed her with cell tissue."

There was no doubt now who the message was from. He tallied the years. If still alive, she must be approaching ninety.

"Is this Vera dead?" he asked.

Maria Moreno appeared to hesitate. "The spirit," she said finally, "has not completely crossed over. It is important you get in touch right away. She lives near Las Vegas, not right?"

Jussek nodded. Vera must still be in Boulder City, perhaps an hour's drive from the gaming capital. But if alive, how could she be communicating, unless through Maria clairvoyantly? What did that do to Maria's belief in her spirit source? Somewhat bemused, he put through a call from Los Angeles, half expecting to be told that Vera had passed on. He was pleasantly surprised when she answered the phone, even though in barely a whisper.

She recognized his voice immediately. "I have been thinking of you," she said weakly. "I have not been well, and I would like to discuss a number of things with you."

"What is wrong?" he asked, realizing it could be anything at her age.

"I've just come out of the hospital. I was in intensive care after a stroke, and lay in a coma for a while."

Her voice wavered. "Come down soon, I will not be here very long."

Obviously, Maria Moreno had responded to the old doctor's unspoken appeal. And if so, she had presumably tuned in telepathically, a far less significant phenomenon than spirit communication.

Jussek was saddened but likewise intrigued. "Is it possible," he asked later, "that the spirit leaves the body of a dying person gradually?"

23

I recalled where people had apparently died in drowning or on the operating table. Then after resuscitation by emergency measures, they remembered an entirely different world than they had known before.

Jussek looked thoughtful. "The soul as an energy form may move out in stages."

"You mean, a little energy at a time?"

"Or a lot."

He regarded me speculatively. "Perhaps Vera de Fernando could throw some light on this problem. She has been a doctor for fifty years, scientifically oriented, and yet she always had a sharp interest in metaphysics, delving into matters that defy scientific explanation."

Before going off with Jussek, I decided to question Maria Moreno. Since she was not aware of what she said in trance, I recounted what had transpired with Vera de Fernando. "There is a strong possibility that you may be merely using extrasensory perception."

Maria Moreno gave me an almost pitying smile.

"Not true, JessStearn," said she, telescoping my name as though one word, "the people come from the other side."

"How can you be sure?"

"Because they tell people things they never knew before, and later they learn it is true. With ESP, the information has to be known by somebody."

"Not necessarily, it could be part of the universal consciousness, what Dr. Jung called the collective unconscious."

She had not heard of Carl Gustave Jung, the humanist and parapsychologist, but she did grasp my point.

"When the spirit turned up in the cemetery," she said, "that was not in the universal consciousness, but a visitation from a soul that wanted the family to know she was not dead. It had not happened before, it was a new experience. She gave her name, the names in the family, and the message to stop crying and not lay any more flowers on the grave." Maria held up an admonitory finger. "And it was all like the spirit of the dead Lydia say, not true?"

It seemed to me that Maria had made a telling point. How could this information have been part of the universal record, when not yet recorded. Still, many clairvoyants accurately read the future without the benefit of guides.

"Some psychics have predicted a future not yet recorded, not already known by somebody." I mentioned the remarkable evening when psychic Helen Stalls of Jupiter, Florida, reading for a tiny group of skeptical newspaper people, in the summer of 1965, predicted, accurately, President Johnson's withdrawal from the 1968 presidential race, Richard Nixon's election, the assassination of Bobby Kennedy, the death in a public place abroad of Ambassador Adlai Stevenson, and Jacqueline Kennedy's marriage to a foreigner on a Greek island.

"And she had no help from the spirit world," I pointed out.

Did she agree then that there was an alternative?

"Oh, no," said she, "it still comes from outside. What does this Helen Stalls tell you?"

"She says the information comes through God."

Maria shrugged. "So God is the keeper of all the guides and spirits. He is everything."

"But she still doesn't name a human source."

"Because the psychics' energy is not strong enough to make the manifestation."

25

"And is that because they don't believe in spirits?"

"They see them, and still don't believe, and so they credit it all directly to God."

The psychic could often see clearly without spirit help, but with this superior guidance the preview was even clearer. Of this Maria was certain.

She tapped her chest. "In here, the future of the person is locked up. It is unknown to them, but not to the psychic."

"Then each person carries his own destiny pattern around with him from birth?"

Maria Moreno gave her childlike smile. "The Bible says our days are numbered like the hairs on our head."

Then what did this do to the Western concept of determinism and free will? "You mean that nothing can be changed?"

"Only reactions can be changed, and that decides our happiness. The person can enjoy living, or be miserable over what happens to him."

"In other words, some see the bottle half-filled, others half-empty."

"Exactly, JessStearn."

This was all very fine, but it still didn't explain a living woman communicating extrasensorily a few hundred miles without telepathy.

Vera de Fernando was in a wheelchair when we arrived. Despite her lack of mobility, she held herself with dignity. There was a certain regality in the way she held her head, and fixed us with a calm, grave look. She was an aristocrat to her fingertips, poised, gracious, concerned about our comfort. Her background was unusual. Born a White Russian, she had moved to Brazil as a child, studied medicine, and married a landed baron, long dead.

He had left her his name and the freedom to practice medicine. She had practiced past eighty, retiring only five years before after a heart attack. She spoke in measured tones, taking time to synchronize her tongue with her stroke-affected brain. I stood a little apart, giving the two the opportunity to speak privately. But I couldn't but notice the gentle pressure on his hand and the suspicion of tears as she said, "Your family is all I have left."

Jussek turned away quickly, but not before I glimpsed the tears in his own eyes.

I gazed at him questioningly, not knowing whether to interrogate her.

"Vera," said he, "my friend would like to ask about the message you sent me."

Her face was gray with fatigue, and I was about to back off when a slow smile transformed the worn features, and gave her a wraithlike, ethereal look.

She nodded, and her gray eyes looked out with a glint of humor.

"Frame your questions," said Jussek, "so that she can answer by moving her head or with few words."

My first question was rather elementary.

"Do you believe in life after death?"

Her head moved forward almost imperceptibly.

"What form does this life take?"

She gave a little shrug of her shoulders.

"She has no more idea," said Jussek, "than the rest of us."

"Do you think humans have a spirit life?"

Her head bobbed.

"And what form would this take?"

She replied in a low voice, "Energy."

"She feels," put in Jussek, "that survival is a form of

energy displacement, from one dimension to another."

Dr. de Fernando's lips began to move. "You do not die all at once."

"You mean the death process is gradual?"

"Near the death state, in a coma, the spirit may begin to leave the body. The envelope of the body is the human aura, and the departing soul changes this aura."

"Into what?" I asked.

She cleared her throat, and sighed a little. "A different magnetic force, which the medium may have picked up on."

She seemed so near death that it was no wonder she was peering beyond life.

Her breathing quickened and color came to her face. The gray eyes had a new light in them.

"You are still very much here," I said.

She smiled wanly. "Not all of me. Unless death is violent, I am convinced as a physician, who is no stranger to death, that the crossing is gradual, the aura lingering on as an ectoplasmic force."

Jussek pondered. "If Vera is right, then Maria may indeed have picked up the outgoing spirit, which still had its tenuous connection with the physical body. It is quite possible that Maria Moreno is capable of picking up both clairvoyantly and from the spirit side."

Dr. de Fernando's slight nod seemed to express approval. "If the surviving spirit is energy, as it must be, then the energy released can be manifested through a medium."

She gave the doctor a slow smile. "We physicians know intuitively that in a single cell of the body is hidden a complete history of the individual's mystique. We must learn to read it properly. In the same way, the aura is a key to the soul."

I was not at all convinced. "You really can't prove any of this, for the simple reason there is no way of proving it."

Dr. de Fernando was sitting back in her wheelchair, her eyes closed, a sweet serenity on her smooth, oval face. If she was partly in spirit, she was obviously enjoying the crossover.

We had nothing conclusive. What Vera thought was certainly not evidence, any more than people once thinking the world flat made it so. I recalled a conversation with the late medium, Arthur Ford, a protégé of Sir Arthur Conan Doyle, concerning his spirit guide, the celebrated Fletcher. "Wouldn't it be a joke on me," he said, "if there were no Fletcher and no spirit world, and communication were a dramatization of my own psychic subconscious?"

"Would it bother you?" I had asked.

His face had lit up mischievously. "I wouldn't give up Fletcher without a fight. He was more of me than I was."

Fletcher had almost got him in trouble. "A few days before the first atom bomb destroyed Hiroshima, Fletcher suddenly announced to a startled audience the very day the bomb was to go off." Since not even the scientists on the project knew what they had created together, this was indeed an awkward revelation. "I was a mighty scared man for several days until the bomb was exploded," Ford recalled. "Otherwise, Fletcher might have gotten me in the dock trying to explain."

Why should spirits know more than they did in the flesh?

"They see things from a different perspective," Ford said. "It's like looking down a mountain to the valley below. You see everything in motion, the direction as well, and given this view, the destination."

What had the mystic Edgar Cayce, the sage of Virginia Beach, to say about spirit communication?

"The soul lives on. In the release of the soul-body from a house of clay the activities in the world of matter are only changed in their relationships to that which the physical body sees in material or three-dimensional form."

He was asked:

"What form does the spirit entity take?"

"That form which the entity creates for itself in the plane in which the existence is passed."

And what was death?

"Death, as commonly spoken of, is only passing through God's other door. That there is continued consciousness is evidenced by the abilities of entities to project or to make those impressions upon the consciousness of sensitives or the like."

One picture was sometimes worth a thousand words. The Rev. Douglas Johnson, a Los Angeles spiritualist, had been sitting in a Pasadena coffee shop when a middle-aged woman sat down at a table nearby. As she entered the restaurant, Johnson saw the image of a man hovering over her shoulder. The impression was so strong that he felt impelled to tell the woman that her husband—for such was his conviction—was trying to reassure her that he was all right.

"I was on the verge of approaching her," he said, "then realized what a fool I might seem. Suppose her husband was alive and well, off working somewhere."

He settled back to his coffee, still not able to get the image of the husband out of his mind. Then, getting up he overheard a waitress say to the woman, "You haven't been in for a week."

The woman replied, "I guess you hadn't heard that my husband died. I just came from his funeral."

As a boy, before he knew what the word psychic meant, Johnson had foreknowledge of his mother's death. He had heard her from a great distance, and when he went to the Minneapolis hospital where she lay ill, she was already dead. "I knew it," he cried, "I knew it."

His friend, Vina Skaug, with whom he once worked at Dayton's department store in Minneapolis, had also lain dying in a Minnesota hospital, when she had a spirit vision that apparently saved her life. "At sixty-two," Johnson recalled, "she suffered a stroke and the doctors felt she wouldn't finish out the night. I hurried to the hospital, hoping to arrive before she died." She was unconscious, breathing sluggishly, and he held her hand for a while, praying for her recovery.

The next day, he hastened back, fearing the worst, and found friend Vina sitting up in bed, smiling.

"Whatever happened to you?" cried Johnson. "You're supposed to be dead."

"I was ready to die," said she, "and seemed to be floating into space. I was beginning to wonder if this was death. Then, suddenly, I was pulled back into the room and there by the bed stood a lone figure, with a beard and a sad smile. 'I have come in answer to that young man's prayers,' he said. 'You will recover, and live for a long time.'"

Vina Skaug had felt a longing for the euphoria she had just experienced. But suddenly, a new warmth flooded her limbs, and in a few days she was ready to leave the hospital, unaided. She was aging even then, and could normally have expected only a few more years at best. But, as presaged, she lived on into her nineties.

Johnson had asked if she recognized the apparition.

"Well, you know who he looked like," she replied.

He regarded her doubtfully. "You mean...?"

She nodded. "That was all I could think of."

Johnson's own life had been fashioned by a spiritual experience. He had been sitting on a park bench, in Minneapolis, wondering what to do with his life. At sixteen he had already had a heart attack and was concerned about physically surviving. Suddenly, as if drawn by some magnetic force, he looked up, and there in broad daylight he saw a tall man dressed in black.

"One day," said the stranger, "you will find the truth you are seeking."

For the next fifteen years he lived in a nightmare of fear, induced by a frightening fibrillation of the heart. Then one day, venturing into a library, he pulled out a book which introduced him to the occult world. "I suddenly felt in tune with the universe," he recalled, "and my fears left me. That very week, I got up one morning and the disturbing fibrillation had disappeared. I had found the truth prophesied by that vision in black."

Maria had never questioned the truth of her spirit communication, and Jussek had been favorably impressed as well. "It's all coming through her. She knows nothing herself. Clarita speaks in a voice vastly different from Maria's, and Pepe is more vivid, as he hunches his back, than anybody I ever encountered. If she were merely dramatizing her own subconscious she would receive messages for only the people getting the reading. But stray names are forever slipping in, with no connection to the sitter."

I remembered now the day singer Janis Joplin had come through. She was only a name to me, and Maria had never been aware of her. I had some hazy knowledge that the rock singer's death had been a big blow to her cult of hippie fans, but that was all.

"She is confused," said Maria, "because it was not her time to go. She is seeking help now, because her soul is still attached to earth because of her suicide. She took drugs, but she wouldn't have taken her life if somebody else hadn't brought her to it. She was overcome by dissatisfaction with herself, while so many thought she was so lucky, having wealth and fame when she was so young."

Maria had moaned a little in sympathy. "The masters say they will give her life light, so she can come back as soon as possible. She did not finish her karma on earth."

Janis Joplin's appearance was certainly not evidential. We had no way of even confirming if her death was properly described. But it did show, as Jussek observed, that Maria was not directly influenced by the presence of the sitter.

Occasionally, because of her rhetorical questions, new light was remarkably cast on the validity of her sources. She had been reading for a Mrs. James Yeno of Venice, California, when Clarita suddenly came up with the name Joyce.

"Who is Joyce?" she asked. "Joyce Yeno?"

"I am Joyce," said Mrs. Yeno.

"They tell me that in a few weeks Joyce will have a problem with blood pressure and a mole on her face."

Joyce Yeno had normal blood pressure. "That's interesting," was her only comment.

But some six weeks later she had cause to recall what Clarita had said. For her sister-in-law, married to Jim Yeno's brother, Joe, suddenly reported high blood pressure, and a brand new mole on her face. And what had this to do with Maria Moreno's forecast?

"Sitting there," said Joyce Yeno, "it had not occurred to me to think of anybody else." But Joe Yeno's wife was also named Joyce, Joyce Yeno, and it was obviously she that Maria's guides had seen.

Both Jussek and I had puzzled over the explanation of Vera's baffling message. Had it come, as Vera thought, from an auralike, odic force that moved out in stages as the body died, apparently restorable when the vital processes revived and renewed themselves? Or had Maria just tuned in telepathically to Vera from Nevada?

We arrived at the solution to our quandary almost simultaneously.

"Let us," said Dr. Jussek, "hypnotize Maria, and see what answer she comes up with to this problem."

"But she doesn't remember what she said," I pointed out.

"Under hypnosis, she can pluck the entire reading out of her subconscious mind."

"Or, in her own trance state."

"True," said Jussek, "but with hypnosis I will be at the controls."

Maria, at first, balked at hypnosis. "My guides can handle whatever you want to know."

Jussek placated her. "We may bring out a deeper dimension of the subconscious, reaching directly into the universal mind."

She looked at him doubtfully, but dutifully stretched out on a couch, and at his suggestion, delivered in a matter-of-fact voice, was soon in deep hypnosis.

"Do you remember Vera?" Jussek asked.

"The woman that sent the message to Dr. Jussek."

"Did you have a feeling that she was dead?"

"The vitality was very low, but she was alive, the body had not yet passed over."

"Then how," asked Jussek, "were you able to pick up her message? Was it clairvoyance?"

She shook her head. "You do not understand how the spirits work. When the person is unconscious, or in coma, the astral body, which is the envelope of the soul, moves out into space. It is similar to the energy form of the spirit. And it is these energy forms that communicate with my guides."

"And these energy forms are spirits?"

"They are the same as any other energy forms from the astral body. The only difference is that when the sick person gets better, they return until he dies, or makes another astral journey."

"And when is this?"

"When they are again close to death."

Maria had justified the spiritual source of her message, but one thing obviously baffled us both.

"How can we be sure then that your message is coming from the living, or the dead?"

Even in this deepest of trances, she snorted.

"There is only the thinnest edge between the living and the dead. And my guides, being in attunement with Vera in the spiritual dimension, were able to tune in to the astral force and pass on the communication."

Remarkably, Vera with her physician's intuition and the astounding Maria had agreed.

3

Mae West: Come Up and See Me Sometime

I WOULD HAVE THOUGHT that everybody had heard of Mae West. She had become a legend in her own time, familiar not only to her contemporaries but the young as well. There was probably nobody impersonated as much, and with greater relish. Yet when I mentioned her name to Maria Moreno, she went completely blank. "What does she do?" she asked.

"Do!" I exclaimed. "Why, everybody knows about her. Haven't you seen her old movies on television?"

Maria shook her head. "I don't watch television."

And in the isolated Mexican villages where she had spent most of her life, there had been no television and no movies, and so no Mae West.

"She is a very famous actress," I said.

She held up a hand. "Don't tell me anything. Does she want a reading?"

The celebrated actress, so long a sex symbol, was actually not concerned about herself, particularly, but was interested in the possibility of contacting a very dear friend on the other side, not only for his advice and counsel, if possible, but to establish at the same time some evidential basis for life after death.

In some respects, the actress was little different from the average mortal who was getting older and wondering whether he had anything to look forward to but the dark curtain of oblivion. Her friend, Jack Kelly of Buffalo, New York, a remarkable medium, had passed on a few years before, and it had occurred to Miss West that if anybody could come back, it would be Jack. He had seemed capable of any psychic wonder.

She recalled the time two Los Angeles detectives had questioned her and her sister, Beverly, about a man wanted for murder, whom they had innocently harbored in their home. Mae had interrupted the interrogation to put through a call to Jack Kelly in Buffalo. Even before she had a chance to explain, he said, "The man they are looking for was picked up in Long Beach, California, twenty minutes ago." The detectives had greeted the information with derisive smiles, but on making a phone call to police headquarters, their chins dropped. "The arrest," said one, "is just coming in over the departmental teletype."

Mae West missed her friend Kelly sorely. "There's nobody around like him," she said. "He could do anything." She was an admirer of the Rev. Richard Ireland, a metaphysician of Phoenix, Arizona, and I had watched him work at her invitation. He was amazing with billets, slips of papers, on which the audience wrote their questions, and he gave his answers with his eyes masked and taped, presumably replying to questions he had not even read. She had already consulted Ireland, but, as with medicine, it never hurt, I supposed, to have a second voice.

She had many questions to ask Kelly, but thought it best, as I did, that the medium not be apprised of her objective, and give her reading blind, so to speak.

"It would be something if she even got Kelly," she said.

I had known the actress for years, and saw her occasionally through our mutual interest in metaphysics. Nevertheless, I knew her as a highly intelligent, down-to-earth individual who, at eighty or more, seemed immune to the usual aging processes. She not only looked far more youthful than her years, but acted and thought young, wonderfully alive to everything about her.

Her devoted companion, Paul Novak, was a handsome, rugged specimen, many years younger numerically, but she seemed a match for him. She was in great shape for her age. She had flawless skin, without any sign of the sagging so common in the aging. Her eyes were brightly blue and sharp, not missing a trick. Her hands were a wonder, small and well-formed, with the soft suppleness of a child's. She spoke softly, almost gently, with a courtesy and reserve that belied the salty, suggestive image of the screen. Though I called her Mae, presuming on years of contact, she addressed me as "Mister," causing me to wonder whether she would prefer I call her "Miss West."

She and Maria Moreno were a study in contrasts. Both were of modest stature, slightly above five feet, but there the resemblance stopped. Mae was fair and blonde, with her hair carefully twirled atop her head, and she still possessed the hourglass figure that had made her name synonymous with the upper feminine torso. Whereas Maria, self-consciously clad in her Sunday best, was more pear-shaped, and her hair had the spun darkness of silk without a streak of silver.

Our meeting took place in the actress's spacious apartment, on the top floor of a building she had owned for some time. We were ushered into the living room, which was a symphony in gold and white—rugs, davenports, chairs and drapes. Dressed in a rich white gown that trailed to the floor, the actress blended in beautifully. Looking around, I remembered my last visit when we had watched home movies of the perennially youthful Honzas in their primitive Tibetan setting. They were shown youngish looking at ninety, with sinewy bodies, smooth, unwrinkled faces and black hair. They were spinning and weaving, tilling the fields, laboriously mending their clothes, living much as they had lived two thousand years ago. I remember thinking what a drag it seemed, when Mae, cupping her hand, said *sotto voce*, "Maybe it just seems like ninety years."

Now we scattered in a small circle around the room— Miss West, Paul Novak, Dr. Jussek, Maria and myself. The two women sat facing each other, and I could plainly see the reservation in the actress's face. I was sure that the proudly sensitive medium had picked up on this as well. She stared stonily ahead, not saying anything, then closed her eyes, and appeared to be meditating. We had been careful not to give her the slightest hint of the reasons for the sitting. I noticed that Dr. Jussek, who had worked in rejuvenating cell therapy in Switzerland, was regarding the actress in frank admiration.

"She's got the complexion of a woman fifty years younger," he marveled in an undertone.

The actress had obviously overheard the remark. She patted her hands against the bottom of her chin, and preened her neck forward the least bit. "I've never had plastic surgery," she said, "it was never necessary."

Maria was so immersed that it was apparent she had not heard any of the exchange.

"All right," she announced, as if she had come to a sudden resolution. "I will give you a consultation."

She inched closer in her chair to the actress, and moved her hands about her head as if summoning her guides.

Mae West looked at her with the ghost of a smile. "I'm ready," she said.

Just as Maria had no preconceived idea of the actress's wishes, so, too, she didn't know what to expect.

So it was quite a jolt, I could see, when Maria, her lids still closed, thrust her hand with an abrupt movement into the actress's stomach, just below the shapely curves which had led to inflated life-preservers being known as Mae Wests.

As the actress flinched nervously, the medium's fingers kept digging. Invoking the spirit of Dr. Jallikete, she announced her Japanese doctor was making a very thorough examination. "He finds," said she in the harsh staccato of Japanese, "that you have chronic indigestion. Not true?"

Mae West nodded uncertainly, still shrinking awkwardly from the probing hand. "Yes," she said, "I do have indigestion, from eating too fast. I'm a nervous eater."

Maria cocked her head to a side. "You don't eat meat?"

"Just vegetables, and occasionally some fish."

Maria's head bobbed in assent.

"Good, eat more fish. You need the phosphorus."

The actress's pale eyes lit up. "So that's what I need," she said with a semblance of her screen smile.

Maria would not be diverted. "Dr. Jallikete fix the stomach," said she, waving her arms in her peculiar windmill fashion. She then resumed her probing of the star's abdomen, as her subject looked around rather helplessly.

"Feel better?" said Maria. "Indigestion go away?"

"As a matter of fact," answered the actress, as Maria removed hands, "I do feel better now."

The examination continued as I sensed the star's growing uneasiness with the course of the reading. I could see that Jussek was amused by the turn of events, but Miss West was obviously on the verge of annoyance, and being a good sport about it.

As I made a silent prayer that Maria would somehow get on to the desired information, she asked, "You have trouble with the eyes?"

Mae shook her head.

A puzzled look came over Maria's face, and she frowned. "But the doctor says you have contact lenses, no?"

Mae nodded. "Yes."

Maria breathed easier. "Then you must have trouble."

At this easy assumption, the actress and Paul exchanged cryptic glances and I groaned inwardly. But Maria proceeded, undaunted.

"The doctor say you have trouble sleeping, getting up in the middle of the night."

Mae nodded, and I saw a new glint of interest in her eyes.

"I have too much energy," she explained. "So when I can't sleep, instead of tossing and turning, I get up and meditate for a while, relaxing, then settle back in bed again." She gave a throaty laugh. "I don't know what it is to sleep a night through."

Paul Novak's interest also seemed to have been captured. He gave Maria an inquiring glance. "What can she do about it?"

"Steep the leaves of the orange tree in boiled water for

a few minutes," said Maria, "and make a tea of it. The blossoms of the tree can also be used in the same way. Drink this tea during the day and before going to sleep."

As orange trees were plentiful in neighboring back-yards, this remedy presented no problems. But I was disappointed, as I knew Dr. Jussek must be, that Maria had not as yet fulfilled the first requirement of a first-rate psychic, knowing why a subject had sought her out and responding automatically to his or her unspoken question. The examination had neared its conclusion, with Dr. Jallikete pronouncing Miss West in extraordinarily good health. "You have the mind and body of a much younger woman," said he through Maria. "You will always be youthful."

The medium placed her hands around her own throat for emphasis, and then said incomprehensibly, "You are like twins here, is that not so?"

Mae gave the medium a piercing glance, as if seeing her for the first time. "That is very true. I was told once that I have a double thyroid gland."

Dr. Jussek, silent until now, leaned over to whisper, "This is astounding. The double thyroid is very rare and it accounts to some extent for her youthful appearance and boundless energy."

I looked again at her hands, one of the first indicators of advancing years. They had a youthful freshness that defied time.

I supposed it was natural to move on from youth to its logical consequence.

"They tell me that you have had many lovers," said Maria, in a solemn voice.

The familiar Mae West come-hither look flashed for the first time, and the actress said in an easy drawl, "That's past, what of the future?"

We had moved from the living room to the bed-chamber, and gazing at the ceiling I could see a massive mirror over the king-size bed. The actress followed my glance and smiled. Her smile was more expressive than a thousand words. She would never be anything but vital.

"You will always be young," Maria said again. "The golden years are golden for you in every way."

Mae seemed pleased despite the fact the sitting was not going as hoped. Even so, we had agreed there would be no leading questions. But it was no longer sticky, as Maria had at least tuned in sufficiently to have reassured the actress about her health, touched her vanity. She was no longer fidgety, and showed signs of enjoying the proceedings. "She is a good showman," she acknowledged in an undertone.

Maria, indeed, put on quite a performance. She gesticulated more than any psychic I had ever known, and she rolled her eyes even in trance, a remarkable undertaking.

Now, with Mae West closely watching, the medium's eyes reached out and came to a stop beyond the actress's head. She seemed to be staring, as if trying to pick out a hazy, ill-defined figure.

We all turned our heads but saw nothing.

"I see a Sarah, Sarah B.," said Maria, "I don't get the last name yet." She turned to Mae West. "She knew you well in a previous life, when both were somebody else."

I didn't know whether Mae West believed in reincarnation, but Maria believed that present associations often materialized out of past relationships, where some karmic debit or credit had to be worked out.

"This Sarah," she went on, "knew you in a previous life. It was long ago, another century." She closed her eyes.

"You also have known her in this life, but not well. She has only one leg. She was a great actress, too. And she was an inspiration to you, even though you never realized how much. She did much of the writing for her sketches, and even rewrote her parts for the stage, like you."

Mae concentrated for a few moments. "I really don't know who that could be," she said finally.

"Think again," said Maria, "and you will remember."

"Sarah B.," Mae murmured as if to herself. And then her face lit up. "Why, of course, the great Sarah Bernhardt. She had a wooden leg, the result of an amputation, and she fancied herself a writer as well."

"You knew her once," said Maria, "for she knows you and has followed your career with pleasure. She was a great actress then in France."

It was apparent that the actress preferred to confine the relationship to this mundane plane.

"I didn't really know her, though I did see her on the stage when I was a child. She was a remarkable performer. They called her the Divine Sarah and she was France's greatest lady."

Maria shook her head. "That is not how you knew her. You knew her when you were Ninon"—she faltered slightly—"Ninon de Lenclos."

"Ninon who?"

"Ninon de Lenclos." Maria seemed very sure of herself. "You admired her writing then."

There was a circle of blank faces. But as I thought about it, the name seemed vaguely familiar. I mouthed it to myself a few times, and then it dawned on me. Ninon de Lenclos, the toast of Paris. But, of course! She had lived through the seventeenth century, and at ninety, still beautiful and alluring, was breaking hearts all over Paris.

"She was a French beauty," I said, "celebrated for her eternal youth and loveliness. Even when she was approaching a hundred, the young men of Paris were head over heels in love with her. Her salons were meeting places for the rich, titled and talented."

Mae's eyebrows went up. "She sounds a bit of all right to me."

Like myself, Gene Jussek had an explorer's interest in reincarnation. "Is it at all possible," he asked, "that the ingredient of perennial youth be passed on from one incarnation to another?"

"Theoretically," I replied, "if the quality of youthfulness were handled properly in one lifetime, it could even develop to greater advantage in another life."

Actually, Mae West could have been a personification of her predecessor, possessing the same ageless allure, a sultry sense of comedy and wit, together with a timeless appeal for the young in heart.

Ninon de Lenclos, living in the glorious reign of Louis the Fourteenth, the Sun King, had entertained the princes who stood next to the throne and the litterateurs, Saint-Evremond and La Rochefoucauld, known for their Gallic wit.

"You know," whispered Jussek, his eyes roving around the apartment, "these furnishings are purely French Provincial."

We had almost forgotten the unseen Sarah. But not so Maria. "Sarah says she knew you well, when you were Ninon de Lenclos, and you were very good friends, helping one another. She was a man then."

Mae, I must say, did not appear impressed. But Sarah had more to say.

"You will always be youthful, just as Ninon was," she

said, "and have lots of lovers."

Mae's teeth gleamed. "I should hope so."

As from a distance, as though conversing with the Divine Sarah, Maria said, "Sarah was not her real name." Actually, she had been born Rosine Bernard and changed her name when she chose the stage. She had a leg amputated in 1915, and courageously pursued her career, writing plays for herself, until her death eight years later.

Sarah removed herself from center stage, without being missed, as Miss West clearly was preoccupied with the current incarnation. Clarita now appeared, as the actress asked, "What do you see in the future for me?"

"You have an offer," said Clarita–Maria, "to appear on the Broadway stage."

"Only this week it came," said Mae.

"You will not take it, since you do not fly. It was because of a fire."

The actress and Paul again exchanged glances, but this time of almost incredulity.

"I don't fly at all," said the actress, "not since 1958 when the plane caught fire in the airport and we all had to be led to safety." She folded her hands in her lap. "What else?"

"You will receive an award from the Motion Picture Academy, not for any one picture, but for everything you have done for pictures. You will finally be recognized."

Mae seemed pleased, but remained silent.

"That would be long overdue," said her friend Paul.

The conversation got back to the everyday.

"You are a Leo, right?"

Mae nodded. "August seventeenth."

"You have a flair for doing things, for being dramatic—" probably the understatement of the day.

"Some people think so," said the actress.

"You are psychic," Clarita says, "and hear voices."

Mae grinned. "You know what they say about people who hear voices. But," she acknowledged, "I do have intuitive feelings that I frequently follow."

"You were in a court action," said Maria, "and the voices helped you."

Mae frowned. "I can't place that."

I recalled her telling me years before of a suit she had brought against two men who had appropriated an original script of hers. "A voice told you to ask them a certain question," I reminded her, "and this won the suit for you."

"That's right," she marveled, "I had completely forgotten."

Clarita was still gliding about. "Clarita says you should watch out for the elevator."

"What elevator?"

"In the building."

It had seemed all right when we had ascended on it earlier. But both Mae and Paul were visibly startled. "The elevator has been breaking down," he said, "and we've been having people over to fix it."

"Watch out," said Maria, "it can break down anytime."

While the session had been illuminating as a test of Maria's powers, we still had not come to the reason for it all—Jack Kelly and his hoped-for appearance from beyond.

"If there are spirits," said Jussek in a low voice, "they don't necessarily do our bidding, or attach the same importance to things that we do."

"The right person," I pointed out, "has shown up on every previous occasion. This will be the first time she has missed."

Mae didn't seem particularly concerned; obviously she had not expected much. I felt slightly chagrined, having wanted Maria to make an impressive showing, as well as providing evidence for a continuing life. But Maria, still in trance, breathing rhythmically, was not yet finished. She was peering now into a corner of the room, as if she were looking for an old friend.

Clarita seemed somehow to express a dramatic quality that was an offshoot of Maria's own temperament. "Clarita," the medium announced, "will now tell you what you have come to hear." She frowned, her eyebrows drawn together. "What does that mean?" she asked, as if talking to herself. "Clarita says she sees a shamrock. This has something to do with you?" She turned to the actress questioningly.

Mae shook her head slowly, then said, to be helpful, "The leaves of the shamrock could mean good luck, like a four-leaf clover."

I pointed out, "The shamrock is the floral symbol of the Irish."

Maria's head had tilted forward. She gazed again into the corner, and then made a triumphant noise.

"Koly," she finally called out, caressingly, as if speaking a friend's name. She repeated the name, changing the pronunciation so that Koly became Kally.

Her pronunciation, because of a strong Mexican accent, was normally imperfect, and she slurred words constantly. She was having trouble with the name, so she proceeded to spell it out painfully. "K-O-E-L-Y," she turned it over on her tongue. And then with a smile, put it all together, "Kelly," she said. "Jack Kelly is standing there."

I felt an instant jolt, and as I looked around me, I could see the others were similarly affected. A quizzical look had come into the actress's eyes, but I could sense the reserve behind the quickening interest. She was not swallowing anything whole.

Maria appeared in rapt concentration.

"Kelly knows," she said, "that you wanted to hear from him. He is interested in your welfare, and he wants to help you. He is watching over you. He is your great friend."

"We were great friends," the actress acknowledged. "He was such a tremendous psychic that the Buffalo police consulted him in murder cases, though they never gave him credit, for fear people would laugh at them. I was playing a Buffalo theater once, when the police begged him to help with this important murder case. In a flash, he named the murderer, and told police where they could find the murder weapon and the killer. They went where he told them, and found it just as he had said." She sighed. "There was nobody like him."

Kelly was still apparently very much with us.

"He is pleased with your spiritual growth," Maria went on, "and wants to thank you for being protective of his family, and writing the book about him."

I had not known that Mae West was in the process of doing a book, though she had a natural flair for writing and had written all her own skits for the stage and celebrated movie roles, including the comedy classics with W. C. Fields.

I looked at her inquiringly.

"I am writing a book about Jack, *The Amazing Mister Kelly*. My royalties will go to Jack Kelly's relatives. They need the help."

Maria appeared to be listening. "That is not the only book. You are writing three books in all."

This seemed highly improbable, yet the actress nodded, her eyes widening a little, as she regarded the medium with an entirely different look.

"That is correct," said she, "there is the Kelly book, another called *The Pleasure Man,* coming out soon, and one about my own life."

"They will be successful, with help from the other side," said Maria. I was later to recall this forecast when *The Pleasure Man* hit the paperback bestseller lists.

As the trance state deepened, Maria's English improved noticeably, and she glided easily from one topic to another. Whenever she mentioned Jack Kelly's name, she smiled, as though she approved.

"He misses his Church of Life," she said, "but there was no way of keeping it after he passed."

I glanced at Mae questioningly. But she had turned to Paul Novak. "He did have a church," said she, frowning, "but I never heard its name."

"I don't remember," said Paul, "but I can check his correspondence. It might be on a letterhead."

"The Church of Life," Maria repeated. "He keeps telling me. He was a good man."

Mae beamed. "There's no question of that. He was a wonder. Once, in Chicago, I heard him predict Pearl Harbor, to the exact day, December 7, 1941, and nobody would believe it."

With this record, it was clear why the actress had sought to contact him. But he was gone now, alas, without having told us very much. But Mae West seemed sufficiently impressed with the sitting to serve us tea and cookies afterward.

"He didn't have very much to offer," I said.

Maria looked up from her tea. "Who is that?" she

51

asked, wide-eyed.

She remembered nothing, of course.

"Your man came through," I said, "but he didn't say much, considering he had bridged the great divide."

"The next time," promised Dr. Jussek, "I will hypnotize her, it should provide a clearer channel."

In the hall we waited for the elevator.

A tiny woman, with a worried frown, fluttered by, heading for the exit stairway, then walked back a few steps.

"Are you going down?" she said.

We nodded.

"Good, I don't want to get stuck on the elevator alone. It's always jamming between floors."

For the second session, Mae West was dressed regally as usual, and she gave Maria a warm welcome. She seemed more expectant than she had before. As Maria left the room for a few minutes, Mae discussed her friendship with Jack Kelly. "He was an amazing man. He could bring in voices, materialize himself at will, and levitate." She had witnessed all these things. "He was the greatest physical medium I have ever seen."

He had died ten years before, at eighty, and she had never encountered a physical medium since.

"They are rare," acknowledged Jussek, "but I find the spiritual work Maria does with her spirit doctors far more impressive, because it accomplishes more good. Materializations and levitations make converts to the metaphysical, since there is no other way of explaining these phenomena, but a psychic's worth should be measured by the good he or she accomplishes."

"Jack Kelly helped many people," she said. "If we could only tune him in, he might be as helpful as ever."

Knowing she was highly psychic herself, and, as we had seen, both clairvoyant and clairaudient, I inquired, "Have you ever felt Kelly's presence since he moved on?"

"After his death, I saw Jack Kelly only once." She pointed to the elegant sofa. "He was sitting right on that couch as I came into the room. I was so startled that I couldn't say a word."

"Couldn't it have been an illusion?" I asked. "He might have been on your mind, and his image appeared. That happens all the time."

She shook her head. "This was different. I had been thinking of him, it is true, and thinking how much I missed him. But he still materialized, and was sitting on that couch as big as life."

It had happened about eight in the evening, right after she had walked into the living room. "I had just turned on the television set, and was sitting at the end of the couch when I heard someone whispering to me. I looked around and recognized my friend, Jack Kelly."

She was stunned. "I can't recall ever being so terribly frightened. I've had many psychic experiences but this was the first where I actually saw something."

She got over her fear quickly, and took a second look at the apparition. "He looked sensational. He was wearing a dress suit and the material was out of this world. I can't ever remember having seen him look so good."

Just a few days before she had been talking about Jack to friends and said, "With all of Jack Kelly's great powers I wonder why he doesn't come in and let me see him. And three days later he did. Jack was saying in effect, 'You wondered why I didn't come. Well, here I am!' "

Jussek sought to explain. "The energy from our thoughts, and from the atmosphere, is enough, some metaphysicians say, to induce a materialization. It is an energy form, substantially."

Maria was now in the room, ready to lie down and be hypnotized. Trusting the doctor, she quickly relaxed and was soon in deep trance. As he had done before, privately, Jussek took her back into the past, regressing her in time into previous life experiences. "If we place her subconscious into a period of great psychic development, it may open an entirely new channel."

Soon she was in Sikkim, where she knew Master Rampa, and seemed to have achieved a high rate of development under this great sage. From there, she moved into a dramatic past experience, as Heidi the little girl in Liebsig (which we assumed to be Leipzig). This was a horrible experience; she lived in a wine cellar, and crouching behind a barrel witnessed the slaying of her own parents. As she mentioned these horrors, I looked up to see Mae West twiddling her thumbs impatiently. She gave an eloquent shrug, and I quickly scrawled a note for the doctor, asking him to return Maria to this lifetime. "Mae West," I wrote, "wants to know about this lifetime or the next one, not the last one. That's done with."

Jussek good-naturedly brought Maria out of hypnosis, and she fell quickly into her natural trance state. The transition was barely perceptible, except that she now sat up in a chair, and instead of lying prone like a zombie, seemed an extension of her own lively self. Soon, Clarita had reemerged, and Maria briefly acknowledged her presence.

Jussek looked at her with a grunt of satisfaction. "She is keener now, I think the hypnosis helped clear her deeper subconscious."

As if to confirm his judgment, Maria held out her hand and pointed to the living-room doorway, using a name that she was not yet consciously aware of.

"Kelly," she said, "is standing right there."

We all turned, but saw nothing.

"You are not in his vibration," the medium explained. "He looks short and stocky, not so?"

Paul Novak nodded. "That is so."

She had the uncanny habit of appearing to listen, and since we heard nothing we could only sit around during this void of a few moments and look at each other foolishly.

She spoke again. "He was in Tibet, in northern India. He tells me that he spent some time there."

It seemed unlikely to me, on the surface, that Welsh-born, Buffalo-bred Jack Kelly could have lived in so out-of-the-way a region.

But Paul was nodding, with widening eyes. "When Jack Kelly was young he served with the Bengal Lancers in Northern India."

"Yes," said Maria, "he had good times then, and he learned about Eastern teachings."

Kelly's interest in the esoteric, and his advanced development, suddenly made sense. The Welsh were the most psychic of people, perhaps because of their insulation by language and custom retaining the gift of the primitives, and this quality had, I was sure, been augmented by Kelly's being steeped in the lore of the East, and the paranormal powers of the ancient yogis.

"It may have even been the other way around," said Jussek, as Paul nodded. "The East intrigued, and he went there, as best he could in those days, to fulfill the burgeoning power he felt within."

Maria was still the listener. "He tells me he had major surgery, and then suffered a bad fall just before his death."

In a voice almost of awe, Paul said, "That is correct."

With all this, we still seemed to be getting away from specific information. "Why," I asked, "is he telling us all this?"

"To let you know he is here, since you didn't see him standing in the doorway." She pursed her lips, as was her custom when the spirit presence was questioned. "He knows why Miss West has tried to contact him, and he wants to help in this very annoying personal problem."

At this, the actress suddenly perked up, and her eyes rested unblinkingly on the medium.

"It is about a ring," said Maria, "a big diamond."

I couldn't understand the actress being so concerned about a mere bauble that she would seek help from a life beyond. But her eyes had flared angrily at the mention of the ring.

"It's a big, pure-white diamond," she said, "and it's worth a small fortune. But that isn't what bothered me—it's that a very dear friend might have walked off with it."

"The ring that you have missed will come back, never fear," said Maria. "It will be returned by the people who took it. They will be afraid to sell it and expose themselves. It was so big it would have attracted attention. And so, eventually, they will return it. They did it to hurt you."

Paul looked up. "Who are they?"

"A man and a woman."

"I would have given it to them," said Mae indignantly, "if they had asked for it."

"They took it out of revenge. You were in a business deal with them, and it didn't work out."

Mae nodded. "Yes, they would have lost the business if I hadn't picked up the payments and taken the place over."

Maria's head wagged wisely. "Friends do not easily forgive those who help them."

Jack Kelly was apparently still hovering about. "Kelly says he cares for Mae West very much, and for her to forget the diamond. It is a very material thing and she has more important interests for her to concern herself with."

Suddenly, the conversation had shifted away from the ring to the imponderables of life that I knew Miss West to be vitally caught up in.

"What," she asked, "is Jack doing on the other side?"

"He tells me," said Maria, "that he has a mission to work with the Masters over there and learn from them. He has reached the sixth dimension, the truly spiritual side, and will not be reincarnated until he has completed his study of all twelve dimensions. There are as many," she added, "as there are signs in the zodiac."

Dr. Jussek was intrigued by reincarnation.

"What determines when we come back?"

"The way we live, the choices, the karma we develop from our actions, good or bad. Some people come back right away," she said. And surprisingly, they were not the good people but the bad. "They are people who have created great crimes. They come back blind, crippled, sick, often born that way."

Gene, having been drafted as an adolescent into Hitler's Wehrmacht, asked with a natural curiosity, "Did Hitler come back already?"

"He is the anti-Christ," said Maria, shuddering a little.

"Is he in hell?" Gene persisted.

"There is no hell," she replied, "except in the minds of men." But Hitler was living that hell, of that she was sure.

In the sixth dimension, Kelly, if it was he, was virtually a fountain of esoteric information. What could he have done in the twelfth? And Jussek was quick to utilize this apparent omniscience. He asked a question that many interested in reincarnation have pondered over the ages.

"Does the reincarnating individual maintain his own identity from one life to the next?"

We all strained forward for the reply.

"There are many bodies, but only one life, he tells me. The soul which is the gift of God continues through countless cycles, which is why there are soulmates constantly working out their karma from one life to the next."

The spirit was an outcropping of the soul, a vibrating force contributed by the individual, appearing as an energy or thought form. "It is this spirit energy which manifests itself when a spirit appears."

I puzzled over the distinction between soul and spirit.

"The spirit is part of the soul, just as a thought is part of the mind. There cannot be one without the other, but the soul is the essence, and the spirit its reflection."

"Are there friends and family in the spirit world?"

She sighed. "Not like here. They are aware of other spirits, but there are no problems or activities of the flesh, merely an exchange of energy."

Paul sought an explanation of what was unfolding before our eyes.

"Why is it that Jack Kelly makes his presence so readily felt here and now?"

"It is a manifestation of energy. In concentrating on him, the people here supply the energy that allows him to manifest himself." She reflected a moment. "He tells me that Mae West had been thinking of him strongly. But when she saw him on the sofa"—we all blinked a little at this—"this energy left her and the manifestation disappeared. Do I make it clear?"

Why then didn't the spirits always appear when somebody thought of them strongly?

"Hah," said Maria, "that is a good question. It is all in bringing in the right vibration, like with electricity, with lights, or radio or television. The energy is there, but it needs the proper signal and frequency—the beam—to channel it. So the medium is the channel."

That was very fine, but many people reported seeing spirits without the benefit of any psychic. I remembered radio personality Arthur Godfrey, an unbeliever, telling me how he had awakened in the middle of the night on a United States destroyer and seen an apparition at the foot of his bed. It was his father, whom he had only heard from a few days before. He said in a normal voice that he had just passed over but that he did not want his son to grieve. He was not unhappy. Godfrey pinched himself to make sure he wasn't dreaming, then he flicked on a light and looked over at the clock. It was 2 A.M. It was some time before he fell back to sleep, and in the morning he was still wondering if it wasn't a dream. But the next day a radiogram arrived. It was from his family: "Father died at 2 A.M."

Maria had a ready explanation. "He must have been close to his father, and he was thinking of him even in his sleep, when the subconscious is open. But also when the spirit is strong, it is able to draw energy from the atmosphere, and forms enough ectoplasm to manifest itself without the earth energy of others."

59

Maria seemed in such rare form, so completely knowledgeable, that we bombarded her with a barrage of questions.

"Why," asked Paul, "are any of us here on earth? What is our purpose in this life?"

I suppose Maria had heard the question a hundred times.

"We are here to help achieve God's mission for us. Then we move on to new and higher spiritual dimensions, until in the end we become companions of God."

"And then we don't have to come back?"

"Our work is done, and we can rest."

There was something Dr. Jussek had wondered about twenty times a day.

"Why does there have to be illness?"

"It is part of our development. Some illness is psychically caused from conflicting vibrations reflecting inner discord, the body and mind being at war. Other illness is materially or externally caused, such as accidents on the highway. But it all has a part in establishing a person's growth pattern."

There were always those ready to tell us that adversity made us strong. But I couldn't help sympathizing with the man whose wife had run off with his best friend, and whose business had failed. "So I'm strong," he had wailed, "why can't I be happy, too?"

All of us had wondered about the significance of dreams, particularly those that seemed to reflect events in our everyday lives. And so Jussek asked:

"Do dreams tell us anything about our lives?"

"There are three kinds of dreams. One is a carryover from past lives and concerns people in those lives. We don't recognize these people, because they do not have the same identity in this life. Some dreams come from bodily indispositions, such as indigestion from eating or drinking too much, and are merely the system's reaction to a bodily condition. Don't put too much stock in these dreams."

Paul laughed. "They must be the nightmares."

"The third kind of dreams," she went on, "are prophetic. They produce revelations to help the individual in managing his life. This is why we often have these situations we describe as déja vu, a feeling of familiarity, both with a person or a place, as if we had seen them or known them before. When the dreamed event occurs, the person has that hazy feeling of familiarity, but since the dream has long since faded from his conscious mind, he doesn't recall having dreamed it."

Ever since my own injection into the study of metaphysics years before, when a random psychic correctly foretold the unexpected course of my life, I had wondered how anybody could foresee an event that had not yet shown any plausible indication of taking place. I could understand telepathy, as a tuning in of minds with radio-like antennae, and even the dredging up of situations recorded in Carl Gustave Jung's concept of the collective unconscious or racial memory. But as Nobel Prize winner Alexis Carrel had observed: Once we understood how somebody could foretell the future, then we might very well be standing on the threshold of solving the riddle of the universe. And so I asked, "How can some people predict the future when that future has not yet occurred or showed any sign of occurring?"

I suppose she had heard this question many times, too.

"Everything is happening at once, and it is all on the same plane. But it cannot be immediately expressed in activity or action because of people's physical limitations as to time and space. But it is already happening in the thought consciousness of the person, which is as one with the greater thought consciousness of the universe. And so the psychic, whose subconscious mind knows no physical limitation of time and space, tunes into the thought consciousness that will be expressed eventually in the conscious framework of time and space."

It was an explanation difficult to comprehend because we didn't fully understand the relationship of the universal subconscious to the individual subconscious, or the impact of precognition on our declaration of free will. What happened to our vaunted free will if a psychic could correctly foretell every event, two days, two weeks, two years, or twenty years from now—as had been foretold by psychic Maya Perez of Balboa, California, in my own life two decades before?

I mulled over Maria's answer, without understanding it, intellectually. The understanding, I was sure, would have to come out of the intuitive faculty governed by the subconscious. And this would require meditation, developing to the fullest the supernormal powers of the subconscious mind. And still the intellect, and the intellectual, would not accept anything outside its own limited horizons.

Paul was sitting across from me on the sofa where Mae West said she had perceived her friend Kelly sitting as big as life. And as the session ended, with Maria stretching her arms and yawning a little, I thought I saw Paul raise his hand, inexplicably, in a farewell salute.

Dr. Jussek's eyes had followed my own. "Did you see that hand wave from the sofa, just in front of the lamp?" he asked.

"Yes," I said, "it was Paul."

Paul looked up at his name. "I didn't wave at anybody," he said. "I haven't moved an inch."

There was nobody else within several feet of the sofa. We all looked at each other a little uncertainly.

"It might have been Jack waving," said Mae West. "He had a marvelous sense of humor."

4

The
Posthumous
Gift

R ITA PITTMAN had enough problems of her own, without taking on her daughter's. She was in the midst
of writing a book, she was trying to sell some property,
and she was still young enough to want to know what to
do about her personal life.

"Ever since Monty died," said she, speaking of her
screenwriter husband, "I haven't had it all together."

However, she and daughter Sherry Jackson, child actress
grown up, had been especially close, and it had been all
she could do to sit by idly during her daughter's longtime
relationship with millionaire Los Angeles sportsman
Fletcher Jones.

"I just didn't think he treated her right," Rita recalled,
"and in all the years she was with him she subordinated
her own acting career to his personal whims."

Sherry had shrugged off her mother's concern. "Don't
worry about it, Mother," she said, "Fletcher loves me, and
said he will always take care of me. Besides, I'm in love
with him, and nothing else matters right now."

He had been alone the day he crashed his private airplane enroute to his four-thousand-acre ranch near Santa Barbara. Sherry had a premonition of the crash and had warned the forty-two-year-old Fletcher not to take the plane up. Typically, he had scoffed, "I could make the flight from Los Angeles with my eyes closed."

All Sherry's hopes for the future—marriage, security, love—had died with Fletcher Jones. "He died," said Rita, "just as he was making financial provisions for Sherry."

Sherry was in a quandary. In their five years together, she had asked very little materially. And now that Fletcher was dead, she was inclined to let any claim on his estate die with him.

Fletcher had told her of proposed will changes, but nothing tangible had apparently been done. He had spoken of working on his will that weekend, but no papers had been found in the wreckage. "If I only knew what Fletcher had really intended," Sherry sighed.

Her mother did not have the same misgivings. "He loved you and wanted to provide for you," she pointed out, "or he wouldn't have decided to put you in his will."

But Sherry was still loathe to file a claim. She had a retiring personality, and being metaphysically oriented, was inclined to minimize materiality and to place her fate in the hands of the God she believed in. She also was fond of Fletcher's two sons by a broken marriage, and did not want to challenge whatever dispositions had been made for them.

And so it was that when Rita Pittman consulted medium Maria Moreno she was preoccupied primarily with her own problems. "Of course, I had no idea what was stirring around in my subconscious, but consciously Sherry's problems were the furthest thing from my mind. I was interested in me, for a change."

As she did with others, Maria encouraged Rita to bring along a tape recorder, permitting the sitter to check over details of the session later at her convenience.

But she really didn't know what to expect. She had been married twice, and both husbands, Montgomery Pittman and Curtis Jackson, were dead. She had no idea who or what would come through, even though friends had said that Maria Moreno was constantly coming up with names and messages of the dead, so often helpful and to the point. She hoped for as much herself. But when Maria closed her eyes, and began wheezing a bit, it seemed like almost a parody of a seance, something for a movie on a quiet Saturday afternoon.

And then, suddenly, her attention was caught. She was riveted to her seat, her eyes glued to the medium. For as the heavy breathing subsided, Maria had begun to spell out a familiar name. She pronounced each letter deliberately, pausing a moment, as Rita Pittman listened, entranced.

"F-L-E-T-C-H-E-R."

"What about Fletcher?" Rita asked in a whisper.

"He is here," said Maria, "and wants you to know that he is sorry."

Rita was speechless for several moments, a rare occurrence for her.

"What is he sorry about?" she finally managed.

"He says that you know."

This was hardly informative.

"What do I know?"

Maria appeared not to have heard.

"I see this man with many horses. He is making money with them, and spending money. Do you understand?"

Of course. Fletcher Jones was a millionaire industrialist,

a computer genius, who had indulged his love for horses with one of the most prestigious racing stables in the country. Only a short time before the crash, his thoroughbred Typecast had made headlines in a $200,000 match race with a rival, Convenience. He had poured millions into his hobby and his Santa Ynez estate, near completion, had plans for stabling two hundred horses.

It struck Rita as ironical that Fletcher Jones of all people should be announcing that he was alive and well on the other side. Nobody could have been more critical of anything dealing with the supernatural. He had taunted both Rita and Sherry for their preoccupation with this field, and said more than once, "When you're dead, you're dead."

Did he have to die before he could learn there was really no death? That was, of course, if it was indeed Fletcher Jones coming through.

Maria, as if to dispel her misgivings, now launched into a description of the millionaire turfman. "He is tall and slim, with blue eyes and light hair. He is restless, yet supremely sure of himself, and expects things to be done as he wants them."

Rita chuckled under her breath. "That's the Fletcher I knew, all right. It was all one way—his."

They had never been friendly. She resented what she considered Sherry's mistreatment. And he was jealous of her closeness to Sherry. "He wasn't building a mother-in-law cottage on his estate, you could bet your shirt on that."

But death presumably had a mellowing effect. "He wishes to discuss something very dear to his heart," said Maria Moreno. "He is sorry he didn't change his will before the flight as the papers he was working on disappeared in the crash. He wanted to make your daughter financially independent so she could feel free to work or not, as she chose, if anything happened to him."

This is all very fine, Rita thought, but what could he do in the circumstances?

And then came the shocker.

"Fletcher says he is ready to do everything he can to help Sherry collect what she has coming from his estate."

Rita pinched herself to make sure she wasn't dreaming. But there was the cosy little room, with a crucifix on one wall and a picture of Christ on another, and Maria sitting quietly with her hands in her lap.

"How will he help?" asked Rita.

"He will tell you," said Maria, "be patient."

She wondered how Fletcher could present himself as he actually looked, when, presumably, he was only an energy form without substance.

"They manifest themselves as an apparition only to the medium, or to the people who provide the energy which makes them visible to them alone."

In other words, as Rita understood it, there was an invisible link between spirit and sitter, which resulted in an ectoplasmic simulation of the loved—or unloved—one.

The practical mother considered her daughter's chances. She remembered Sherry saying that Fletcher Jones had jotted down his will changes on a yellow legal pad, which he had carried on the plane with him.

"What happened," she asked, "to the yellow pages?"

Maria nodded. "He is very upset about this. He wants you to find these pages and show them to an attorney."

Rita shrugged helplessly. "Sherry inquired, and Fletcher's executors denied there were any such papers. They could have been destroyed in the crash."

"He says she could keep asking about these papers."

"Can he advise her what to do?"

"He says to get a good lawyer, and take legal action against the estate. He left a fortune, and wants her to share it."

Rita recalled Sherry's love for Fletcher's two children. "I don't think she would sue the family."

" 'Sue the estate, not the family,' he says. He left the bulk to charities."

Although surprised by the change in him, Rita was able to accept an ongoing Fletcher Jones. Both she and Sherry had long believed that life was continuous and death only an interlude.

"It was more a question," said Rita, "of extracting useful information."

As the session ended, she realized there had been very little for her. But she was pleased for Sherry. However, Sherry had no wish to revive any painful memories with protracted litigation. But Rita did not give up easily.

"After all, Fletcher's wishes should be important to you. You could very well be disappointing Fletcher by dashing his hopes for you."

Sherry's chiseled features looked properly pensive.

"With this desire for retribution unresolved," Rita persisted, "his spirit may have to remain earthbound, tormented by remorse, until it purges itself of the wrong done."

Sherry was as anxious as her mother to see Fletcher make a peaceful transition. And her curiosity was aroused. Would Fletcher Jones communicate with her, as he had with her mother? Even so, she was not sure she wanted to open old wounds.

Her mind turned over the justice of her cause. She had

made thirty or so movies before she was ten, and had been featured on the Danny Thomas television show for six years. But much of what she had gained professionally had been lost after she had subordinated her career to Fletcher's demands. Was it any wonder then that her mother had quoted Fletcher as saying: "Let Sherry base her claims on the losses suffered through neglecting her own career at my insistence."

Nevertheless, Sherry still could not make up her mind. Meanwhile, the statute of limitations for filing a suit was running out. Her mother kept urging her to at least see Maria Moreno. "If Fletcher had all this to say to me, how much more should he have for you?"

Ultimately, curiosity won out and Sherry agreed to an appointment, without committing herself to any action. Rita made the arrangements, but Sherry's identity remained a secret. "Maria did not have her name," said Rita, "nor did she realize our relationship. We were determined that the reading would not be influenced in any way."

As she sat down, facing Maria, Sherry resolved that Maria would get no clues out of her.

Clarita appeared first, as Maria profusely acknowledged her presence. "It is the gypsy Clarita," she announced, "who wants you to know that what she tells me is from the spirits on the other side."

Sherry made no comment.

Maria's head bobbed, as if in conversation.

"Robert, Robert, on this side, who is he?"

"My brother," said Sherry.

Maria shook her head. "Your half-brother, they tell me."

"That is right," replied Sherry, quietly impressed.

71

"He has problems."

"Everybody has problems."

Clarita gave way to Dr. Jallikete, and he began to examine Sherry, physically and emotionally.

"You are anemic and allergic to penicillin. Keep a balanced diet and be careful of antibiotics." He continued. "You have a cyst. You must see a doctor and have it removed."

Maria's doctors apparently had other things to do that day, and Dr. Jallikete moved on, to be replaced by a more personal counselor. "Keep away from a singer named Andy [not Andy Williams], who keeps calling from Las Vegas."

Sherry had already decided this for herself.

And then came the injunction: "Be careful with the steering of your car. There will be an accident, but you will be safe."

While all this was interesting, the communication she was hoping for had not materialized.

"Curtis is here, you know him. He wants you to know how much he loves you."

"My father's name was Curtis Jackson. He died in 1948. I hardly remember him." She refused to be bowled over by anybody but Fletcher.

"But he remembers you, and feels very tender for you. So that you know who it is, he tells you a family secret; he was adopted into his own family as a child."

Only a handful of people had known about this, but, still, it had nothing to do with her being there.

Maria had been speaking casually until now. Suddenly, her voice vibrated with a new urgency. "They tell me you are being protected by someone you once loved deeply, now on the other side."

Sherry felt a chill down her spine.

She asked her first question. "Who is protecting me?"

"This man you once rode a motorcycle with, but who now tells you not to ride any more as it could be dangerous."

Who else could it be but Fletcher? They had cycled all over his ranch together, over the hills and gulches, sometimes racing to express the rivalry that marked their relationship.

"Pepe is here," announced Maria, "and he will try to help you with your business affairs. You must think of business for your own protection. You still have an ache in your heart. You loved one another, even though you sometimes ran away because he was violently jealous."

It was not necessary to name Fletcher. The description of their relationship was sufficient, a love-hate affair issuing out of Fletcher's desire to possess her completely.

"You were his common-law wife, his wife in everything but name. And he promised one day to make it up to you."

Sherry's eyes misted over. She had clung loyally to the man she loved, despite the unkept promises. She shook herself, trying to feel his presence, but there was only Maria there, clearly in trance and about to speak.

"Fletcher Jones," she said, "you know him?"

Sherry managed a barely audible, "Yes."

"He wants you to know how sorry he is that he didn't take better care of you. He has decided that you should have a million dollars for the sacrifices you made. And he wants you to have it, even if it means suing his estate."

Tears were streaming down Maria's face. "He will look after you at all times. He is sorry about his moodiness, and he is crying now because he was cruel to you."

A lump came to Sherry's throat. But she was soon distracted. Maria had taken Sherry's hands in her own, and the water was dripping from Maria's palms onto hers.

"They are tears from Fletcher," explained Maria, "just as my tears are his."

It was another of those inexplicable materializations of energy from the atmosphere.

Apparently recovering quickly, Fletcher recalled a discussion that only the two knew about. Just before his death, he had asked her to submit a record of the money she thought she had lost through devoting herself exclusively to their relationship. He had also asked her to itemize her monthly expenses, and he had put the totals together for his proposed settlement.

"I had these figures down on the yellow paper," Maria quoted Fletcher, "and had approved them. But they disappeared when the plane crashed. I had planned to discuss my plans with my attorneys, after I got to the ranch."

Sherry was heartened by this sign of Fletcher's interest, but she still didn't know what to do. She preferred that the decision come directly from him. But Pepe first had a warning for her.

"The people you think close friends are not real friends," Maria was saying. "They will say things to hurt your cause. Watch out for them. You have a new boyfriend, is that not right?"

"I met somebody after Fletcher died."

"Be careful to keep everything quiet or the executors will try to show that you were not true to Fletcher."

"It is a year since Fletcher died, and I have been very lonely."

Maria's Pepe was unimpressed.

"They have detectives following you, to prove there were others in your life. So far they have found nothing."

"That's because there was nothing," said Sherry indignantly.

Fletcher, obviously, had more to say to her than to her mother.

"He doesn't want you to grieve," said Maria, "but to take courage and behave wisely. You must fight for the money and the stock he wanted to put aside for you. The executors will try to keep you from sharing, since organizations they favor stand to profit. If you listen he will try to help you. But you must be careful about your personal life."

"How will he help, not being in this world?"

"By the sheer force of his will, he hopes to influence the executors to look more kindly on your claim."

She was not to worry about his sons. "Your suit has no bearing on the trust funds set up for them before my crash." He made specific references to his principal beneficiaries. "It can only affect the funds left to the Salvation Army, the Boy Scouts, and some hospitals. So go ahead and sue."

Fletcher had died in November, 1973, and Sherry's suit just got in under the deadline. She sued for a million dollars.

"She was only doing," said her mother, "what Fletcher told her to do."

Her friendship with Fletcher's children continued. For a high school graduation present, she gave the younger son some gold cuff links that Fletcher had ordered especially for her. "I knew Fletcher would like that."

After the suit was started, I questioned Sherry on whatever might be thought relevant to her action.

"Confidentially," I asked, "how close are you to this new boyfriend?"

She hesitated a moment. "Until the case is decided, I wouldn't want it broadcast about, but I've finally come around to dating somebody regularly."

"What happened about the cyst?"

"I went to my doctor and after checking around a little, he found it."

"Did he remove it?"

"He's keeping an eye on it. So it was very good that she picked up on it." Her dark eyes twinkled. "However, it may never be operated upon. Maria said they were coming up with a medicine that would painlessly dissolve this type of cyst."

Sherry had already had her auto accident. Something happened to the steering mechanism of the car, as Maria forecast. The vehicle skidded off a California freeway, missed several passing cars, then jumped a ditch before it came to a halt just short of an abutment.

She was spared by a miracle. "If I had hit that abutment, it would have been curtains. But I wasn't even hurt."

"Do you believe you were protected?"

"What else can I believe?"

She hoped she was on the proper course. "Everything that Maria Moreno said coincided with our last day together. Fletcher told me not to worry, that he was taking care of me, and I'm not worrying."

Rita Pittman had been as entranced with her daughter's reading as with her own. She had hoped to hear from her husband, Montgomery Pittman, a movie writer, and found it intriguing that neither of her husbands had come through, though Curtis Jackson had apparently communicated with Sherry.

Rita hadn't given up hope. "If one person survives in spirit, then all must." There was no reason why Monty and Curtis shouldn't appear, if Fletcher could do it.

"Monty was such a voyeur," she observed, "so inquisitive, never quite accepting the psychic and survival, but still very interested."

And so Rita went for another appointment with Maria Moreno. As usual, Maria began with a question or two, as if trying herself to determine the presence which had just made itself known.

She wagged her head a few times, then characteristically cocked it to one side before demanding:

"Who is Jack?"

Rita searched her mind. "I don't know any Jack."

"Jack is here, and says he knows you well." Like so many entities flowing through Maria, Jack seemed contrite for past misdeeds. "He is sorry, and asks your forgiveness."

Rita still couldn't place Jack. But she was amused that he was feeling remorseful. That was the story of her life, people always regretting things when it was too late.

Maria tried again.

"He was in a terrible car crash, and died in it."

"But of course!" How could she have been so dense? She was obviously blocking. Jack had once been her name for Curtis Jackson, Sherry's father. After their marriage, she had called him by this affectionate diminutive, reverting to Curtis only after relatives stuffily expressed disapproval of such disrespect for their family name.

"Jack," she savored the name, "was an alcoholic. You

know what that must have been like."

Curtis had been a total unbeliever, so it was rather ironic that he should now manifest himself through the medium.

He seemed ridden with remorse.

"I could not help myself," Maria quoted. "I was really sick. Please forgive me."

How familiar it all was. As she had done a hundred times, Rita responded on cue. "Tell him I forgive."

She had loved Jack as a mother loves a helpless child. She had mourned his passing, even as it liberated her, suffering additionally through having foreseen his death.

Two weeks before the crash that killed him, she had awakened at night, sobbing.

Curtis had abruptly sat up in bed.

"What's wrong?" he asked. "Tell me about it."

She was reluctant at first, but he insisted. "Once you talk about it, your fears will evaporate."

And so she finally blurted it out. "I dreamed that you will be dead in two weeks."

He took it well. "At least," he smiled, "you were crying."

He had tried to reassure her.

"When one door closes, another opens."

"Yes," Rita rejoined, "but there may be a long period between doors."

"I'll just tell God that I never stepped on a spider or hurt an animal."

That was all that had been said. And now Maria was saying:

"He knew that he was going. It came to him from a dream."

Startled as she was by this echo from the past, Rita took

comfort in the thought that Jack had made it across the divide. "He had to see it to believe."

"He was a good man," put in Maria, "he never hurt an animal."

"Nor," added Rita, "did he ever step on a spider."

She had been waiting for Monty, and for Fletcher. Instead, other names kept popping up, of people known long ago.

"Carl is here, can you place him?"

"Uncle Carl Stephens lived near my childhood home in Moberly, Missouri."

"He liked to play the guitar."

Rita smiled. "You couldn't stop him."

"He mentions the Argonne and Château-Thierry."

"He talked incessantly about World War I."

Rita's older sister, Bernadine, had taken her life in a fit of depression.

"I feel her vibrations," said Maria, "she had a hard time with her nerves."

"Yes," said Rita, thinking back sadly over the years. "She was given shock treatment, and never recovered."

"She is still confused," said Maria. She was another who had discovered that suicide only leaves the gnawing problems still to be dealt with.

"Mack is here, too. He reminds you that he was more than a father to you."

"My only father from the time I was six years old. He was my stepfather."

Her mother was in the room as well. "She had a massive heart attack," said Maria, breathing spasmodically, as though reliving the agony. "But she was ready to go. 'I don't know why they are keeping me here,' she would say."

She had heard her mother make this remark a hundred times.

"How is mother now?"

"She is happy, free of pain, and close to your step-father."

Apparently, some kept up communication, and others floated their separate ways, biding their time for the eventual return in new and brighter raiment.

The sitting ended without Monty or Fletcher appearing. Rita was disappointed, but sophisticated enough to know she had no jurisdiction over the spirits.

"It is not enough to want something. You have to let it happen in the good Lord's time."

She was at home several days later when the telephone rang. It was Maria Moreno. "You must have a reading immediately. I have never called like this before, but a message came for you."

The medium had awakened from a sound sleep, drenched to the skin. As she changed into dry clothing, Mrs. Pittman's name kept ringing in her ears, and she felt she must see her. The wetting came as a message.

As she listened, Rita had attributed the phenomenon to perspiration or a nervous kidney. But Maria had pointed out that the blankets as well as the pillows were sopping wet. And there had been nobody else in her apartment.

For the first time, Maria eagerly awaited her own reading. "I never got such a message to call anybody before."

As usual, she quickly put herself in trance, and went on with her message.

"Monty, Monty," she called out, "he did it. He materialized the water. Do you know this Monty? He says he knows you. He keeps laughing, like he is enjoying a big joke."

"Do I know a Monty?" said Rita. "He was the world's greatest practical joker."

"He asks if you remember Bonnie Jane." Maria snapped her fingers. "She died just like that."

"Yes, she was killed in an automobile accident."

"So young, they tell me, such a pity."

"She was a lovely girl, only twenty-two."

Bonnie Jane's mother had been Rita's best friend, and it was surprising the girl hadn't come on directly, instead of through Monty Pittman.

"Apparently," said Rita, "this was Monty's way of getting into the act. He should have been an actor instead of a writer."

Bonnie Jane seemed tuned in. "Her father is paralyzed," said Maria Moreno, "and she knows that he will not live much longer. She knows she can't help him, and so is more concerned about her brother Larry. Is that not his name?"

Bonnie Jane's father had been bedridden for years, following a stroke, but Larry's problem was new to her.

"Exactly what is wrong?"

"He should stay away from a young man named Paul. He is a bad influence."

"Can you be more specific?"

"It is a business situation, and could result in charges of fraud. He must be careful, or he will become involved with the authorities."

There was no more from Monty, and Bonnie Jane quickly passed on. The session was over, and with all the billing from Maria, it was still innocuously anticlimactic.

Rita dutifully telephoned Bonnie Jane's family. Larry came to the phone. "You won't believe any of this," she said, "but tell me if it relates to any of your activities."

Larry listened for a while. "I know a Paul who's trying to run me out of business. He's pulled every trick imaginable by a competitor, but I don't see how he can get me in trouble."

He did not seem impressed. Subsequently, Rita received a call from Larry's mother. "Larry," she disclosed, "was involved with another Paul. Thinking over what you told him, he got out of the deal, thank the Lord."

All in all, the incident had not seemed important enough to justify an apport, the projection of an object, water in this case, without apparent physical means.

But Rita Pittman did not agree. "You are forgetting one very important thing."

"And what is that?" I asked.

"I now knew that Monty had made the transition into a dimension of happiness."

"And how did you know that?"

"When I learned he was dousing people with water. He was always happiest when he was bugging me."

With no more word from Fletcher Jones, Sherry's suit kept running into snags. The executors were not about to capitulate to a young actress who had nothing to show for her claim but her unsupported word. The suit had touched off investigations designed to minimize Sherry's relationship with the millionaire turfman. "You would have thought she was a criminal," said a horrified Rita.

Rita was now more concerned about Sherry's state of mind than the estate. "It is more important that she be happy. She has a whole life ahead."

She had not liked the developments in the case. "I didn't think Fletcher was good for her alive, and I'm not so sure he's good for her dead."

Sherry found her way back to Maria Moreno. For one thing, she wanted reassurance that it was actually Fletcher in communication with her. And for another, as the trial date neared, she was plagued by the prospect of having her personal life raked up. Also, because of her affection for Fletcher's children, she dreaded getting into the thick of her stormy life with Fletcher. By nature, quietly introspective, she had cherished a personal life separate from her professional image. "There were many things Fletcher and I didn't agree on, and this suit was one of them."

As yet, Maria Moreno had no conscious awareness of Fletcher Jones, or the ensuing litigation, and so it could be safely assumed the reading would be untainted by suggestion.

There were none of the usual preliminaries. "Fletcher is here," said Maria right off. "So that you will know it's really him, he reminds you of the small scars on his face from scratch marks as a boy."

Sherry started the least bit. "Yes, he told me they came from chicken pox, which he picked at when he was little."

"Good, he says, that you know who you are listening to."

Fletcher got on with the case. He mentioned her lawyer's name, then said, "Your attorney must fight hard. Don't accept a trust fund or a small settlement."

The conversation got back to their relationship, and how much he enjoyed their last trip to Europe, just before his death, and his plans for their life together on the Santa Barbara ranch.

"I had been drinking the day of the crash, but I felt I could fly that plane blindfolded. You were right in refusing to go along with me."

Maria's face took on a troubled look.

"Again he wants you to know how sorry he is that he was so rough at times. He is crying now because he was so mean to you."

Sherry thought of the times she had left him, only to return on his promise to be good.

She sighed. Her own inner voice was in conflict with what others thought best for her. How seldom she had been her own person. She had been in pictures before the classroom, packaged and plumed for the screen, too busy for the carefree adolescent romances so many girls enjoyed. And then, stardom in her grasp, she had fit her life into Fletcher's, constantly compromising her own freedom. It was time she took command of her life. Hadn't even the reincarnationist Edgar Cayce held that the only life that counted was the present? For if this life experience was not significant, then no lifetime was.

Fletcher's was suddenly a small voice, dimly and darkly perceived.

"He is not happy with what they are doing with the money," said Maria, "and he does not like his sons living in want."

Sherry nodded mechanically. "The children don't get their trust funds until after they become of age, and that's some time off."

"He wants you to know that he is watching over you."

"I've been helping them whenever I can," she said.

The sitting ended in an emotional stalemate, with Sherry more perplexed than ever. "My whole philosophy, based on metaphysical studies, is that one has to go on with his life. You can't live in the past. In the present we meet challenges, and establish our karmic pattern."

Fletcher had presumably seen the situation clearly, identifying his beneficiaries, telling her how to proceed, and naming her lawyer. But with all this, her doubts had not been dispelled. She had no heart for the suit.

I was not at all surprised when her mother called to announce that Sherry had settled the action out of court.

"Was it a good settlement?" I asked.

"Not what she should have had."

"She must not have taken the advice very seriously."

There was a certain resignation in Rita Pittman's voice. "That had nothing to do with it."

"Then what did?"

"It would have been a messy trial, and she just couldn't handle it. She didn't feel the money was worth all that to her. She didn't want them trespassing on precious memories."

I wondered how Fletcher Jones would react to Sherry's decision.

Sherry's mother was not terribly concerned.

"He could have avoided all this," she said a little waspishly, "if he had considered her wants while he was alive."

Had Rita not accepted the voice as Fletcher's?

"Of course, it sounded like Fletcher all the way. Always promising, never quite coming through."

5

Marilyn Monroe Onstage

I HAD NO IDEA that Paula Petrie knew Marilyn Monroe. Actually, the Hollywood realtor had called on behalf of her husband, Jack Petrie, a musician, who was terminally ill.

"I understand," said she, "that Maria has wonderful healing powers."

"She attributes it all to her spirit doctors," I said.

"However it happens, I would like her to see Jack. The doctors have given him up."

But Maria was out of the country, and by the time Paula Petrie did reach her, Jack Petrie was dead. And so now with a widow's problems, she arranged a sitting for herself.

"I was so desolated that I didn't know what to do. I was working for an advertising agency, but needed a change. California wasn't the same without Jack. I had an urge to go back to his home in Hannibal, Missouri, and live as a recluse. I was still youthful, but the thought of marrying again was repulsive to me."

She didn't know what to expect of Maria, but she had an open mind. And it was just as well. "Imagine my hus-

87

band coming through, telling me he loved me and didn't want me living out my life alone!"

Paula's dark features brightened. "I went there not believing, thinking I had nothing to lose. She picked up the name Jack, described him to a T, caught his personality. Jack wanted me in the real estate business, where he had worked before his death, though his first love was music. When she said he would help me join his old firm, I wondered what I was doing there, listening to such drivel. As a matter of fact, she even told me who would get in touch with me, Joe Castagna, and spelled it out. And it was Joe Castagna, the owner of the firm, who offered me the job. He had been a friend of Jack's."

"And I suppose Jack influenced him?"

"That's what Maria suggested."

Eventually, said Jack, she would be in advertising and real estate at the same time. It didn't seem likely but Maria had been right about everything else. Obviously, something of a supernormal nature was going on, but the source was not as obvious.

"What made you think it was Jack communicating?"

"When something comes through that only that one person would know about, you must consider very seriously the identity of the source. Maria, speaking for Jack, described his operation for lung cancer and the last days, when he expressed his undying gratitude for my help."

"This attitude," I said, "could be safely assumed."

"She heard beautiful music, without being told he was a musician. It made me wonder whether gifted people could tune into energy forms conveying sounds, tastes, and even smells. I had vowed never to marry again, but he kept repeating, as in his last days, that I should find someone."

Jack was not the only visitor. An actress he knew quite well, who prodded him to play the piano at their small parties, also manifested herself. Her name was Norma Jean.

"This Norma Jean," said Maria, "has a smiling face and beautiful blond hair. She has a message for you."

A shiver ran down Paula's spine. Norma Jean Dougherty was the name she had for Marilyn Monroe. What other Norma Jean was there?

"Even after she became famous," Paula recalled, "we still called her Norma Jean. The name represented a feeling of family for her."

In observing Maria, I had frequently noted a connection between sitter and spirit. But even so, why would the famed actress, dead tragically at thirty-six, appear to Paula Petrie, when there were so many others she knew better?

Paula Petrie smiled. "I was probably the only one who had gone to a medium."

They had met in the early days, when Marilyn, as Norma Jean, was a struggling bit player, living at Hollywood's Studio Club.

"She had been dating Freddie Karger, who composed the music for *From Here to Eternity*. We ran into each other at the home of Anne Karger, Freddie's mother, who was my godmother. We were never close, but we were friendly, and we shared the affection of Anne Karger. Marilyn regarded her almost like the mother she never had. At Sunday gatherings at the Karger home, Marilyn would let her hair down. She was like a little girl, naïve and gullible, terribly trusting. She seemed happy and gay, but underneath the childlike façade there was a horrible fear of going insane. Her natural mother had been mentally ill and she was obsessed with the fear that she may have inherited this weakness."

Even after Freddie Karger married actress Jane Wyman, Ronald Reagan's former wife, Marilyn remained close to the Kargers, regularly visiting Anne Karger, and Freddie's sister, Mary.

"She thought of them as family. Occasionally, she would call us and ask Jack to play at a party. She enjoyed his music so. She would get up and sing while he played. In this way, we kept in touch during her rise to stardom. She enjoyed talking about how she flunked her first screen test. She had a hard time getting into movies, but she enjoyed her success all the more, contrasting it to all the earlier rebuffs. But she was a natural, and nobody could keep her down. She had gorgeous violet-blue eyes and a keen sense of fun. She was so warm-hearted that anybody with access to her could play on her sympathies. She never forgot Norma Jean."

Paula had rejoiced with Marilyn as she broke into movies in *The Asphalt Jungle*, got fully launched in *All About Eve*, and then burst into stardom. She continued to see Marilyn during her marriage to Joe DiMaggio, but lost sight of her after the marriage to Arthur Miller.

"She should have stayed married to Joe. She needed sheltering."

As were so many, she was shocked by the news that Marilyn had died in her Los Angeles home, an apparent suicide.

"It was incredible, so young, so beautiful, so talented, so full of life."

Marilyn smiling, laughing, twirling gaily at a party,

kept flitting through her mind, but with time the pictures faded. She had not thought of Marilyn for some time until Maria's message hit her between the eyes.

"Yes, I knew a Norma Jean," she said, her lips suddenly dry.

"She is here," said Maria, "and she is glad to see you."

"Tell her," murmured Paula, "that I am glad she is here."

Paula had wondered why Marilyn, with the world at her fingertips, had taken her life. True, she had three broken marriages, but she had lost none of her winsome charm.

So often the spirits seemed to be just passing through, but Norma Jean had a special reason for communicating.

"I want the world to know that I did not commit suicide."

As Paula repeated these words, she smiled half-apologetically. "I couldn't help wondering why the world would know about this through me. I had no way of knowing that anybody would ever be writing about it."

Marilyn's death had been coupled with persistent rumors of a broken romance with a personage high in government. Hours before her death she had tried vainly to contact him. She had been drinking heavily and was depressed. Considering her emotional state, suicide had seemed the likely cause of death.

But Paula Petrie had felt compelled to ask, "How did it happen?"

Maria cleared her throat, then continued in the first person, as if to point up Norma Jean's authenticity.

"I woke up dazed, in the middle of the night. I forgot I had taken some sleeping pills a short time before, and took some more. I just wanted to black out. It was an accident. I was a religious person, fundamentally, and would not deliberately take my own life, no matter how often I talked about it, or seemed to try it."

With all her drinking, her death could very well have been accidental. Sleeping pills combine with alcohol for an accelerating, synergistic effect, offsetting any tolerance to the barbiturates, and frequently prove fatal.

"I had my problems," she continued, "but I knew this wasn't the way out, and I know that even better now."

The spirits of suicides, as with Bishop Pike's son, invariably professed regret for their action. It had solved nothing and only served to keep their souls earthbound longer than customary.

"She says," Maria slipped out of the first person, "that she had too much to live for, and quitting does not end one's problems."

Maria had breezed along, accepting Norma Jean and her friends as she found them.

Her head had a familiar birdlike tilt. "Who's Joe? She wants to know how Joe is."

"That would be Joe DiMaggio, her former husband. He was deeply devoted even after death."

As she recalled this intimate interlude, Paula seemed almost embarrassed.

"I really didn't want to pry into her personal affairs. I felt like a Peeping Tom."

Before Marilyn's death, there had been considerable gossip about her and both President John F. Kennedy and his brother, Senator Robert Kennedy. But apart from her appearance at White House functions, there had been nothing of a tangible nature. I wondered how closely Maria's communication had touched upon this delicate subject.

"Did you ask about her friendship for the Kennedys?" I asked Paula Petrie.

"I didn't dare. But Norma Jean did say something odd."

"And what was that?"

"I could tell you some juicy secrets, but the tape recorder is going, and it wouldn't be good for the country."

I gave Paula a questioning glance. "Couldn't you have turned the machine off?"

"I was in such shock it never occurred to me."

Norma Jean quickly got off on a tangent. And Paula was just as well pleased, for the conversation now centered on her.

"Take seven petals from seven different kinds of flowers and carry them in a small cardboard carton for luck."

Paula was inclined to laugh this off, but as she thought about it, she realized that seven was indeed a very significant number for her. "I was married on February 7, Jack's birthday was April 7, and we met on October 7."

Paula looked at me uncertainly. "The strangest thing happened the next day. I awakened from a dream with a bouquet of carnations in it. All that day the smell of carnations filled the house. Other people smelled them as well."

The scent was so strong that she went to the garden outside and smelled her sweet peas, but it was an entirely different fragrance.

At my silence, Paula gave a nervous little laugh.

"This may sound bizarre, but it happened. I wouldn't ordinarily accept something like this. I only went to Maria as a last resort."

"But what was the significance of the carnations?"

"It was one of Marilyn's favorite flowers."

"Even so, where was the smell coming from? Do we have spirit flowers, as well as spirit actresses?"

"It was a sign confirming the visit."

As I was mulling this over, she looked up with a smile. "You know, I am a very practical person. I was with an advertising agency, and I am doing very well in real estate. But there may be more to life than meets the eye. Psychic phenomena can't be dismissed just because we don't understand them."

She was still a little uncertain. "A Kay, or Kathy, also came through, without my placing her. She was a pretty girl who just dropped by to say hello. She had died, violently, at twenty-seven. I could not identify her. Later, I played back the tape and realized it must be Kay or Kathy Dalton. She had been killed in a car crash two years before."

Still thinking of Norma Jean, I had nothing to say.

"Oh, there was more to it," Paula said quickly. "Just then the phone rang. It was Jack Dalton, a friend of my husband's, who lives in Detroit. He was Kathy's husband. He hadn't called in a year. 'I just had a strange feeling that I had to talk to you,' he said. 'Nothing specific. It was like somebody wanted me to call you.'"

After a moment's hesitation, Paula mentioned she had been to a medium and Kathy had come through.

Dalton was immediately intrigued. "I had been thinking of her quite strongly," he said. "Could there be an other side?"

There was no more then about Norma Jean. But I had noticed on repeat sittings that the same spirits often came through with additional information. What might Norma Jean say with the tape recorder off?

To this session, Paula arrived with a friend, Merle Fortier, an enthusiastic devotée of Maria's. She delivered an unsolicited testimonial, as we waited for Maria to come into the room.

"My blood pressure was up to 230, and her Dr. Dermetz operated spiritually on my veins, inserting an imaginary valve to relieve the pressure."

Her regular doctor made his checkup the next day, and found the pressure down forty points.

"Keep taking your medicine," he said, cheerfully.

Merle had not mentioned Maria or Dermetz to her doctor. "He would have thought I was out of my mind."

By this time Paula was working not only for Castagna Realty but for her old advertising agency, Doyle Dane Bernbach, in television programming, just as Maria had forecast.

"It's amazing," she said, "how she sees these things."

I lightly recalled the smell of carnations.

"Any other signs recently?"

"You won't believe this one," she said. "But Merle was a witness." Paula, coming out of the shower, had been startled by a big M on the bathroom mirror. It had not been there a few moments before and the bathroom door had been locked from the inside.

"It looked as if a big stalk had been used to daub the M on the mirror."

"It might have come from the steam," I said.

She shook her head. "No, it had been evenly put on."

The big M kept appearing and disappearing, until she sent off the tape to me.

"Now what do you make of that?"

I had no idea what, if anything, it signified.

"She may have just been letting me know," said Paula, "that she was still very much around."

"It couldn't have been an accidental design," Merle Fortier observed, "the M's were deliberately lettered. We both saw the M. It had not been there a few minutes before, and nobody else was in the house."

Maria had now appeared and quickly went into trance. She put her hands to her head, and said in obvious surprise, "I feel somebody touching me. He is sighing, so sad that you have suffered another loss. It is your husband Jack."

"Does he say who this was?" Paula asked.

"Anne, you knew her very well."

"Yes, my dear godmother, Anne Karger, passed a week ago."

I remembered Anne Karger as Marilyn's dear friend and confidante, but had seen nothing about her death.

"I see her in the corner," said Maria, pointing across the small room.

We all looked and saw nothing. "With a camera," said Maria, "you could take her picture."

It would have to be a camera, I felt, that picked up ectoplasm.

"She complained of cramps in her legs," Maria went on.

"Yes," nodded Paula, "she did have problems with her legs."

I ventured a question. "Is there anybody else in spirit who knows of Anne's passing?"

The answer came back promptly. "Norma Jean and Patty." I looked questioningly at Paula.

"Patty was Anne Karger's daughter. She died some time ago."

Paula had a very long face, and I couldn't help but wonder why people grieved so over the dead if they felt they lived on.

"When a friend moves away," said Maria, "don't you miss him?"

"That's a rather good analogy," observed Paula.

"Anne sees other beautiful souls, like Judy Garland," Maria continued, "and she is pleased that Judy has gained the peace she never knew on the earth plane."

How could an energy form be happy or troubled, if such was spirit?

"Thoughts and energy are the same in this vibration," said Maria. "The individual souls are a personification of the person and never die. In passing over, a person loses the limitations of time and space, for death frees the energy forms produced by the soul. But he still projects himself and his own personality."

During the Mae West sitting, and now again, I found myself unbearably sleepy, hard-pressed to keep my eyes open. As my head nodded, Maria opened her eyes and gave me a cryptic smile.

"What's so funny?" I demanded.

"We take from you."

"Is that why I first get cold, then drop off to sleep?"

"You are like a medium, so they take your energy."

Before I could comment, she slipped back into trance.

"Joe, Joe, Joe," she repeated, "three Joes she is asking for." She fluttered her hands. "Norma Jean is here. 'Joe, Joe, Joe,' she says. 'How are they?'"

"I can get two of them," said Paula, "Joe DiMaggio and his son, Joe, Junior, she was terribly fond of him. But not the third."

"How about Joe Schenck, the head of Twentieth Century Fox, who gave Marilyn her break in *All About Eve*?"

"Oh, yes," Paula recalled, "he was her big booster, and a close friend as well. They often dined together after Marilyn finished at the studio."

The next message caused my heavy lids to open.

"You could feel Norma Jean's energy, not right? She spelled out her name for you."

Paula looked at her incredulously. "Only the initial M."

"Not something else?"

"The smell of flowers."

Maria's face was wreathed in a happy smile. "Yes, she tells me about that."

Why weren't these initials NJ and not M?

"She liked her name Marilyn Monroe," said Maria. "She picked it for herself."

Paula thought it time to question the gossip linking Marilyn to the Kennedys.

Maria shook her head sadly. "People say a lot of things about her but she doesn't want to become involved. She recognizes the beautiful soul of her friend, and she is in communication with it. She wants to be in peace."

"Tell her," said Paula, "that there is no tape recorder and she may say what she pleases."

"Her mind is confused. People say she committed suicide, but like she said, it was an accident. She was married three times, and had many romances, but the only man she loved still holds her memory dear."

"That," said Paula, "would be Joe DiMaggio. Every year, he puts flowers on her grave."

She did not inquire about her third husband, playwright Arthur Miller, nor her first, Jim Dougherty. But she was concerned about Miller's father, for whom she had a genuine affection in life.

"She wants him to know that she cherished his kindness."

"How about Miller?"

There was no answer.

"After her death," commented Paula, "he took her apart in his play *After the Fall*. And if I know Marilyn, she would rather not be critical of anybody."

Maria was having a field day. "I see her walking arm in arm with a handsome man with a mustache. It is Clark Gable." Her voice rose excitedly. "He died before her, she is saying, and she is sorry for it."

Marilyn had starred with Gable in his last picture, *The Misfits*. There had been endless delays because of Marilyn. Gable had fretted impatiently, and overtaxed himself on location. His wife Kay, as I recalled, had rebuked Marilyn after Gable's heart attack.

"Norma Jean worshipped him, and wouldn't knowingly have hurt him," said Maria.

Gable, Garland, Jack Petrie, all had taken their bows. But Norma Jean was perversely circumspect about the Kennedys.

"Both died in a sad way," said Maria, "and it made her very sad."

"Who does she mean by both?"

Maria hesitated. "The President of the United States."

"Would that be John Kennedy?"

"And the other?"

Norma Jean's tongue was strangely silent.

"She doesn't want to hurt anyone."

How could naming Bobby Kennedy possibly hurt him?

"She says that she did nothing wrong. She had great respect for President Kennedy. And it makes her uncomfortable to talk about him now."

"Does she see a second man?" asked Paula.

"I will ask her. But I see only her head now. Her energy is withdrawing."

"Just ask who he was?"

Maria smiled thinly. "She says they were both in Washington, and you should know who they were."

"Can't she tell us?" I put in.

"She says you ask like an interrogator. She says they care for him on the other side and want to see his position preserved."

"But he no longer has this position."

"In the hearts of people he does. She was infatuated with someone people have great respect for and she doesn't want to damage his reputation. They did nothing wrong."

Marilyn had made a last call trying to reach the man she cared for.

"Couldn't this person have helped her when she was lonely and ill, needing a few words of encouragement?"

"Nobody responded when she called, but there was nothing mysterious about her death. She will say nothing to harm anybody in spirit, as she wouldn't in life."

And now came a hint of the saddest chapter in Marilyn's life. "Her dream," said Maria, "was to have a baby of her own. But whenever it seemed possible, something happened to block it. She says she had a miscarriage shortly before her death and this disturbed her greatly."

There had not even been a whisper of anything like this.

Maria sighed heavily. "She wants to see everybody happy. Life on the other side is better for her. The things that happened to her now seem unimportant. She had no

desire to create any mysteries. But let people find out
things for themselves. She doesn't want any sensations.
To achieve her own evolution, she has accepted the good
and the bad. She has new goals now, and everything
before is like a dream. There is only one thing she wants
established."

We all looked up, eagerly

"And what is that?"

" 'I took the pills,' she says, 'without realizing what I
was doing.' "

6

The Guiding Spirits

D R. JUSSEK pursued the idea that under hypnosis Maria Moreno would be even more formidable. "I have the feeling that she would then become a clear channel, with all language barriers removed, and any vestige of the conscious mind effectively displaced."

Maria had no compunctions about being regressed.

"You put me to sleep?" She smiled in amusement. "What's wrong with the way I go to sleep?"

"Nothing," the doctor explained, "but I have a feeling you will establish stronger contact with your spirit world in this way."

Maria stuck out her chin.

"Why should that be?"

He did his best to explain, pointing out the different functions of the conscious and subconscious mind. "Normally," he said, "even in trance, the conscious mind has some distracting effect on the subconscious brain."

He planned to regress Maria to a past life experience to trace any possible connections between herself and her various guides. "It seems to me" he said, "that if there is anything to reincarnation these physician guides of hers must bear some special connection to Maria's own past."

And so, with Maria lying on her couch, her eyes closed, he soon put her under. "You are hypnotized so deeply that you will not feel this needle when I stick it into your arm." He pressed in the needle, and from her relaxed state it was obvious that she felt no sensation.

Unlike some hypnotists, engaged in time regressions, Jussek did not pick out a specific period, trusting that Maria's subconscious would automatically fasten on a relevant experience.

"Go back into a past life," he commanded at random. "You are ten years old."

She remained silent.

He repeated his suggestion several times before her lips moved.

I leaned forward eagerly for whatever wonder she had for us.

"Barrels," said she, "barrels."

"What about barrels?" Jussek grimaced.

"The cellar is full of barrels, I am hiding behind the barrels."

"What is your name?" he asked.

She spelled it out. "H-E-I-D-I."

"How old were you then?"

"I was a child."

Oddly, her Mexican accent had disappeared, and her voice was clearer than I had ever heard it.

"I live in a village," she went on, "it is cold." She shivered. "We live by the fire, there is a special furnace."

"Are you dressed warm?"

"It is still cold."

"What place do you live?"

"Croatia.' She spelled it out, referring to a Middle Age

104

principality in the Balkans, now part of Yugoslavia.

"Who are your mother and father?"

"My father was a Russian. He wasn't Croatian." She spoke proudly. "He was a White Russian."

She groaned, and held her hands to her heart. "Dear God, they stabbed my father in the heart."

There was no sadness in her voice, only the horror of a bad dream. The murder had taken place down amid the barrels, and she had been a terrified witness, playing among the barrels when the murder suddenly made her own life a hazard.

I found it especially interesting that she should zero into this particular experience again, for I had often heard from reincarnationists that only the significant incarnations were remembered, in hypnosis or out of it. As Jussek questioned her, perhaps we would see something out of each recalled experience that had important bearing on her present life.

Jussek, as a scientist, was anxious, of course, to put the regression into a definite framework, relating to time, place, circumstances. However, if there was no time or place in the universe, only that expedient to self-regulation, we would have to accept her psychic information on its own terms, not ours.

"There is no reason," I said, "for the spirits to put themselves in a convenient little box to accommodate the technicians."

Jussek nodded. "I understand, but we still need some sort of recognizable yardstick." And so he continued with his effort to assemble meaningful, factual information.

"How old were you?" he repeated.

"Ten or eleven years old. I never saw my father again. An old lady took care of me."

"What year was it?"

She hesitated. "Seventeen hundred thirty-three."

Jussek pondered. "Was this your last life before this one?"

"Oh, no, I had others. But something happened to my body in that life." She moaned softly, "The cemetery. They say my mother was Croatian. My father left her. And then he was killed."

As Heidi she had a truly terrible time. "They chained me, and locked me up for the rest of my life."

"But why did they do that?"

"It was for money. After my father and mother were gone, they buried me in a secret place. They hated me."

"And then," there was a sob in her voice, "they killed me. I saw the lady when she hanged me. My father's mother, my own grandmother. They said I was bad."

Jussek looked at me across the couch. "You see, even then," he said wryly, "what people do for money."

"It may all be in her head."

"Well, it came from somewhere. Something doesn't come out of nothing."

Indeed, it was difficult not to watch her twisting and turning, moaning and groaning during this recital, without crediting the reality of her remembrance. We were made uncomfortable, without any enlightenment on any significant connection with the past. Jussek, unconcerned by any tragic history he may have inadvertently dug up, continued to explore the theory that some gifts and aptitudes are carried from one life experience to the next, as certainly the great Mozart must have done to be able to compose serious music at the age of three.

"At this time," he asked, "did you have any psychic powers?"

How unlikely this seemed, hearing the pathetic tale of the fugitive orphaned child hiding among the barrels, to save her life from the evil adults who had designs on her inheritance—or so I had tailored the script in my own mind.

But, improbably, she replied, "Yes, but my family were orthodox Catholics. It was blasphemy."

Jussek seemed somewhat encouraged. "She could have been one of those children who was forever being put down because she talked about the things she had seen. That may have been the excuse they used for locking her up."

"At least, she saw her father's murderer."

He grunted. "That wasn't psychic."

The questioning had not even inferentially turned up anything about Maria's spirit guides. But Jussek was patient, persistent and direct, when indirection didn't succeed.

"Does Pepe," he asked, "mean anything to you?"

She shook her head. He then inquired about Clarita, Dr. Dermetz, Jallikete and the rest. The answer was the same shake of the head.

"How can she use them," he marveled, "when she doesn't even know who they are?"

I pointed out the obvious. "As Heidi, at this stage of time, she may not have been conversant with any of them."

He took her back further in time, to the fifteenth century.

She spoke in barely a whisper. "There is an epidemic, black bodies lie in the streets, and I have the disease. It is the plague."

Maria had not had an easy time.

"Life can be very cruel," Jussek observed, asking then, "Where is this?"

"Liebsig," said she, "in Istria."

This was intriguing, for the unlearned Maria had touched on a bit of obscure history. In the Middle Ages, when it was under the rule of Muslim Turkey, the Bohemian state included Serbia, Dalmatia and Istria. Jussek himself, though schooled in neighboring Germany, was not aware of this background, nor would I have been had I not chanced to look into this recently. Leipzig took its name from the original Slavic settlement of Lipsk.

She had known the black plague.

"Did you die from this?"

She shook her head. "I was left with scars. I died of old age."

"What language did you speak?"

"German."

Her name was Teresa and she was a teacher of astrology. "I taught the symbols."

Jussek's interest perked up.

He asked again about Dermetz, Jallikete, Clarita and company.

As she shook her head, I was beginning to wish we had forgone this project.

"They called me a witch," said she, "but I dealt with oracles. I gave prophecies to the people." She made a low guttural sound. "They didn't burn me," she said proudly, "like the others."

Only a few years before, still in the fifteenth century, the Church had burned "heretics" like the Slav patriot-priest, Jan Huss, at the stake, and the practice continued with witches and other heretical figures who violated Church dogma.

"Who were the enemies that wanted to burn you?"

She started to writhe and groan on the couch.

"The people wanted to burn me. But the Duke saved me."

"What Duke?"

"The Duke of Orange."

We checked quickly and discovered that this Dutch protector of Protestants had taken jurisdiction of civil affairs in Austria, ending Catholic Church persecution of nonconformists and free thinkers.

"My friends got the Prince of Orange to help when they arrested me for witchcraft."

Jussek looked up. "You see, she was psychic also in this previous life."

"A witch," I said, "a purveyor of black magic."

He shrugged. "They didn't call them psychics in those days, but what else were they?"

Teresa's father was a German physician, a prominent Protestant, her mother an Italian.

"At least," said Jussek, "her father in this experience was a doctor. He might even have been Dr. Dermetz."

"Or Jallikete."

"Hardly," said he, "since he was German and Dermetz sounds German to me."

Under hypnosis, we discovered that her English not only became clearer, but her vocabulary improved, and she used words that she ordinarily didn't even know the meaning of.

Jussek did not think this particularly strange. "After all, in hypnosis, she has spoken languages she was not familiar with in this lifetime."

"Perhaps," I said, "she was a writer or a professor in a prior existence."

"I hope not," he said, "I'd like to keep her pure and simple. The simple ones make the best psychics."

"Now Teresa," he said in a cajoling voice, "you are living in that time again. Your father's name was what?"

Slowly, "Herman ... Herman...."

"Herman Dermetz?" said he quickly.

She shook her head. "No, Herman Wald."

He gave a gesture of disgust. "Just when I thought we were getting somewhere."

"Go forward in time," he said, "until you can tell me who was Clarita or Dermetz."

Her head moved from side to side, but she said nothing.

"Who was Dr. Dermetz?" Jussek persisted.

"My father."

"But you said it was Herman Wald."

She seemed to be trying to remember. "But later, in another life, he was Dr. Dermetz. Twice he was a doctor."

"What happened to Dr. Dermetz?"

She sighed. "He died in 1910, before I was born in this life."

Maria, we knew, had been born in 1915, and so this at least was mathematically plausible. Granting reincarnation, and living spirits, did the spirit of Dr. Dermetz recall his relationship to Maria when he was Herman Wald and she was Teresa?

"In her subconscious mind, it is as real as anything she has experienced," said Jussek, "and so it becomes a reality in itself, accounting for the personality and knowledge attributed to her spirit doctor, Dermetz."

In hypnosis, she seemed to float from one life to another, and still retain knowledge of herself.

"How did you find out," Jussek asked, "that Dr.

Dermetz and your father Herman Wald were one?"

"They were not one, but one followed the other and I knew that he had been my father."

"But how did you know this?"

"We were in spirit the same time, and our souls communicated. There are no secrets in the soul world, on the other side. Once we were father and daughter, another time husband and wife, working off our karma."

"Now what kind of doctor was Dr. Dermetz?"

"He was an alchemist." And he had many lives, commencing in ancient China in this rudimentary beginning of modern chemistry, which first dealt with the transmutation of baser metals into gold and the restoration of youth in man.

"Where is this Dr. Dermetz now?"

"On the other side," she naturally replied.

"Does he tell you how life is over there?"

She seemed not to have heard the question.

"Would he tell you if you asked him?"

Her head came forward. "I will ask him."

She paused for a few moments, apparently in rapt concentration. And then she answered obliquely.

"He is prepared to come back to his material life. He will finish the consultations with the medium in a few years and say goodbye then because he is prepared to come back to earth."

"Can he tell you when he comes back and where?"

"He says he has only two or three earth years in consultation with the medium. Then he must go to another, more advanced dimension to prepare for his return, as there will be much need of him."

Jussek's questions came like rapid fire. "How will he be prepared in this extra dimension?"

ters will teach him about his new role in
anity, telling him of his contract with des-
ot work like a medium, but must develop
....nel. He will spend nine and a half months
with a master and the soul on the other side will go
into a state of pregnancy to loosen its consciousness of the
soul and prepare to enter the material body. That is what
he told me."

"But why must he lose this soul consciousness?"

"If he is burdened with all the weight of past lives,
he cannot function as a free individual working out his
karma."

"But he does remember something?"

"The information, the skills, but not the personalities,
and he develops outside these personalities, perfecting
himself until he no longer has to come back, but remains
in the twelfth and highest dimension, a companion of the
Lord."

Jussek and I looked at each other silently and shrugged.
What was there to add?

He now took her forward in time, in search of Clarita,
Pepe, Jallikete and company.

Suddenly, she began babbling in a strange tongue,
nothing we had heard before, not Chinese, Japanese, Russian, Greek, or any of the Romance languages or their
derivations.

She came from a family of nomadic shepherds living
in Nikosia at one time.

At the mention of Nikosia, Jussek smiled. "But of
course, Nikosia is the principal city of Cyprus and it was
under the rule of the Turks for a while. She was speaking Turkish. Isn't that amazing?"

But she was not Turkish herself, and neither was her

112

family. They had moved in and out of countries with roving bands of gypsies.

"There were lots of gypsies," said she, "and we would sit around the campfires at night and keep warm."

I could see Jussek's eyes light up. "If you remember," said he, "Clarita was a gypsy."

He turned back to Maria.

"What was your name?"

She shook her head. It wasn't going to be that easy.

"How old are you?"

She shrugged. "We came from Romany, and lived in Spain and France, near Lyons. It was at the turn of the century."

"The twentieth century?"

"During the revolution, in France."

"Ah, the French Revolution," exclaimed Jussek.

"Do you remember any leaders from the revolution?"

How would this obscure little gypsy know of Robespierre, Danton, Marat, and the rest?

But, surprisingly, she nodded.

"The man I love."

"And who was that?"

"De la Porteur. But he was not a gypsy."

"Was he French?"

"Yes, and he didn't love me because I was a gypsy."

It became obvious she was not talking about the French Revolution, but a period long before that, for this was not a full-scaled revolt but an insurrection of the mob. They had marched through Lyons in the south of France and through Paris, to the very walls of Notre Dame de Paris, the colossus of a cathedral in the middle of the Seine. And they had followed the banner of the demagogue poet François Villon in the rallies for freedom in the fifteenth-century reign of Louis XI. It had been a march of beggars, with the gypsies in the forefront. Her friends must have been legion.

"Do you remember any of the people?" Jussek asked.

Her face became a mask. "There were many."

"Somebody you know now in spirit?" he urged.

She fell into a long silence, then muttered, twisting a little on the couch. "He was a little man, but very powerful, midget-like, a dwarf."

"Can you name him?"

Her eyes remained closed, but her face seemed cast in the glow of a smile. She finally spoke. "Pepe, the hunchback," she said slowly and her voice grew sly and mysterious. "I must be careful how I talk about him. He is a very strong man, not to be fooled with."

"And how did you meet him?" Jussek inquired.

"He does not like me talking about him, for the people did not treat him very well, and he hated during his life. But he has learned better on the other side."

"But who was he?"

She smacked her lips. "He was Quasimodo, the Hunchback of Notre Dame."

There was disappointment in Jussek's voice at mention of this fictional character. "You mean the hunchback in Victor Hugo's novel?"

"Victor Hugo," she explained, "took his character from a real-life Quasimodo, just as François Villon was a real-life poet. But the poet is better known than the bell-ringer, who is known only to a few, while the many know the poet through his poems."

"But what then made the bell-ringer so wise?"

"Being a hunchback, he suffered a lot, and learned from suffering. He saw the people in the Notre Dame, the priests, the bigwigs, everybody, and he saw how they conducted themselves, when they thought nobody was there. For he was considered a nobody, and they paid no attention to him, as if he didn't exist. But he did, and he learned much to compensate for his deformity."

That brought on another interesting point. As I understood the reincarnation concept, physical imperfections were not transmitted from one life to the next, nothing but aptitudes, mental, spiritual and emotional qualities, and certain distinguishing mannerisms. Benjamin Franklin, a believer in reincarnation, had said he would return one day with a new suit enclosing his altered personality.

But Maria had an explanation.

"The astral body, which is the vehicle of the soul, materializes the spirit force, the energy, and this spirit, which is not the soul, but a reflection of it, can manifest itself in any shape that it finds most effective."

"And Quasimodo likes staying a hunchback."

She shook her head. "Not a question of liking. He wants to be recognized as Quasimodo, for then all know who he is. It is his karma to elevate what François Villon called the swine of the earth."

The gypsies had not stayed on in Paris. I suppose that's why they were called gypsies, for they were always moving on. Or was it the other way around? In any case, Quasimodo remained, and they resumed their roving life.

"Were you persecuted, and driven out?" Jussek asked.

"We crossed from France to Spain, and then back again with bands of gypsies, singing and dancing around the campfires."

"What did you do as a gypsy?"

"I read the palms."

Jussek looked over at me again. "Three lives, and three times psychic, each in a different way."

"But that tells us nothing about her guides," I said. He resumed the questioning.

"And after Spain?"

"We went back to Romany." We took this to be Romania, since Romany was the language of the gypsies. "And that's when I die."

"Did you have a sickness, any heart disease?"

"I just fall dead, from natural causes."

Her companions had given her the traditional gypsy funeral.

"They turned my bed around, and began singing and chanting, and they turned the dirt where they buried me eleven times. I saw my own soul leave my body."

"But how do you see when you have no body, no eyes?"

"We can see like you see the insects. You are big, they so small, that they don't even know you are there, unless you interfere with them. But I see far away, with waves of energy. But I missed my very special daughter. In many reincarnations we were close together."

"Can you go back in time and tell me where you saw your daughter again?"

"We were both Christians, but she was my friend then, and not a gypsy."

"When," persisted Jussek, "were you mother and daughter again?"

He was pursuing some thread of thought that eluded me.

"In Siam," she replied, "in the seventeenth century."

"And what was her name?"

She hesitated. "I knew her in many incarnations."

"But what was the name you remember her by?"

She shivered a little.

"When she was a gypsy. I called her Clarita."

Jussek's face was crowned with a smile. "That takes care of Dermetz, Pepe and Clarita," he said. "But it's Rampa I'd like to know more about, he's the most intriguing of her masters."

"Perhaps the master diagnostician," I pointed out with a smile.

"Do you remember the master Rampa?" he asked briskly, now on surer ground.

"In Sikkim," she said, "long, long ago. He was from Tibet."

Sikkim was a tiny principality in the Himalayas, of some 2800 square miles, and 120,000 people, dragooned out of obscurity some years before when a Boston-bred society girl married the local rajah. It bordered on India, Nepal and Tibet, and was not the most accessible place in the world.

Maria was the daughter of a wealthy merchant in Sikkim, and apparently not involved in the mystic until her meeting with Rampa.

"Where did you live in Sikkim?" Jussek asked.

Her answer, in a voice not nearly as slurred as usual, sounded like Bangkok.

"Bangkok, that's in Siam or Thailand," I said.

"She seems to be confused," Jussek agreed.

She repeated what again seemed to be Bangkok.

Jussek had listened closely.

"It's more like Gangtok," he said.

I was ready to concede the confusion. But later, in the atlas, we discovered a Gangtok. It was the chief city of Sikkim.

The uneducated Maria had either swallowed an encyclopedia, or there was a Sikkim in her subconscious past, Jung's collective unconscious, even her reincarnated past—who could say?

Her incarnations, under hypnosis, seemed to have a way of running together, though she kept each properly placed in time, in relation to the people she knew in each of them.

"He taught you many things, is that right?" Jussek asked.

She nodded. "He's still on the other side. He follows me to all the places."

Jussek's medical background pushed forward. "How does he diagnose an illness and know someone is sick?"

"He was Japanese and Chinese before, and studied with the masters in Tibet. He taught me to open my sixth sense, and the third eye, the pineal gland."

"Is that how he does it, with this extra dimension of the mind?"

"In Sikkim, he gave me the esoteric teachings, to develop my faculties for when I returned to earth. And we make an agreement that we work together for the human race."

"You don't cure or diagnose yourself, but work through him?"

She nodded. "We make a compact."

"Did this Rampa have any connection with Dr. Dermatz in any lifetime?"

She shook her head. "Dr. Dermetz was my father, in one lifetime. But you must know," and her voice took on a special urgency, "there is only one life, through many incarnations. It is all the same life, growing, advancing, going back, depending what the person does. So Dr. Dermetz had one life, and I have one life, and he was my father in one growth period."

"Then Rampa was not always Rampa, what else was he?"

"He was a doctor, a Japanese doctor."

"And what was his name?"

I could see that Jussek, his eyes gleaming, anticipated the answer.

"Dr. Jallikete," she said softly.

Jussek gave me a triumphant look, and it was a triumph well deserved, considering the patience and skill required for the extraction.

"You meditated then, and concentrated, with the third eye?"

"To influence the third eye. That is where the psychic power is focused, there and in the solar plexus, developed by meditating to form the kundalini." This was the snakelike coil of energy that Eastern mystics sent spiraling from navel to top of head by disciplined meditation.

"What is this compact you mention?"

"He said that I had to come back. And when the time was ripe, he would use my channel to heal, and to give the answers about life to the people ready for this communication."

"And they are ready now?"

She nodded quickly. "There is great confusion today, and people are seeking new solutions."

"Where did his knowledge come from? Rampa must have been very well known for you to study with him."

"He studied in the Himalyas, in Tibet."

"And why was this such a special place?"

119

"They know the secrets of the oneness of the universe, and they are free from the demoralizing discords of civilization."

"But why the Himalayas?" he persisted. "There are other mountains, the Andes, the Alps, the Rockies."

She paused. "When the floods came, drowning Atlantis and other lands, the Himalayas were the highest mountains, and the masters went there."

At Mae West's, there had been an effort to explore the brooding riddles of existence through Maria. And now that she had tapped an apparently boundless world, Jussek saw this as a signal to proceed with a similar line of questioning.

I really didn't know myself what validity her answers had, but certainly if she were right about so many other things that could be proven, there was little reason to suspect that her source was wrong on abstractions not so easily susceptible to proof.

Jussek was no different from so many of us. In the middle years, so often disillusioning and disenchanting, he wondered how truly different he was from the lowly insects. The ants, bees, even the termites, lived out wonderfully programmed existences as complex as our own at times. Were our lives any more important than theirs in the universal scheme? For we, too, considering this sphere an end-all, sank in time into a dark abyss of oblivion, stirring hardly a ripple on the sea of life.

What happened to the skills we had honed, the love we had given and received, the life struggle, the successes and failures, the joys of mating and the thrill of parenthood? What happened for some to effect the spiritual ascent through meditation and dedication, by which they hoped to reach a plateau of universal understanding and fulfillment? Did it all become as nothing, with the body scattered over the sea or buried in the cold, damp ground?

Jussek didn't think so and neither did I. For nature was too providential to waste anything. The life force, the energy, the spirit, the soul that separated us from the insects and other life, was like the Eastern maya, the mystical substance of Mother Earth, neither created nor destroyed. Like the God force that had spawned us, it was a continuum that in its infinity we could not grasp, just as the insects could not understand the earthquake that swept them away. It was just too big for them to see all at once.

In the face of all the magnitude of life and its mystery, I understood the simplicity of Jussek's next question. No matter how it was phrased, it had to seem trite in the asking.

"Will the master tell us what life is all about? Is there any substance to life after death?"

She shrugged. "The master says that death is the reality. When we die, the physical body is removed, but the astral body survives as the vehicle of the soul and we begin the soul life on a different dimension."

For me, there was still no reality about the soul life. What happened to the simple pleasures in this presumed existence, a hearty breakfast of bacon and eggs with dear ones, the excitement of a football game, a sentimental exchange with a lover, the thrill of skiing or racing a car. Was all this to be considered unreality? I certainly hoped not. To no longer appreciate a good movie, nor enjoy a beautiful poem, or the charms of a lovely woman? Was all this unimportant?

Fortunately, Maria's master shared my sentiments.

"Death prepares you for life," said she. "The soul

121

develops more in the other dimensions, and as you advance, you do more with yourself in the next life."

But, of course, advancement was not always general, for certainly the anti-Christs Hitler and Stalin were hardly improvements over Attila the Hun or Tamerlane.

"The choices you make on earth determine the dimension of the soul. And the higher the dimension from which you start the soul life, the greater the advancement." She paused. "But it could become a lower dimension, too, if Christ's word is not followed." And that of course was to love one another, believe in life everlasting, putting love for God above all things.

As a scientist, and pragmatist, Jussek strove for a realistic framework for even the soul.

"Does the soul," he asked, "have a certain location? Are they all in one place, or in different places? Are they close to their families, for instance?"

"No," said Maria, "it is a different environment. No family attachments. The highest master, Jesus, told the Sadducees that there was no marriage in heaven and all were like the angels. Otherwise, there would be large families from previous lives."

"Does the soul know when it has to enter the body again?"

"The more evolving they have to do, the sooner they come back."

"But how do they find the body?"

"They have universal laws on the other side, and they select the body as they would a house."

"But it may be the wrong house."

"Not if they follow the principles of reincarnation. That is what the Master Rampa says."

"He is talking through you?"

Her head nodded. "The soul is not in the embryo of the mother, but enters only when the baby is born."

Jussek and I exchanged quick glances. For what did this do to the Catholic Church concept that the embryo was a living soul? As a Catholic, opposing birth control, Maria would have been mortified that she was a channel for such heresy. Jussek, too, was a Catholic, and the reply had given him something to think about.

"Who determines this?" he asked.

"The same God who determines the laws of Creation with his supreme intelligence. To be happy we must harmonize with these laws."

"But how can we be sure what they are?"

"By coming back, and by using the psychic force, the intuition."

"And how do we do this?"

"With the soul energy, the astral body, which can investigate and explore all other astral bodies."

"And where does all this soul energy come from?"

"From God," she replied simply.

"And if we tune into this universal energy, then are we in a state of spiritual fulfillment, or samadhi?"

"Right," said Master Rampa.

Jussek now took the full plunge. Like myself, as a boy, he had constantly asked his elders about this God he was forever being whipped with. And so with a tingle of anticipation, I greeted the question.

"What is God?"

"The five senses," she replied, "have natural limitations to understand what is God. We try to think of him as a physical body, but God is the Universal Intelligence, the Supreme Energy, never created, never changed, but has always been. He is in every solar system, and every galaxy, for he is the infinite, the word and the way. He is the first cause of everything. He is that Jehovah who told Moses, 'I am that I am.'"

Out of this God-head or God-spirit came the universal energy, with which the individual energy merged to gain the source of all healing and creative power. The spirit, tangibly, was a vibration flowing out of the soul, just as the rain fell from a cloud, or a thought burst from the brain.

"My master declares the spirit is in everything, in animals, plants, the atmosphere. But the soul is a gift of God, only to people, and that is why we say that man is created in God's image. God does not have a body like a man, with arms, legs, head, torso, but in man's soul is a reflection of God's perfection. The closer we are to this perfection, the more Godlike we are."

Jussek was still not satisfied.

"Was God here forever, or did he start with the beginning of this world?"

I couldn't help wondering how Master Rampa would get out of this one.

"Before the material planet was the invisible planet. The vibration was made ready for it."

"Would you describe God as a form of vibration?"

She answered the question with one of her own. "Can you see the vibration of electricity in the wires that result in light?"

It was difficult, as Maria had said, for finite man to comprehend the infinite God. We had no intellectual frame of reference to work with. There would have to be a moment of clear intuition, a vision such as St. Paul experienced on the road to Damascus, or perhaps the unifying oneness of samadhi known by a handful of

Eastern masters, or Jesus on the Cross, dying to the Resurrection and life everlasting. The answer p. lay in meditation, tuning into ourselves and the universe around us to know that we were one. And in the function of that oneness, not in some manmade definition, lay the answer that was God.

"No words," said Maria, "can explain who is God."

Dauntlessly, Jussek pursued the thread of his inquiry. "Does God know everything that is going on in this world and in every one of us?"

Nothing could faze the hypnotized figure. "God is suspended in the universe, looking into everything that is happening, inside and outside. Like the Bible says, He marks the fall of the smallest sparrow."

"If we want to be close to Him," Jussek persisted, "what do we have to do?"

I thought I saw the ghost of a smile on Maria's lips.

"Obey his laws."

"How do you recognize these laws?"

"By understanding ourselves. In our own physical bodies we have the conscious mind, which we deliberately control, and then the subconscious and the unconscious minds, which work in tune with God's law. The digestion, breathing, the circulation, sight, tastes and hearing, these are all unconscious, all ordained by the higher law. The subconscious, like the unconscious, is automatic, and rules the intuition. By taking care of the body, we fulfill the law of the unconscious, improving the health. By meditation, thinking spiritually, improving the mind, we fulfill the law of the subconscious. And this also improves the unconscious functions, and brings greater health and happiness."

Maria's law appeared to downgrade the conscious mind,

the intellect, the darling of the savants and the intellectuals.

"This is the limited mind," she explained, "it only sees before its nose."

I was ready to pit Maria's gift against the narrow intellectualism of the laboratory, and give serious thought to her information, even when it went against the grain of traditional knowledge. I could not say for sure she was right, but neither could I say she was wrong. And, in all candor, neither could anybody else.

The enigma of life on other planets, reflected in the growing preoccupation with Unidentified Flying Objects (UFO's) could not be readily clarified by the intellectual mind. But Maria was tuned into the universal subconscious of her spirit guides. And so Jussek asked a question which attained new reality with our landing on the moon.

"Is there life on other planets?"

She did not hesitate.

"God created only one planet where there are living people as we know them. But the master says someday we meet people of another intelligence, and a different environment, but not in our constellations."

As I understood the answer, there was other life, but not in our solar system.

"Is this life more advanced?" Jussek asked.

"They are more spiritual. This planet is like a school, a learning place. Here we suffer and grow."

"Are we happier in the physical body or in the spirit, the soul body?"

"Outside the body, we find a peace of mind that is completely different. Here, we have peace for just a little time, then problems again."

"Is there a heaven and hell?"

"The master says this is only in the mind."

"But," said Catholic-bred Jussek, "doesn't the Catholic Church teach a heaven and hell?"

And the Catholic-bred Maria replied, "The master says it is mostly symbology."

"When Christ speaks about the demons, is that a state of mind, too?"

"He was making a parable of it, what the individual creates in mind and body."

The symbology of the Book of Revelations had intrigued Jussek, as it had countless others, and he inquired about the significance of the seven seals.

"These," she said, "are the seven chakras of the body, the seven sacred glands—pineal, pituitary, thyroid, adrenals, thalamus, solar plexus and the gonads. We have a universe inside our body. The solar plexus is like the sun, radiating the kundalini to the head through perfect concentration."

"And when you concentrate like this," asked the doctor, "what changes take place in the cells?"

"In perfection concentration, you achieve a state of meditation, which stimulates the pineal and suprarenal glands, and opens the brain like the petals of a flower."

As happened so often, I tired quickly during the sessions, my own energy apparently drained by the medium.

Nevertheless, curiosity drove me. "What will the people on that other galaxy be like when we finally make a landing?"

Jussek smiled grimly, without passing on the question. "How do you know they won't land first or"—his voice pregnant with thought—"or that they aren't already here?"

127

Maria remained still, breathing evenly, for under hypnosis she responded only to the one who had put her under.

"Then why haven't we seen them?" I asked.

"She said they were of a different intelligence and environment. They may even make themselves invisible, pure energy forces which materialize at will."

I scoffed, "Then why haven't they let us know?"

"Perhaps they have."

"Come now, how?"

"The flying saucers."

"They may exist only in the minds of the viewers."

"That may be what she is telling us."

I suddenly realized what he meant. It was like seeing an apparition. Only he could see it, for whom it had meaning.

"But someday," said Jussek, "they may have something to tell all of us."

Some thought that through the flying saucers we were being warned of a worldwide holocaust, on the ruins of which the Prince of Peace would return to bring the salvation squandered for two thousand years.

Jussek had turned back to Maria. "Is the Messiah returning to preach his gospel?" he asked.

She shook her head. "Jesus Christ will not come in person, but will send the Holy Ghost, man's spirit in God, and God's spirit in man. This is the bond between God and the soul of man, and the vehicle is the Paraclete, the astral body."

"Then how will we recognize him?"

"He will come as a Christ consciousness. And then we will know that He has rejoined the infinite of which He was a part to begin with."

"And of what does this Christ consciousness consist?"

Her voice came slowly, but forcefully, and had I not known she was under hypnosis, I would have felt that she was making a conscious plea for understanding.

"It is fourfold. Recognition of God in man, and man in God, purging of the vessel of the body through meditation and love; communication through the individual made more susceptible to the emanations of God, and unification with the central source of all power, the divine Father beloved of Jesus."

I could see that Jussek was clearly impressed.

"I tell you," he said, "she is some kind of wonder."

Having been released from her hypnotic trance, Maria yawned and sat up.

"Did I say anything?" she asked.

7

Walking
My Baby
Back Home

"WHY," I ASKED, "did you go to Maria Moreno?" Dottie Colbert's eyebrows came up. "Why? Because
I wanted to talk to Harry Richman, that's why."

I vaguely remembered Harry Richman as the Broadway song and dance man, who had played the piano
for Mae West and the Dolly Sisters, and run his own
nightclubs for a while.

"He was the entertainer's entertainer," Dorothy elaborated, "and the dearest man who ever lived."

"What made you so sure," I asked, "that he would
be around?"

"We had been very close," she said, "and after his death
I constantly felt his presence around me."

As Dorothy Harmony, she had been the beautiful
blond dancer in Richman's nightclub act, and after she
married actor Robert Colbert, the star of television's *The
Young and the Restless*, Harry virtually adopted the
family and made them his heirs. And so it was no wonder
she felt close to him. But as I looked around the Colbert
beach house in California, I couldn't help but see why

Dottie had experienced his presence. His memorabilia were all over the place. There was the famous Harry Richman piano, the famous walking cane with which he strutted across the floor, singing one of his own famous compositions, *Walking My Baby Back Home*. And the famous straw hat, which he doffed so debonairly. There were cartons crammed with his hundreds of songs, diaries, pictures, with and without the glamor girls that chased after him, and yellowed newspaper clippings, telling the front-page story of his pioneering two-way flight across the Atlantic with pilot Dick Merrill shortly after Lindbergh's solo flight from New York to Paris.

The stack of material was formidable. "You could almost write a book," I said.

Dorothy looked pensive. "That's what Harry said."

"You mean before he died?"

"No, while I was at Maria Moreno's."

"Did he tell you how to write it?" I asked half seriously.

"Everything but," she said. She looked helplessly at the clutter of papers. "I wish I knew how to begin."

I laughed. "Why not try the original source?"

"That's an idea," she said. "But it's so difficult to get an appointment with Maria. She's either traveling around somewhere or booked up for weeks."

"Maybe you can tune him in directly because of your psychic closeness."

Dorothy's blue eyes snapped. "Stop putting me on. I'm not a blooming idiot. I did and do feel this intangible closeness to Harry. The night my mother died, on November 4, two years to the day after his own death, in the midst of my grief, I felt I had a message from Harry."

"What kind of a message?"

She looked up at the likeness of Harry Richman on the wall. "For no good reason, nobody was near it, that picture fell off the wall."

I looked at her doubtfully. "What does that mean?"

"He may have been trying to tell me something. After all, I'm not a psychic, I don't have channels he could tune into."

"But what does a falling picture signify?"

"Just thinking of him, being near and responsive, remembering how he had been a father to me, so warm, so kind and so gentle, was enough to lighten my mood."

We had been chatting together in her comfortable living room, looking out on the rolling Pacific, interrupted occasionally by her six-year-old son, home from school with a cold, and by her husband, a big, attractive, graying man in his forties, who seemed intrigued by the recording of the sitting that Dottie had promised to play back for me.

She fiddled around with the tape recorder. "Of course, the tape doesn't do the sitting justice," she said. "It was a beautiful, exciting experience." She turned to her actor husband. "You could use that Maria in your show, she's about as dramatic as anybody I've ever seen."

She had gone to her appointment with actress Mara Corday, who had been married to a television star, Richard Long, and was still mourning the personable actor's untimely death at forty-seven. "Mara was just as curious about Richard coming through as I was about Harry, so we went together, taking our tape recorders, and wondering if we weren't being a little ludicrous."

She had never visited a psychic before, so she had no idea of what to expect. She got no reassurance from Mara, who was also up in the air over the prospect of a possible message from beyond the veil. As the two ladies from the world of glamor and sophistication got the first glimpse of the short, stout peasant woman with the broad face, their earlier misgivings were confirmed. But Maria gave them little time to ponder or retreat. Her eyes flicked from one to the other, and she said, bluntly, "I give separate consultations."

Sitting in a straight-backed chair, opposite Dottie, who didn't know what to expect next, she was soon in trance. Dottie marveled as her voice, manner, expression, and even her body underwent a drastic change.

Dottie had not had long to wait. "Who is Harry?" she asked. She reached out a hand as if to touch him. The movement stopped suddenly as if it had reached its mark. Her face relaxed in a smile for the first time. "He has a good sense of humor," she said, apparently savoring whatever it was she was hearing.

"The best," said Dottie, "there was nobody with his feeling of fun. That's why people loved him."

She broke off the chronicle and turned to me. "He was the favorite of singer Al Jolson, who he lived with at one time; Texas Guinan, Walter Winchell, Ed Sullivan, Ruth Etting, and all the Broadway and Hollywood personalities of the thirties and forties. While other people jammed their shows, the celebrities lined up for Harry's."

Maria had wasted little time in identifying whoever it was that was making her smile.

"He was a very popular singer and dancer," she said. "And he worked with Mae West, not so?"

Dottie's eyes had bugged. She had no doubt that Harry was coming through. As much as she cherished Harry's name, she knew that he was more or less a forgotten relic in the seventies. Moreover, how would Maria even

134

have begun to know that there was any connection between them? They did not even have any mutual acquaintances.

Maria's dark brows knit together.

"He tells me he helped you with your career."

"I worked with him for years," Dottie responded. "And loved it."

"He did not forget you," said she. "He left a will made out for you."

"He left me and my husband everything he had."

Harry was apparently concerned about the house in Santa Monica that he had left the Colberts. "When you rent out, he says, it is very important that you get a lease. Otherwise, you may lose by it."

Dottie laughed as she thought about it. "He was so right. I've had so much trouble with tenants, and these wouldn't sign a lease."

He had also left them considerable desert land in Nevada. "Your husband and you were named equally in the will," Maria said, "and he is concerned now about the desert property he gave you. He wants you to do well with it. He loves you both."

Dottie's eyes had teared then, and they grew moist now in recollection. "He was more than a father to me. He worried about me all the time, and about Bob as well, and he adored the two children."

Harry's encore via Maria included Bob Colbert as well.

"Tell Bob to stop smoking. Otherwise he will become ill. You must throw away his cigarettes." Harry apparently showed the omniscience of so many of the spirits coming through Maria. "He will have big throat problems down to his esophagus," said she. "He has a hernia there."

This was indeed bad news for any actor who had lines. But it was news to Dottie, for Bob had never complained. "Not that I know of," she replied cheerfully.

"If he feels bad," said Maria, "he must go to the doctor immediately."

Bob was crossing through the room at this time, husky, tanned, and smiling, looking as fit as anybody I had ever seen. "He looks fine to me," said I with the practiced eye of a writer.

"That's what you think," Dottie rejoined. "One week after the sitting Bob got a test, an upper G.I., and found out that he indeed had a hiatal hernia of the esophagus."

"And so what did they do, operate?"

"Horrors, no," said Dottie, "but he gave up smoking, thank God, and now he sleeps with the pillows propped a certain way to favor his throat."

Suddenly, Maria had begun groaning, and agonized moans issued from her throat. She clutched herself, as she cried, "Oh, my head, oh the pain in my arm."

"Before my very eyes," Dottie turned to me, "she simulated the very stroke that Harry had suffered. It was frightening in its vividness."

Maria sat transfixed, as if paralyzed, just as Harry had been the last months of his life, before succumbing to cancer at age seventy-seven, two and a half years before. Dottie relived that nightmare once more. It had been shattering to see this vital, magnetic figure reduced to the helplessness of the wheelchair. Until this last mortal illness, even after a heart attack in 1964, he had been gay and indomitable, continuing to get around in public and mixing with people.

"He has a powerful vibration," said Maria, and Dottie couldn't help but smile her agreement.

"Nothing curtailed his interest in people," she recalled. "We took him to the Santa Monica pier one evening for dinner, and he was fascinated by the pretty young hostess. He got to talking to her, and learned that her husband was sitting at another table and invited him over. They got to chatting and Harry said, 'You and your wife make a lovely young couple.' The man was dark, slender and remarkably fit looking, and his wife was a bubbly twenty-seven. But the husband looked at Harry, who was then well over seventy, and said, 'I'll bet you, Mister Richman, I'm older than you are.' " His wife reached over and gave him an affectionate kiss.

Harry Richman looked at him incredulously, and laughed. "Are you kidding? I have neckties older than you."

"Whereupon the man replied, with a tender glance for his wife, 'I am seventy-seven years old.' "

"After a long pause, Harry said, 'Prove it.' You should have seen his face when the husband showed him his driver's license. Seventy-seven it was."

Harry drew back and gave the man a long look. "Tell me, how do you do it?"

"Yoga," said the man, flexing his arms, and stretching in his chair, "yoga twice a day."

Several days later, Dottie was preparing lunch for Harry at his place and noticed his refrigerator crowded with containers of yogurt, a substance with the texture and taste of sour cream.

"What are you doing with all this stuff?" she asked.

"Eating it," he said, with a wry face. "I thought it might do for me what it did for that other old guy."

Dottie laughed so hard that she had to sit down.

"Yoga, not yogurt," she cried. "It's an Indian system of

exercise for body and mind."

"Thank God," Harry said, "I couldn't stand another mouthful."

After telling this story, Dottie looked at me with a suspicion of moisture in her eyes and said with a catch in her voice, "How can you keep a man like that dead? He's got to be alive."

Everybody that I had seen dead had looked very, very dead.

"I know that he was there, in Maria's room, with me," Dorothy said breathlessly. She put on the tape recorder to stress her point, and I could hear Maria saying in her sonorous voice, "He tells me that you must put things together and do his life story. 'Tell her to do it,' he says, 'before they forget me.' You must do this book, as he left you all his papers and documents, with his letters and writeups, so that you could make a beginning."

Dottie, with her active mind, quickly jumped ahead of the book.

"If we did a movie," she said, "who would play the part?"

Maria's voice almost broke with a laugh. "He is laughing, and he says, 'Don't take Jimmy Durante. Look for some handsome man to play the part. That is your job.'"

Comedian Jimmy (Schnozzola) Durante had been an old friend of Richman's, and Durante's comic appearance in the role had long been a running joke between them.

Cami, Dottie's nine-year-old daughter, had come in to practice on the piano, which had been Harry's gift, but her mother waved her off for a few minutes. Looking around again, I admired the collection of canes, and singled out one which looked like a gnarled shillelagh.

"The great Scottish comedian Harry Lauder gave that to his friend Harry Richman as a token of his esteem."

Her eyes were glistening again, and she rubbed her hand over a blue sapphire ring she was wearing.

"That's a beautiful ring," I said.

"It's more than that, it's a keepsake." She looked at it wistfully. "Harry gave it to me, and Maria said that Harry was blessing it, and told her that when I had problems I should put it on, and I would be helped."

She acknowledged my doubting glance.

"I suppose he intended it as a signal," she said.

Astonishingly, Harry had known that she was not wearing the ring at the sitting.

"Harry wants to know," Maria had said, "where his ring is."

"In my purse," Dottie replied.

"He wants you to put it on your right hand." She complied, with her hand trembling the least bit. "All right, you now have it on, now put your right hand straight out in front of you. He is blessing the ring, so if you have problems or need good luck in anything important in your life, remember to put the ring on."

It was through Clarita that Maria was in contact with the energy force representing itself as Harry Richman. And he seemed in no hurry to depart, dropping a few philosophical pearls as well as personal advice.

"He was intetrested in people of all faiths," Maria said. "It didn't matter to him what religion anybody was, and it still doesn't."

"He was almost as Christian as he was Jewish," Dottie observed. "He frequently went to Mass and had a string of rosary beads which Cardinal Spellman had given him after his trans-Atlantic flights with Dick Merrill. When he lay dying, he was attended by two priest friends. He was my daughter's godfather. And on his grave, we put the inscription: Beloved brother, godfather, friend.'"

Maria mulled over this for a few moments, then said as if she had just been given the word, "He was born of Russian Jewish parents. He talks about the Russian people quite a bit. He is a beautiful soul."

Maria now closed her eyes and gave a little shudder. "He didn't want to be buried in the ground," she said. "He desired a crypt."

"True," said Dottie, "and so we got a surface crypt for him. I'm glad he knows about it."

More fortunate than some spirit entities, the singer was in communication with friendly spirits on the other side.

"You know Al Jolson," said Maria, referring to the celebrated blackfaced jazz singer.

"They lived together for a while," Dottie replied.

Maria's head nodded. "They're singing together right now. I can hear their beautiful voices."

Jack Benny, another old friend, was there, too. He had recently joined them, and they were communing together in this Broadway Valhalla, where the élite apparently came to meet.

But it was not like it was here. "The earth mind thinks in terms of a circle of friends, but there they communicate from what we would think of as a distance."

Looking at her ring, Dottie now recalled another sign she had received not long before.

"Ask Harry," she said, "if he visited my house in November after my mother died?"

Maria nodded wisely. "He says he will give you many signs from time to time." She suddenly sat up at attention. "Lean forward," she whispered, "and touch his hand. Don't be afraid. He is holding it out for you."

Dottie, as if hypnotized, tentatively extended her hand, and then thrilled as she felt her hand taken warmly and pressed, just as Harry had often done in a moment of affection.

This recollection was too much for Dottie. She turned off the tape recorder and faced me with dewy eyes. "I don't know how I can describe the feeling," she said, "but the hand on mine, clasping it warmly, felt just like Harry's hand, and I could sense the love and affection in his touch."

The potent force of suggestion, the subtle hypnotic effect of the sitting with a powerful medium, Dottie's own impressionability and the wish to believe could have all been factors in Dottie's susceptibility.

She refused to be put down. "I felt it, I really did," she maintained. "And I hadn't expected to. It was crazy, and I'm not a kook. Moreover, it was in broad daylight, 1:30 P.M., and all I had was a cup of coffee."

Harry was never one to linger after he had made his point. Before anybody could say Harry Richman, he was gone, but not without a parting message.

"He says love each other, and believe in God and religion."

There was certainly nothing wrong with that. And for Dottie, a practicing Catholic, it was certainly on the beam.

I couldn't help but wonder a bit at this close attachment between Dottie and a considerably older man which obviously carried to the grave and beyond. Dorothy had wondered, too, and Maria, in touch with her spirit guide Clarita, had a very simple explanation.

"You were not soul mates, but in a past life he was your father, and your subconscious remembers when you met, though the conscious mind has no recall of this.

"Keep close to this beautiful soul," she went on, "and you have good things to remember for the rest of your life. You must understand that life here is so short, that your big mission in the future is to believe on the other side. Have assurance that this beautiful soul comes to visit you very often."

I thought about this for a while. "If you believe all this," I said, "then you must get on with the book that Maria says Harry wants. And you could very well be guided in this."

I mentioned the time a medium had called me at one in the morning to tell me that Edgar Cayce had come to her, and expressed gratification that I was doing a book on him, a book I had discussed for the first time with my editor only that afternoon. "He will help you as you are writing it," she had told me. Call it suggestibility, or what you will, but I finished *The Sleeping Prophet* in three weeks, and watched it promptly climb to the top of the bestseller lists.

"But I'm not a writer," Dorothy said.

"You will find a way."

Harry had certainly dominated the scene. I wondered why there had been no communication from Dottie's own natural parents, for whom she professed a special close-ness.

"But there was," she protested. "I just got caught up with Harry because I had felt his presence, and wondered what he wanted me to do with all the material he had left me."

Her father, William—known as Charlie for some rea-son—and her mother, Anna, had both appeared through Maria, but not at the same time.

Anna's manifestation had certainly been dramatic.

"Smell the beautiful perfume she sends you," said Maria.

At this, I looked at Dottie inquiringly, trying to keep any suggestion of irony out of my voice. "Where could it possibly come from?"

She nodded vehemently. "I may be going batty," she said, "but there was a sudden aroma in the room and it smelled like gardenias. It was my favorite scent."

With Paula Petrie, and Marilyn Monroe, it had been carnations, and now it was gardenias, a flower which had always suggested the cloying scent of funerals to me.

I supposed if the spirits could manifest themselves in apparitions and the like, there was no reason why they couldn't draw on the same principle of energy in nature, and reproduce the biogenetic factors that resulted in this apparent physical phenomenon.

While the scent was still fresh in the room, her father had chosen to pass through. He had not had much to say at first, and this perhaps was in character. It was enough for Dottie that he turned up, and she presumed that he was in the same sphere as Harry and her mother.

"Your father is here," said Maria, "he knows that you're sensitive and have had a lot of disturbance in your life recently. You must take care not to have a nervous condition."

At this pause in the reply, I looked at Dottie questioningly. She seemed very normal, blonde and beautiful, to me, with a ready smile or laugh on her lips.

"I had quite a time," she said. "Mother died, and Harry died, and Father died, and it just seemed like one thing after another. I missed them terribly, and used to sit and cry a lot. But things seem better now, since the sitting with Maria. I am calmer and feel closer to them all."

"They are concerned for you. This is what they are telling me," Maria had concluded. "They will protect you always."

It had been an unforgettable experience for Dottie. When she came out of the small room, where she had been closeted with Maria, she looked at her friend, Mara, and let out a deep breath. "Amazing," she said, "absolutely amazing."

Mara had been waiting expectantly. Her husband Richard Long had died a short time before, and wherever she looked at home, there was some remembrance of him. She had many problems on her mind, settling the estate, the children deprived of a father they loved, and what to do with herself. But mostly she wondered about Richard. She had been a well-known actress herself in the fifties and sixties, but had retired from the screen after her marriage to the successful television performer. Richard was that unusual Hollywood phenomenon, an actor who could work whenever he wanted to. He had been in many TV series, including Barbara Stanwyck's "Big Valley," but turned down more roles than he accepted. He seemed to get very little zest out of living.

It had been Mara's only marriage, but Long had been married previously to actress Susan Ball, who had died of bone cancer. Her early death may have made him morose. He had died fairly young himself, at forty-seven, of heart failure.

"He seemed to have a death wish," Mara recalled, "and yet he didn't believe in life after death. He would say, 'When you're dead, you're dead.' "

But Mara, religiously oriented, believed there was more 'twixt heaven and earth than man realized. "I just wanted to know if Richard was alive and comfortable on the other side, and if the transition had been easy for him, since he didn't have the assurance of knowing there was something after death." She had been impressed by the sitting beyond anything she could have expected. The tape from Maria's seance had come almost to personify Richard for her. When it was temporarily mislaid, she had gone into a panic, for it represented a communication that had become very meaningful and dear to her. Maria and her guides had apparently tuned in perfectly. In every word or expression, in outlook and demeanor, he was the same plain-spoken, often abrupt and dogmatic man who had helped make their marriage a stormy if loving one.

As usual, from the outset, Maria had picked up on the name of the desired person. "She hooked onto Richard right away," Mara recalled, and Maria smiled as she said, "You thought of leaving him?"

"A hundred times," laughed Mara. "We were always battling about something or other."

Maria frowned as if listening to two voices. "Yes," she nodded agreement with Mara. "He is angry even now, and I hear him say in an exasperated tone, 'What do I care about clothes?'"

Mara laughed, in spite of the seriousness of the occasion. "That is just like Richard," she said, "for I had been wondering what to do about his wardrobe. He recently had twelve suits given to him that he wore during a recent picture. But, typically, he practically lived in a pair of comfortable old corduroy trousers."

As with other visitations, there was a desire on the part of Maria—or the spirit—for the sitter to know that it was indeed his dear, departed on the other end of the line. And Richard, apparently, made sure of this.

"He says to tell you that he is glad that the money from the Veterans Administration was finally signed over to you."

Mara's surprise was plain. "That was pretty much a family matter," she said, "and it was some time before one member of Richard's family signed the necessary papers over to me. Richard," she added, proudly, "was an Army sharpshooter, but could never kill anything."

"You still keep his golf bags," he says.

"Yes, in the bedroom."

"He has a little scar near one eye."

"Barely visible," agreed Mara.

As in life, the ridiculous and sublime were often not very far apart. The conversation jumped about aimlessly, without any seeming pattern. The medium now reviewed the actor's final agony in the days before a death he frankly welcomed. Life was not that joyous or meaningful for him. He was not so much complaining, as inventorying the last days, so she would know that death was virtually a blessing. "He speaks of a bad back," said Maria, "the kidneys suddenly did not work, and the artery in the left ventricle of the heart did not function properly."

"That all happened," said Mara.

"His eye bothered him just before the end."

"Yes, he had scratched the cornea and it was very painful."

Maria continued with the inventory. A chronically bad back had affected his leg. He suffered from arterial sclerosis and had been told he had three years to live.

Who else but Richard would have known his own symptoms so well?

Mara's dark face sharpened in wonder.

"That's exactly true," said she.

Maria described his dying in detail. "He had to sleep in a semireclining position the last three years of his life, with an oxygen inhalator nearby because of the fluid in his lungs." Her voice came in rasping gasps. "He could hardly breathe," said she, simulating his final agony. "But he never complained, joking until the end."

"Yes," said Mara, "he was a gallant man. He turned to me just before he died, and said with a smile, 'The show is about over.'"

From the last agonizing days, it was not much of a jump to death and the funeral. "He liked what you did," said Maria, "throwing his ashes over the Pacific."

With cremation, she added, the entity that comprised the soul and spirit apparently did not stay earthbound for any length of time. "Once cremated, the soul is free, not so much attached to the earth as when it is buried."

"Yes, he wanted to be cremated," Mara said. He had been meticulous about every detail. "In Richard's will he planned his entire funeral right down to a wake at the Colbert home. He wanted to buy his friends a drink. And over one hundred people showed up."

The actor had not been afraid to die. His philosophy was simple, if somewhat sophisticated. He believed that we were all here for a little visit, and that we might as well make this as pleasant as possible, taking whatever pleasure we could on the way. And with death, the trip ended in the bliss of oblivion.

Believing in God's will and rebirth, Mara had been concerned that Richard might be in for a rude awakening.

"Did he have a good transition?" she asked.

Maria had her head cocked in that familiar tilt. "He

147

says his transition was like passing into a deep coma, floating in space, marvelously happy, with peace of mind and no pain. His soul is now distant from his body."

His body was of course scattered over the sea, but before deciding on cremation he had considered a burial plot decorated brightly with flowers.

"He loves flowers," said Maria, "pansies."

"They were the only flowers he liked," Maria concurred.

She fidgeted with her hands for a moment, hesitating over a personal question, but not wanting to appear selfishly oriented on a momentous occasion. But the practical woman finally won out.

"Does he have any message for me?" she asked. "I really don't know which way to turn at times."

Richard was apparently in a helpful mood.

"Don't worry so much," he says. "You are too nervous. And don't cry because you lose energy this way and make yourself sick."

"He says that when you cry, it makes him cry, too."

On hearing this, she promised to dry her tears immediately.

"Don't mourn for me," the voice said, "but live your own life. Be realistic. In time, you will find a good man to take care of you."

Mara shook her head in disbelief. "I'll take care of myself."

"You don't have plans, but when the children grow up, you'll be ready to make your own life. He knows that."

She made a little face. "No, thanks, Richard was enough to last me the rest of my life."

"And he wants that you should go back to work, and

keep your mind occupied. You will be successful."

Mara was dubious about resuming her career after so many years.

"Who would want me?" she asked.

But Richard was encouraging. "The doors will open."

And so she called a Hollywood agent, Alex Brewis, and told him she wanted to get back into pictures.

Richard seemed to have called the turn. Almost immediately, she was hired for a stint on the "Joe Forrester" television series, with other shows in prospect, and people were made aware of her without any effort on her part.

She had been listening to the Johnny Carson talk show, when Don Rickles twitted the television comedian about the ruggedness of his wartime service. Carson laughingly rejoined, "I lay there in my bunk and looked at pinup pictures of Mara Corday."

All of a sudden, Mara realized with a surge of new hope that she was not dead, professionally. Out there somewhere, there was interest in her, as Richard had suggested. It was great for her morale.

There was more practical advice.

"Richard says not to sell the house right away, keep it until you can calmly decide what you want to do. Make sure that everything about the house is legal, and be careful about his insurance money."

It sounded so much like Richard that Mara couldn't help but laugh. "He never felt that I could do anything right."

Richard was also concerned about future California earthquakes and their effect on his family. "He's worried about a landslide destroying the retaining wall back of the house, and causing cracks in the walls and floors. Remember the last time, he says."

Mara nodded thoughtfully. "We did have a slide a few years before in which the hill behind us tumbled into our backyard."

"Eventually, you will sell the Encino house, but paint it first," he says, "and don't buy a two-story house and keep away from the hills. But don't panic. You are being protected, and you will find a good buyer."

I couldn't help but wonder whether the buyer would also be protected, but it was obviously too late to ask.

If anything, Richard showed more concern in limbo than he had in life.

"Was there trouble with the gardener?" he asked.

"I just got rid of him," Mara replied.

"He says to watch out for a leak in the swimming pool."

And sure enough, on investigation, Mara located the leak and had it repaired, cutting down appreciably on her water bill.

How wonderful for a widow caught up in a tangle of unaccustomed problems to have a husband counsel her from beyond the grave.

He was presently concerned about her health. "Drink more water, he says, living off it like a plant. And take papaya with it for your skin."

As a purifier, water and papaya juice could only be helpful.

Richard had died but six months before, and his spirit, invoked by Maria, still seemed entangled with the mundane.

"He remembers when the two of you went to London together, and enjoyed things."

Mara nodded. "Yes, Richard made a movie there."

"And how he wants you to go to Chicago for a family

affair, is that not so?"

Mara's eyes widened. "Yes, there's a wedding, and I have been thinking of flying to Chicago."

In eighteen years of marriage, the Longs had quarreled constantly, their intense feeling for one another causing these eruptions. But this same love had also kept them together, when it appeared that a separation or divorce would have been preferable. She had wondered often how they had managed together all those years.

"Could we have been soul mates?" she now asked, soul mates being karmically disposed to one life after another together, working out their cycle of problems.

Maria didn't answer directly. "There is no such thing as coincidence," she said after a while. "You were too close to each other in a previous life, and the problem of that life carried over. You quarreled constantly, for you were very jealous."

"In this life or the last?" asked Mara.

"In both," said Maria. "This is a consequence of previous lives. You were close friends, but you fought a lot." And since the problem had not been resolved karmically, the lesson never learned, they would have to work it out in some future experience. "Richard," she added, "is not jealous, not where he is."

Mara didn't look particularly happy.

"I must be a very hard learner," she said with a grimace.

But if Maria were correct, Mara would have all of eternity to relive her mistakes with Richard Long. They would never be parted. All this she had felt intuitively, and now came the reassurance she had been looking for.

"You will not be separated for long, since you are soul mates."

Maria's eyebrows came together in the familiar frown. "You were divorcing, right?"

"I tried, but I couldn't. Some sort of magnet seemed to keep us together." She laughed uncertainly. "It had to be something I had little control over. During the first year of marriage, I left him eleven times, and in the second year ten times. I filed for divorce four different times." She sighed. "But there was something I didn't understand that constantly drew me back."

If the spirit that was Richard was in the room, it could hardly have heard this unmoved.

"Have you forgiven him? He wants to know."

Her eyes misted over. "Tell him yes. Does he know if we'll meet again somewhere, sometime?"

The head bobbed quickly. "Yes."

"Will he come back?"

"Yes."

Mara's head dropped, and she was in a world of her own for a few moments, until roused by a sudden cry from Maria. The medium seemed almost startled herself. "He was standing close to me," said she, "and at first I thought he had gone away. But then he hit my guide, Clarita, on the arm. It was an expression of his energy, just to let us know he had been listening."

She got back to the message.

"He also wants me to tell you," said Maria, "that he is always sober where he is now."

"Thank God," murmured Mara.

Listening, it was difficult at times to tell whether the information was coming through Maria or her guides. But the medium explained that she was only the relay point. And when Richard was telling her something, that meant he was merely putting out the thought, sending out a vibration, and Clarita was bringing it in through the medium. So, in effect, the message could be said to be channeled through Maria, and Clarita and the rest of the guides were but super-catalysts.

But Mara, like others, was primarily concerned with the authenticity of the source—in this case presumably Richard. The insight into her life, the continuing involvement with her future, and the correctness of details, previously unknown or known only to an intimate few, were enough to make her seriously consider the existence of her late husband in spirit. Above all, Maria seemed to have captured and transmitted the mordant, ironic personality of her husband. It almost made it seem that he was actually in the room, talking, and so when Maria mentioned the physical contact with the guide Clarita, Mara was not inclined to dismiss this out of hand.

The spirit of Richard, so it seemed to Maria, was truly trying to make amends for the past. He was concerned, so said Maria, not only about his wife, but the three children, particularly eighteen-year-old Carey.

"Carey," said his mother with a shrug, "has the same problems most teenage boys have today."

"The younger boy," said Maria, "has foot trouble. He must wear arch supports."

Mara found herself nodding.

"He likes sports, and lifts weights to develop his muscles. He is more settled."

They are good boys, said Richard, and would turn out all right.

Mara couldn't resist a grin. "Just like Richard, glossing over the problems, content to let things work out for themselves." He knew she would worry it through.

It had not been an easy marriage, at any time. "He did

153

wrong things to you. You had to pay for something you did to him in another life."

"What could I have possibly done?" asked Mara.

"You fooled around in a previous life."

"Well, I was certainly loyal in this one."

"He is sorry he hurt your feelings. Nothing so bad as hurting feelings of people who love you. The hurt does not easily pass."

Mara's face had grown pensive.

"He has had a change of heart," Maria went on, "and would like the children instilled with religion. If they don't shape up, you can get help from his older brother, Robert."

"They're fine," said Mara, "both the two boys and the girl."

"He's pleased that Valerie is working and buying her own clothes. And he says you should tell her what she needs to know."

"Yes, she's doing well," said Mara, impressed that her seventeen-year-old daughter's name should have come through, along with the others in the family. "We communicate."

"And he's concerned about the residuals on his television and motion pictures."

The concern was justified. "I have not been receiving any of these royalties," said Mara.

"Then you should check on them." She paused for a few moments. "He drank very much."

"With his friends," Mara agreed.

"And he had many friends?"

"The Colberts were close friends, and there were others in the industry."

"And he thanks Dean Jones for praying for him at the

end. This is another friend?"

Mara nodded.

"He wants to be remembered to Gregory."

"That is the younger boy."

"And let Carey do what he wants with his career. He will make out all right."

From family, Richard passed on to friends, expressing concern by name about one of their dearest associates, Mike. "He is worried about Mike's health," said Maria. "He says to tell Mike he will have eye trouble, and also to check his stomach. Watch out, too, for congestion in the lungs and kidneys."

Mara couldn't help wondering how Richard in spirit had suddenly become a diagnostician, but Maria had been so right about everything else that she didn't question her now. No sooner did she arrive home than she got on the phone to friend Mike. "It might be a good idea," said Mara, after the first pleasantries were out of the way, "if you had stomach and eye checkups."

Mike whistled in amazement. "Who have you been talking to? My stomach has been bothering me, and I just came from the ophthalmologist."

She hesitated about going on further, not wanting to completely dismay the poor fellow, but then as casually as possible, she said, "You might as well have your lungs and kidneys checked too."

He seemed to stiffen on the other end of the line.

"What are you, some kind of doctor?"

Richard, if it were he, was not weighing his concern, but was apparently reviewing a long list of friends and relatives.

"Who's Thompson?" Maria asked. "He's asking about him."

Mara had stopped being surprised. "That would be Marshall Thompson, Richard's brother-in-law. He made a lot of movies, and was the star of "Daktari," the television series about African game life."

"He has not been too happy lately," said Maria, "but Richard says he will soon be busy again, making documentaries. He will travel a lot, to London, Italy, Mexico City. He suffered from a broken contract, is that not so?"

"Perhaps," said Mara, "I heard something like that. He has been working on a series of his own lately.

Mara had profited tremendously from the session. Her belief in the hereafter had been reconfirmed and she had been reassured that Richard's rejection of the Christian doctrine of life everlasting had not diminished his own chances for salvation. It had been a very sobering experience, and gave her much to think about. She had always known that jealousy was not a very attractive trait, but had not always been able to conquer that green-eyed monster.

Even though Richard was no longer around to be jealous of, Mara was working on improving herself. Nevertheless, it had given her a start, near the end, when Maria had called out in a voice of surprise that a lady named Susan had suddenly appeared. Maria had calmly, if none the less dramatically, lifted up a leg, and pulled it back to her body, as if to demonstrate that the visitor only had one leg.

Mara had been understandably dumbfounded. For Richard's first wife, Susan Ball, had had a leg amputated because of her bone cancer.

"She's beautiful," said Maria, sighing over the dusky beauty of the fragile young starlet who had passed so unaccountably in her twenties.

Shaken to the core, Mara could not help asking, "Does he see Susan now?"

Maria shook her head. "They are in different worlds, in different dimensions."

The session got Mara to thinking about herself and life. She had been desolated by Richard's death, thinking of the things she might have done and hadn't. But now she saw a chance of atoning for it in the vague hereafter that Maria Moreno had given her reason to believe truly existed. She hoped, too, for Richard's sake that he would develop spiritually where he was. How much easier their life together would have been if there had been anything he believed in, so they could have been joined on solid common ground.

Would his present experience, reflected in Maria's communication, carry over to their next earth life together? Would he remember what he seemed to have forgotten from any life he had experienced before?

"Have hope," said Maria, "he will be a new man."

There were already signs of that in the concern expressed through the medium. "He says you need peace of mind," Maria had said. "He says it is important for you to keep up your appearance, to work hard in your field and keep the mind occupied."

There was no question but that the reading with Maria had lightened Mara's load, both as she considered this plane and the next. She had seemed almost cheerful as she talked about her prospects, in marked contrast to the depression that had previously weighed her down.

Weeks after the reading, I called to check on the accuracy of some of Maria's predictions.

"She was right on everything," Mara Corday said.

"And so you are going ahead on all fronts?"

Her laugh came rippling over the phone.

"You heard what the man said. He's still running the show."

Dorothy Colbert's problem was not quite as simple. Mara could launch herself, both in her personal and professional life, but Dorothy was certainly not a writer, and didn't know where to begin on the Richman project. "What's more," she said, throwing up her hands, "he wants a movie made of the book."

"Maybe," I said, "he could play himself."

"Don't be funny," said she, "when I'm being serious."

"If you're so serious, why don't you ask him?"

"You mean see Maria again?"

"It can't be any harder to come through twice than once." I thought of my own apparent advice from the dead Edgar Cayce. "And while you're at it, ask what kind of book it should be."

Eventually Dottie managed an appointment. And she was not to be disappointed. Wherever he lived, in the psychic consciousness of Maria Moreno or the world of the spirit, Harry Richman came promptly on center stage.

"He comes often and chats and looks for people to talk to," said Maria. "He is very friendly. He says he has given a lot of thought to the book, and it should be nostalgic. It should deal with the thirties, with Broadway at that time, as well as himself. It should be a very colorful book, and in that way it could be a bestseller."

"A bestseller?" Dottie fairly screamed. "Who is going to write it?"

"You should make the selection, he tells me. Pick somebody with sincerity, who will write with heart."

"That's Harry," exclaimed Dottie, "he always said heart was the most important thing. You had to have heart."

"Don't hide nothing," said Maria's Harry, quaintly employing a double negative. "Everybody makes mistakes and I made mine. I made millions and lost them, squandered money like there was no tomorrow, and got taken by people I thought my friends. But I have no regrets. Get all my romances into the book, too. That should make people sit up and take notice. Sex wasn't discovered just yesterday, but don't make it crass and obvious like they do today, leave something to the imagination."

"Should he want his friendship with Al Jolson in the book?"

"Get all his friends in, even Harry Cohen."

Maria had looked up questioningly, and Dottie explained. "Harry ran Columbia Pictures, and Harry Richman was one of the few people he counted as his friend."

"He is with Harry Cohen as well, all races and nationalities are together."

Dottie pursued her quest.

"And how should the songs be handled in the book, the "Birth of the Blues," "Red, Red Robin," and the other songs he wrote?"

Maria held up a finger. "He says you should be careful in using songs because of collaborators and their claims."

"In the book or the movie?"

"In both. The right people will come to you. It will be published and it will be a big success." She then invoked the colorful spirit guide who specialized in business and

159

commercial ventures. "Have confidence," she said, "for Pepe will help with the book."

Dottie breathed easier. "I'm glad somebody's helping because I can't do it alone."

Maria laughed. "Harry says you will never be alone."

Like so many inhabitants of the corrugated California coastline, Dottie Colbert was bewitched by the possibility of a sudden, cataclysmic earthquake, which could conceivably destroy large populated areas and wash the mainland into the sea.

And so when Maria Moreno had so glibly spoken of future landslides, it had made her wonder whether Harry Richman could be as prescient in his plane as Richard Long. After all, he had been up there somewhat longer than Richard, so to speak, and might know better how things worked.

And so she demanded of Maria.

"Ask Harry when we can expect an earthquake affecting the beach."

Maria moistened her lips, and hesitated, as if this were something she wanted to consider along with Harry. She finally gave a grunt of satisfaction.

"Harry says don't waste energy worrying about earthquakes. The earth is moving every minute of the time, and so there will be earthquakes at different times. But he doesn't want people to panic."

Dottie was clearly a thyroid type anyway, a bit on the nervy side, and now her adrenalin was really up.

"I keep hearing these Cassandra-like predictions of earthquakes and I have to know for sure. How about June of 1976, on the Malibu beach?"

Maria shook her head. "Don't worry," says Harry. "It

will be a while." And, as usual, she was right.

I had even more comforting words for Dottie. "Edgar Cayce, the sage of Virginia Beach, said the killer quake wouldn't hit till the latter portion of a 1958–1998 period, when it would destroy most of Los Angeles and San Francisco."

"And when," she asked, "would that be?"

"Not before 1978 obviously, and probably not until 1998."

She looked at me questioningly. "And why 1998?"

"Because the destruction is obviously climactic and would climax his earth-change predictions."

"Great," she said, "I'll stick with Harry."

The Richard Long odyssey was by no means over. As so often happened in Maria's readings for other people, spirits unknown or associated with them frequently came through. And so it was that the entity Richard Long announced that he would like to communicate with his wife once again through the medium. Apparently, as so many other presumed spirits, he was not capable of producing the energy that would allow him to manifest himself directly.

Mara was understandably excited. The first session had been so detailed, she hardly knew what more to expect. But she felt herself tingling with expectancy when she sat down in Maria's little room. And she was not disappointed. This time the spirit of Richard Long had no time for mundane matters, for the cracked walls or the garden, mud slides, or careers, or friends. He had a special message he wanted to deliver to his dear wife. And that message was not long forthcoming. "The soul," he said, "never dies. I want you to know that." And then Richard Long, the agnostic and atheist, the firm un-

161

believer of anything metaphysical, made his final valedictory. "Where I am," he said, "I have discovered that there is a God, and with that discovery I have found that which I never knew before—peace of mind."

8

The Avenger

THE LOOK in Dave Tillotson's eyes disturbed Maria Moreno.

"He hates," she said.

"He is a cop," I pointed out, "dedicated to finding his mother's killer."

She gave a little shiver. "But hate destroys."

"He could use some help. He has been searching for his mother's killer for twelve years, and has made it his whole life's work."

"That is the problem, he is destroying himself."

Since his widowed mother's brutal slaying in her gift shop in the heart of the Los Angeles black section, Tillotson had offered, first, a six-thousand-dollar reward, then one for ten thousand, and now twenty thousand. "I can't bear the thought of my mother's killers walking loose," he said.

In his flaming desire to bring the killers to book, the fifty-one-year-old police lieutenant had retired from the Los Angeles Police Department after twenty-eight years, and was concentrating on that one mission.

Little by little his friends dropped away, and his wife

left, but Tillotson had his pursuit as his constant companion. He was never lonely. His face grew hard and his eyes were like gimlets. He went after the same leads his colleagues on the police force had, until these leads ran cold, and he had nowhere to turn but the response to his cash offer, and the metaphysical world.

Maria had gained a few impressions of the murder from just reading the skimpy newspaper accounts, but Tillotson had been impressed because she dealt with information the police had never released.

"She told me," said Tillotson, "that my mother's wristwatch, her eyeglasses and a hearing aid were all strewn on the floor. And she was able to describe the killers. She almost seemed to recapture that black day in September, Friday the thirteenth, 1963."

And so a sitting had been arranged, with the fond hope that Maria would name the killer or killers. She had already said there was more than one man involved, and with this Tillotson agreed from the sparse clues available.

The meeting had not gone well. The sensitive medium reacted strongly to this strong, taciturn man who reminded me so forcibly of Victor Hugo's classic manhunter in *Les Miserables,* the incorruptible, relentless Javert.

Tillotson, I was sure, had no idea of the impression he had made. He spoke briefly, almost curtly, pinching off his words. His face was expressionless, save for the pale-blue eyes like agates. He had brought along the mother's wristwatch, to help Maria with her psychic impressions, via psychometry.

Maria took the watch with a smile. "This is not how my impressions materialize. I do not get anything myself, it is my masters who tell me."

But she held on to the watch, as if to please him, closing her eyes.

"Your mother," she announced, "had varicose veins." This was by no means unusual for a seventy-seven-year-old woman. "The left leg," she particularized.

Tillotson nodded.

"She had a problem with the femur, the thigh bone." She had broken her pelvis in a fall.

Maria seemed to be reconstructing the crime.

"She had been eating," she said, "when the men came in from the back and beat her to death."

Tillotson's eyes were hooded. "The remnants of her lunch were scattered on the floor."

Maria was still holding the watch. If she were psychometrizing—tuning in to the odic force of the individual through a possession—then she was clearly closing off alternative sources of a far more provocative nature.

"Where is your information coming from?" I asked.

Tillotson frowned at the interruption.

"From my Master Rampa, who lived in Sikkim and gained his wisdom among the wise men of Tibet."

"Is Rampa in spirit?"

She airily waved a hand. "Yes."

"And he is giving us this information clairvoyantly?"

Again she nodded.

I couldn't help but wonder why Master Rampa, in spirit or out of it, should know more than the Los Angeles Police Department.

"He is very advanced," said she, "and has developed his powers through many lives."

Tillotson appeared a little restive.

"Did my mother know the persons who killed her?"

The answer was not what he expected. "Rampa teaches love."

Tillotson was not deterred.

"How many of them were there?"

The information would not be tailored to the questioning.

"The master tells me she had a fire in the store, and it was done on purpose."

I looked inquiringly at Tillotson.

"Arson was suspected, but it was never definite."

Her eyes still closed, she seemed to be listening.

"Yes, yes," she nodded, she turned back to us. "There were three men, two of them climbed over a fence back of the shop, and broke in through a rear door. The third stood by a car, waiting. They hit her with a hammer, eleven, twelve times, crushing her skull. Her glasses and hearing aid were scattered over the floor."

Tillotson's craggy face was as impassive as ever, but the blue eyes appeared even harder if possible. "Nobody but the police," he said, "knew about the eyeglasses and the hearing device. It was never reported in the newspapers."

"The hammer was in the store," Maria said, "and they picked it up, one holding his arm around her neck." She paused a moment. "They were activists, black cultists, not interested in money. They didn't take anything."

Tillotson nodded almost imperceptibly. "The money was carefully hidden. All they took was her life." He motioned to the watch in Maria's hand. "They didn't even take that."

His voice rose a decibel. "Two weeks before she was killed, somebody came in with some Black Muslim literature and threatened her when she wouldn't buy it. I tried to get her to close up the shop, but she had been there so many years."

"She took precautions," said Maria, "she could see the people before she let them in."

"Yes, she kept the front door locked, and could look into a rear mirror, and see who was outside."

"There were two small narrow rooms, with the shelves crowded with crockery, glasses, porcelain ornaments, some things from Korea and other countries. She enjoyed her work."

"She liked people," her son said softly.

"Yes," said Maria, "she got along with the black people in the neighborhood. Her body was discovered by a black lady from the post office nearby. She had come in to buy something. She called police."

Tillotson's head came up.

"How did you know that?"

"She told me."

"She?" I broke in. "I thought Rampa was speaking."

She smiled. "The mother is here now. Rena, Alexandrena."

"Alexandrena was my mother's name," said Tillotson. "Friends called her Rena."

"She is asking after Mimi and Elizabeth."

Tillotson was noticeably startled. "Mimi is my cousin and Elizabeth my aunt."

Certainly if anybody could describe her killers, it would be the victim.

The same thought may have crossed Dave Tillotson's mind.

"Can you describe the three men?"

"They were all black. One was very dark, with wide

nostrils, thick lips. He was wearing a cap, like a baseball cap."

Tillotson seemed intrigued.

"They were looking for a man with a cap."

"Another man," Maria went on, "husky, with a mustache, about thirty-seven or thirty-eight, was an activist in the black revolutionary movement."

"Was this the man who did it?"

"Willie, that is the man to look for. He is tall and skinny. He climbed the fence, and cut his shoestring. He was wearing tennis shoes."

I sensed a growing excitement under Tillotson's professional mask. He said quietly, "The police thought one of the men was wearing tennis shoes, and they found a torn shoelace."

I could imagine the two men climbing the fence in broad daylight, stealing in on their defenseless victim, and viciously raining blows on her gray head. It was not hard to understand Tillotson's anger.

"Are the killers still alive?" Tillotson asked grimly. He drew in a deep breath. "I can't rest while they walk the streets."

"They have been in prison for other activities, but they are not dead. Look for a man with crossed eyes and a limp. He didn't do it, but he knows the killers."

"The police talked to scores of people, but if any of them knew anything they didn't let on."

"They were afraid of the activists," she said. "There was a liquor store, and a barbershop, and a beauty parlor nearby—is that not right?—they all knew something but they were frightened."

"A black police sergeant was in charge of the investigation," said Tillotson, "and he had a breakdown."

"Consult your own activities, and go through the records. All three have records against whites."

Maria seemed to have picked out one of the killers. "Can't you check the files for a Willie, tall and skinny, known to be a black militant?" I asked.

He groaned. "Even if you did, what would you have? You need an informant to come forward with an eyewitness account or the killers' own story. I put up the twenty thousand dollars, hoping it might bring somebody out of the woodwork."

"Have you had any luck from the announcement in the newspapers?" I asked.

"I got one phone call, from an Eddie White. He said he called to make sure the offer was bonafide. He said he knew the murderer, and would call back to arrange a meeting. I never heard from him again."

Maria held up an admonishing finger.

"Be careful of this man, he was trying to find out how much you knew."

"Could he have been one of the killers?"

"Somebody who knows them well. Be sure nobody knows where you live."

"If they make an attempt on me," said Dave Tillotson calmly, "I will have brought them into the open."

"They are dangerous," said Maria solemnly, "and have killed other people."

She listed the prisons the men had been in. They were scattered all over the state, from high-security facilities to institutions for the criminally insane.

"Are they in prison now?" Tillotson asked.

She shook her head, then asked surprisingly, "Are you married?"

"Separated," he replied shortly.

"Try to have a happy life with somebody you love."

Tillotson shrugged. "I must find my mother's killers. She was a good woman. She never harmed another human being."

"She is not on this plane anymore, but you are," said Maria. "You must think of yourself."

Tillotson was not to be distracted. "Even my superiors urged me to give up, and let the case take care of itself. In all my years as a policeman I never knew a case that solved itself."

It did not seem to be an ordinary break-in. The murderers had exposed themselves in broad daylight, taking the risk that somebody at the front door might nail them in the act.

"They tiptoed in," said Maria, "She didn't notice, because she was hard of hearing."

But what could she have done anyway, this frail, elderly lady, half-blind, and deaf, who had stayed on in a hostile neighborhood because she felt no hostility herself?

Could it have been a case of mistaken identity?

Maria shook her head. "They knew what they were doing. They had been spying on her for a week."

"Why," murmured Tillotson, "would they go to all this trouble to kill a poor, defenseless old lady?"

"For hate, revenge," came the surprising answer.

"Revenge? She wouldn't hurt a fly."

"But her son was a policeman."

Tillotson leaned forward. "How would they have known that?"

"She was proud of you. You were her only son. You were very close?"

"Yes, very close." For the first time, he showed signs

of emotion, his lips coming together tightly. "My father had died several years before, and I had looked after her."

"It was to get at you," she repeated.

"Then why," I asked, "wouldn't they have made a direct assault on the lieutenant?"

"This hurts him more."

Tillotson's jaw tightened.

"Would I know the men who killed her?"

"You had contact back in 1959, '60, '61. Clarita said look to your own activities."

Tillotson made a gesture of helplessness. "Besides my work with the police department, I headed a security service for a large chain of stores. We grabbed hundreds of people, shoplifters mostly. But I had very little contact with them personally."

"Is there any way of checking on them?" I asked.

"There were one hundred and twenty-five thousand arrests in my precinct during this period. There's no way of checking it out, even with a computer."

There were no Sherlock Holmses, no Hercule Poirots, with miraculous deductions leading to quick solutions. Only a few meager clues and a cold trail.

"The only chance," said Tillotson, "is to get somebody to talk. You could never get a conviction with circumstantial evidence, nor even an arrest. That's why a witness is so important."

And so he had kept upping the reward money.

At first, there had been quite a few calls, but with time, the interest had dwindled until there was only the one caller. Tillotson seemed obsessed with him. "How much does this White really know?" he asked.

Maria sighed, "Be careful, that man told you lies."

"He said he worked at a certain place, they never heard of him."

"Give nobody your address, she, Rena, told me that."

"If she knows so much," I asked, "why doesn't Dave's mother come right out and name her killers?"

"They are on a different plane and help in the way they think best." She looked over at Tillotson. "Did you break your spine years ago?"

He nodded, startled.

"Your mother tells me."

She murmured now, "Herriot, Herriot, does that name mean anything to you?"

"That was my mother's maiden name. It is French."

"She mentions the old recipes, still sitting on the file cabinet—rhubarb stew and pie."

He shook his head in wonderment. "She loved rhubarb."

"She's smiling now because she loves you, and thanks you for having purchased her grave plot before she died."

Tillotson nodded silently.
You discussed her moving out of the store two weeks before her death?"

"After she had been threatened over the Black Muslim literature. But I couldn't budge her."

"She had a big easy chair she loved to relax in."

"That is right."

"She is showing me a picture of her wedding day, and a bracelet she loved."

"And she wore it," said Tillotson, "until her death."
Maria put her hands to her head.

"She rolled her hair in a bun on top of her head, and wore it that way during the day."

Tillotson's face softened once more, but for only a moment.

Maria rubbed her hands together. "She had arthritis in both wrists, very painful."

We had a pretty good portrait of the dead woman, perhaps a self-portrait, if Rena was truly in spirit. Even so, it was Tillotson who interested me. He seemed to exude a single-mindedness that would not be thwarted or blocked. His affection for his mother seemed almost a compulsion, yet Maria had seen more hate than love in him.

A moment before, I had thought the memory of his dear mother might be easing his cold resolve. But there was a fanaticism about Tillotson which brought him back, inexorably, to his consuming quest. The killers were never out of his mind.

"Can you tell us more about the husky man?" he now asked.

"He killed two years before in the same neighborhood," Maria promptly replied.

That seemed like a lead to me.

"Not really," said Tillotson, "since it was obviously never pinned on him, or I would have heard."

"This man was prosecuted for selling drugs, and was put away for molesting white people. He frequently bothered her with his hate literature."

"There," I said, "is a clue, the visitor and the killer one and the same."

"Even if true, it isn't anything you could prove a murder by. That corroborating witness is all important."

He turned to Maria, and again asked, "Will I hear from this Eddie White?"

Maria's face grew grave. "If he calls to milk you for information, better to forget it."

"Then I am to let my mother's killers run loose, free to laugh and play and enjoy themselves?" His voice rasped coldly. "I'll see them all behind bars yet."

Maria went on imperturbably. "She says for you to put an advertisement in the black papers, announcing the reward. And remember Willie."

"Which is he again?"

"The tall, skinny one, with buck teeth, tennis shoes and the baseball cap. They called him Kookie, too."

Tillotson still looked unhappy.

"Where are the three men now?" he asked.

"One just got out of prison." She named the place. "Another was in a state hospital."

It seemed to me, with these clues, it would have been relatively simple to come up with some line of inquiry.

Again Tillotson shook his head.

"Even a computer wouldn't help. The computer doesn't know any more than we do. It just assembles it faster."

Tillotson's unhappiness seemed to trouble his mother more than her own death.

"You are not happy," Rena said. "Remember what you learned when you performed as a dancer."

I regarded the grim-faced cop in disbelief.

"You were a dancer?"

"As a boy," he replied almost sheepishly, "Mother had me taking dance lessons." The program had been church-affiliated, and so perhaps religiously oriented.

But Tillotson wasn't to be diverted.

"Will I find my mother's killers?" he asked.

Maria shuddered a little and opened her eyes.

"The masters are all gone," said she. "I cannot help it."

As she came to, she seemed vague about another session and I finally told Tillotson I would call him.

We watched for a moment as he trudged off, his shoulders bent forward a little, his body stiffly alert. He was a good friend and a bad enemy.

Compassion and dismay mingled in Maria's dark eyes. "He hates too much," she said.

"How," I asked, "does one love his mother's killers?"

"It does no good to hate."

I wondered whether murder was out of Maria's depth. But Dr. Jussek's German-born wife, Maya, upheld Maria's gift. "She has her own objections, but it's certainly not lack of ability."

Since Maya was normally skeptical of psychics, her attitude came as a surprise.

She spoke from experience. "Gene had suggested a reading with Maria, and I agreed, to please him. I did everything to disguise my identity. I used a different name, wore no rings, and wouldn't cooperate when she asked a question."

Her father, Charles Rhotert, a distinguished lecturer at Oxford, had died quite suddenly, ending an unusually close father-and-daughter relationship. But when Maria asked who Charles was, she said it was only a friend.

"Oh, no," said Maria, "he is here, and he tells me he is your father, and he loves you very much."

Maya still held back. "I incorrectly answered whatever questions she asked, until she just started describing my father's last days, which had been a mystery to us. He had taken ill with food poisoning one night. We had called a doctor, who was his closest friend. The doctor gave him an injection, and said he would be all right in the morning. The next day my father was dead, and it was assumed that ptomaine was the cause. It troubled me through the years, since it didn't make sense that he should die this way."

Maria provided the solution. "She picked up on every detail of his illness and then mentioned the injection. She said this had killed him."

"What was injected?" I asked.

"Morphine."

"But why was it fatal?"

"Apparently, it was contraindicated in my father's disorder."

"Did you believe it to be your father speaking through her?"

"Naturally, I can't say for sure, but who else would have known all that happened? Of course, once she put her finger on it, we realized that's how it had to be. It couldn't have been anything else."

Meanwhile, I had prevailed on Maria to continue the readings with Tillotson. "You may be able to help him," I said.

We had already received first names, descriptions, names of prisons and other institutions where they had served, and still it wasn't enough. All that remained was for Maria's contacts to fully name and place the killers.

"You'll never win the twenty thousand that way," I twitted Maria.

She fixed her eyes on me solemnly. "I wouldn't take that money. It is blood money, and I wouldn't want it."

"Don't you believe in justice?"

"Justice yes, but not revenge." She held up a finger. " 'Vengeance is mine, saith the Lord.' "

Tillotson turned up with a darkly attractive brunette,

his estranged wife. He seemed more relaxed than before, more communicative. He even smiled once or twice.

Some change was taking place, and I assumed it had to do with his reunion.

Maria seemed anxious to begin. Tillotson handed her his mother's eyeglasses, shattered in the attack, and the remnants of a hearing aid. She had no desire to psychometrize, and shook her head.

I had sensed Tillotson's rising interest in the proceedings, though his chief interest still plainly lay in the killers. I wondered if he gave any credibility to his mother as a living entity, and I watched him closely as Maria explained his mother's presence to him. She was presumably speaking for Rena.

"We are normally far from this planet, but with the proper energy form we can instantly go places where ordinary people can't."

Tillotson didn't blink an eye. But his features sharpened as Maria indicated for the first time that the elderly victim had put up some resistance. "She screamed, then ran, but was struck down by the thin man, Willie. Not hearing the men, she wasn't aware of them until they attacked her. She recognized the man with the baseball cap. He had once come into the store, pretending he wanted to buy something. The husky man was with him. He carried a can of beer, gulping it down rudely, as he questioned her."

" 'Who is the owner?' he had asked. Did she have any family?"

She replied she only had the one son. Upon finishing the beer, he tossed the can on the floor and left with his partner. He apparently had the information he wanted.

Rena had not been concerned about being robbed. "She had the money well hidden between two boxes," Maria said. "She tells me she kept very little in the cash register."

Tillotson nodded, asking, "What did the killers do with their clothes?"

"They washed the blood off with oil. Your mother knows now how it was done."

In each reading, Maria, or Rena, seemed to provide new details of the murder. It was almost as if she were jogging her soul memory. Now, she told of a fourth participant in the elaborate plot. This had been a woman. She had acted as a decoy to draw attention from the street front during the break-in from the rear. She had sauntered up the block, shaking her hips, to draw the attention of passersby to herself. She had apparently succeeded, for nobody had entered the store, or looked in, until it was too late.

I marveled that so much planning should go into the death of a harmless old lady.

"Did not the Black Muslims have quarters around the corner from the store?"

Tillotson replied: "Three hundred people were questioned, all of them black, but nobody knew anything about the murder, or so they said."

Maria had still another warning for Tillotson. "The killers are involved in civil insurrection. They will stop at nothing, so you must be careful. Your mother is telling you this again. Don't give out your phone number or your home address."

How had the old lady, if it was she, remembered so much of her own murder?

"She did not die immediately," said Maria, "her soul lingered as the life ebbed from her. She died in the ambulance, but the soul remembered."

The man who had known no peace in the years since his mother's murder leaned forward and asked softly, "Will she find any peace with her killers still running around free?"

"I hear her voice, and it is the voice of a very peaceful woman. She has her peace and wishes you to find the peace you need."

Tillotson seemed moved for a moment. "Thank her for me," he said. But he was still the pursuer, hot after his quarry. "Are the killers still together?"

"They separated, but they won't talk because they feel like brothers."

"Then how will it be solved?"

"The man with the limp could be the informer. He knows everything. He wants attention, and can hardly contain himself. Advertise in the black newspapers, but don't go to see him. Some day you will see this man with a limp in the newspaper, questioned for another crime, and he will tell what he knows about the others." She paused. "Let the masters decide in their own way. They know best."

"But when?" demanded Tillotson.

"You can't forget, can you?"

Tillotson looked at her uncertainly.

"Would she rather I forget?"

He no longer seemed to question where the information was coming from.

"She says that in her religion, which she taught you, she recognizes the power of forgiveness, just as Jesus said

179

long ago on the Cross: 'Forgive them, Father, for they know not what they do.' "

I stole a look at Tillotson. There seemed to be a new light in his eyes. "Tell her," he said softly, "that I understand."

9

Taylor Caldwell Has A Visitor

I HAD NEVER SEEN Janet Taylor Caldwell in finer form. She was gay and charming, brimming with high expectations, in marked contrast to her forlorn air on an earlier visit, when she was still grieving over Marcus Reback, her husband of nearly forty years.

"I was a real sad sack then," she grinned. "I thought I was about to die, and didn't much care."

She had snorted disdainfully when psychics had forecast that she would marry again, write many more books, including a long-awaited masterpiece on Jesus, and enjoy a full, hearty life.

"Not a chance," she had protested, "I just can't wait to leave this vale of deceit and deception."

Now in Malibu once more, she cheerfully blew cigarette smoke in my eyes and discussed her forthcoming world cruise, without the new husband she had recently divorced.

Though almost totally deaf, she had no trouble understanding me. "I'm picking up your vibration," she explained, while plainly reading my lips.

Since she had just contracted to do a book on Jesus,

another prediction appeared to have materialized.

She plucked reflectively at her underlip. "Perhaps I should have another psychic reading. There's a lot happening around me that I don't understand."

Maria Moreno was in Mexico, but I knew of another medium, Hollywood's Dorothy Vallas, who was quite impressive.

Janet wrinkled her nose. "I don't believe in spirits. When you're dead, you're dead. Don't you have any ordinary down-to-earth psychics?"

And yet years before, an English spiritualist, apparently tuning into her dead father, had given her an encouraging message in a moment of darkest depression. Attributing the information to Arthur Caldwell, he had told her the precise day her first book, rejected by the publisher only the day before, would eventually be published. It had heartened her greatly, and it had materialized on the promised day. Marveling at the time, the novelist had since considered an alternative. "How do I know it wasn't clairvoyance, pure and simple?"

"Because of the emotional content," I replied. "That was part of the equation. You had a need, and someone apparently responded to it."

"That's all conjecture," said she, with a wave of the hand. "Anyway, why should a spirit be more knowledgeable dead than alive?"

"He's presumably in a superior dimension."

Her eyebrows lifted increduously. "That's all so much hogwash."

Taylor Caldwell notwithstanding, there was no doubt in Dorothy Vallas's mind where her information came from.

"Spirit is very tangible," said she. "It's that etheric

substance of a person, the envelope of the soul, which survives when the physical body dies."

"I've never seen anything like it," I said.

"Then you have never seen a materialization?"

Taylor Caldwell showed a glimmer of interest. "Materialize what?" she demanded.

Dorothy's blue eyes twinkled. She spoke slowly, enunciating each syllable, so that the novelist could lip-read, if she cared to.

"A materialization isn't necessary. Spirits will manifest themselves in response to the energy given off in the sitting. In a pure materialization, an apparition, which is essentially an energy form, takes the form of ectoplasm given off by the medium, and serves as the spirit guide."

Taylor Caldwell smiled tolerantly.

"And I suppose that's how we get ghosts."

"Not exactly," smiled Dorothy, "though they, too, are energy forms, which, essentially, is what spirit is."

"Why a materialization?" I asked, "when spirit presumably manifests through you?"

Dorothy laughed good-naturedly. "Merely to convince skeptics, and I long ago tired of that role. It's completely draining and no more helpful."

Physical phenomena appeared to interest most people.

"How do you know," I asked, "that the materialization is truly a projection of the medium's energy?"

"There's a loss of the medium's body weight, sometimes as much as twenty pounds, which corresponds to the weight of the materialization."

I wondered how the scales were managed.

"The apparition is capable of motion," she said evenly.

Janet lifted her eyes in mock horror. "Let's not have one of those," she cried.

183

Dorothy shook her head. "Actually, as a medium, I am only an instrument between spirit and people. No apparitions are necessary. The spirits take over my subconscious mind to deliver their messages."

In manner or appearance, there was nothing spooky about Dorothy Vallas. She was an attractive middle-aged lady with a fresh countenance and benevolently maternal expression.

"I have given myself over to God's will," she said, "for Him to use as His channel."

Janet's eyes gleamed mischievously. "God is quite capable of speaking for Himself."

Dorothy gave her a placid smile. "He does."

At various times, she heard voices, clairaudiently, and made prophecies of general interest. She had publicly forecast the resignation of President Nixon, the uprisings in Portugal, and the time and place—September 9 in San Francisco—of the capture of fugitive Patty Hearst. Why these couldn't have been ordinary psychic predictions, I wasn't quite sure.

"I get nothing myself," Dorothy said, "I'm a channel —nothing more."

She took a seat opposite the novelist, their knees almost touching.

"Spirit," she announced, "takes over my body, my mind, my voice, using my vocal cords for their messages. They use not only my energy, but the energy of all in the room, to manifest as energy forms."

The novelist studied her lips, frowning, "I don't have any energy to spare."

"Will you do a materialization?" I asked.

She shook her head. "No, we're only trying to be helpful here, not win over converts to spiritualism."

I thought Janet had made a good point before.

"Why should a spirit know more about our lives than we do?"

Dorothy Vallas had heard the question countless times.

"They're not earthbound like we are, they're in the Universe, sharing universal knowledge."

Janet viewed the proceedings as she would a theatrical performance.

"Do they dress for the weather," she chuckled, "and who gets their meals?"

"They're on a different level or dimension, a different frequency," Dorothy said patiently. "That's why the ordinary person can't see or hear them."

She had experienced her first awareness of these energy forms at the age of eleven. She was crossing a Los Angeles street with her mother, and suddenly turned, saying, "Uncle just passed away in a St. Louis hospital."

Word came that evening that her mother's brother had died at that precise time.

She was not bothered by the novelist's skepticism.

She drew a deep breath, signaling a friend, Lee Atkinson, a publicist, to record the proceedings.

"I will not go in trance," she advised, "but will tune in clairaudiently."

The novelist shook her head. "I can't hear you."

"You will," she said. "They will see to that."

"Will you have guides?" I asked Dorothy.

She nodded. "Oh, yes, they will be all around me."

"And who," I asked, "may they be?"

She shrugged. "Whoever comes through. It varies at different times, and with the subject."

"Will they be somebody she knows?"

"Not necessarily, but likely those interested in her career

and her message."

Janet had been following the exchange with a frown of annoyance. "Whatever are you two chattering about?"

"Your message," I bellowed, cupping my hand to my mouth.

She grimaced in exasperation. "Please lower your voice."

"What is your message?" I asked in a modulated tone.

"That the world is a terrible place, and we are all better out of it."

"Oh, no," Dorothy demurred. "With *Dear and Glorious Physician* and *Great Lion of God*, seeing the Christ through the eyes of Luke and Paul, you have brought millions of people closer to the principle of everlasting life."

"I'll have to put an end to that," Janet smiled.

Knowing the novelist so well, I was aware that she frequently played the devil's advocate, privately cherishing what she publicly disavowed.

"One life is enough," she said with an exaggerated sigh.

Sensing her isolation after Marcus's death, I did not take this seriously.

Dorothy had closed her eyes. "The spirits are all around me," she said, waving her hands.

Suddenly, she held one hand to her ear.

"There is one voice I hear above the others. It is seeking to express its love for the one who remains in this dimension."

Janet gave me a devilish look. "Here we go again," she said under her breath.

The medium lightly tapped the novelist's shoulder. "He is reaching out so that you will know it is he. He is

186

referring to you lovingly. 'Trust me, Small One,' he is saying, 'when I tell you that I am close.' "

Janet's head drew back involuntarily.

"Why," she exclaimed, "that was my husband's pet name for me."

"Small One," I marveled, "why, you towered over him."

"That's the point," she said. "It was a little joke between us. Nobody else knew about it."

Dorothy kept staring at the ceiling, straining forward as if listening.

"He has learned to be humble, and regrets that he caused difficulties by claiming credit that was rightly yours."

Janet's interest was piqued. "It's too bad," she said, "that he wasn't humble when it counted."

"It still counts," Dorothy said, "for he is now trying to atone for his mistakes, and is surrounding you with purple light."

Janet's hearing appeared to have improved remarkably. "What good will that do?" she scoffed.

"It will protect you from people seeking to harm you."

"I need a guard around the clock," Janet shot back.

"You have had trouble working lately, and he will help you with a book you are trying to finish."

The novelist held up a finger. "I could use some help. For the first time in my career I've missed a manuscript deadline. There's so much confusion around me I can't hear myself think."

"He will clear that up, and the discordant influences will melt away."

Janet responded to a sympathetic audience. "Everybody

is bothering me: lawyers, accountants, bankers, business agents, literary agents. There seems to be a conspiracy to keep me from working. That's one thing about my husband, he didn't let anybody interfere with my work. He knew where the rent money was coming from."

She turned to Dorothy with a grimace. "How do I know he has anything to do with all this? It's obviously absurd."

Dorothy's eyes were serenely shut.

"He asks your forgiveness. He truly loved you, but he was influenced by an older woman."

Janet's head wagged. "Nobody ever influenced him. He always had his own way."

"In his youth."

"Oh, that would be his mother, I suppose. But there's nothing unusual about that."

"That influence always stayed with him."

She regarded Dorothy doubtfully. "This doesn't sound like the man I knew."

"He's seen his mistakes, and knows that you are in a constant state of shock, with a new marriage and divorce, nuisance suits. Some of your own representatives working against you. But all this will be removed, as if by a cleansing, with help from the other side."

Janet's look of incredulity was marvelous to behold. Her brow was furrowed and her eyebrows had tilted expressively. Her lips had turned upward, revealing two gleaming rows of sound, white teeth.

"I can't swallow all that," she said. "God knows, I've never had any help before. Where is it coming from?"

"From within you. They are working on that, and you will find new direction."

Janet snorted. "At my age? Don't make me laugh."

Dorothy reached out and touched her hand. "You will see, have faith."

"Faith in who?"

"God."

Janet sighed audibly. "It always gets back to that."

"You will have help in the spiritual plane."

"I need somebody to help me against all the vultures on this plane."

"It will be provided. But you must start working on yourself. The wounds others have inflicted have blocked your hearing, but this will improve, as Christ's light surrounds you."

Janet's lips smacked together. "I thought it was a purple light."

"It is all the same. Your husband is doing Christ's work."

"That's fine, for an Orthodox Jew."

"There is no sectarianism in spirit, only the will to do better at the highest level."

Dorothy brushed Janet's knee lightly. "You have been having trouble with your legs. When your husband puts you in this purple light, he will call on a spiritual doctor to help you."

"Help me from what?"

"You have had a feeling of fear since you were ten, stemming from your previous lives."

"My childhood was a horror, it didn't have anything to do with any past life."

Under hypnosis, regressed in time, Taylor Caldwell had been, in turn, the mother of Mary Magdalene, an Irish scullery maid, a physician in the Greece of Pericles, and a servant girl ravaged by the rakes of the Hellfire Club in pre-Victorian England. She had hanged herself, thrown herself off tall towers, died ignominiously and prematurely. But she had always been a woman, through many regressions.

"I was never a man, but unlike those woman libbers, I recognize man's superiority and revel in it."

"Actually," said Dorothy, "you don't like women and there's a very good reason for it."

"They're an inferior race," said Janet, harping on a pet theme. "Men are like old wine, women are sour grapes."

Dorothy shook her head. "You were a general in the Middle Ages, in the Crusades, and you were betrayed by a woman at that time. You have disliked women ever since."

"What nonsense," said Janet. "I was never a man."

Presumably in past lives, the author had shown a remarkably detailed recall of people and periods, which she had drawn on to make her novels so remarkably vivid and realistic.

"You once planned to do a book about the Crusades, on Saladin," I said of a project that had been launched and then abandoned.

"Coincidence. An impulse I quickly dismissed."

"The inclination still came from somewhere."

"I get so tired of reincarnation."

"Then why"—I recalled a recent side trip to Palm Springs—"did you tell writer Bill Hisey that you had known each other in England in 1771?"

Dorothy Vallas, enjoying the break, smiled in silent amusement.

Janet cocked her head, bird-fashion. "I must have been out of my mind."

190

"That would put you back in the Georgian days of the Hellfire Club, when you were presumably ravished by the gentry."

She let out an incredulous guffaw. "I hope I enjoyed it." More seriously, she turned to Dorothy. "What's going to happen to me? That's what I want to know."

Dorothy seemed not to have heard. "You had a problem with a ring recently. It seems to have gotten away from you."

"It got away all right, somebody stole it."

"They say it has not been sold."

"Who are 'they'?" Janet demanded.

"The spirits."

"And whatever happened to my husband?"

"He's still hovering about."

"Oh, I see, he's getting help."

"The person who stole that ring is not well."

"I would hope not," said Janet.

"But you were reimbursed for it."

"Oh, there was insurance, some twenty thousand dollars."

"Your husband says it will eventually be recovered."

Janet's tone reflected her mistrust of the entire proceedings. "Hasn't he anything better to worry about?"

"In the next two months, November and December, you will get everything in order, and your eyes will be opened. You will finish your book with a minimum of confusion, and will put your trust in somebody reliable."

Janet snapped her fingers. "So everything is fine, just like that."

"No, the answers will flow through you, and the animosity around you is going to end. As a child you didn't have the love you needed, and this has been the pattern later on as well."

"Nobody gets the love they need," scoffed Janet.

"They do," said Dorothy, "when they give love."

"And where did that gem come from?"

Dorothy leaned back in her chair. "Marcus," said she, naming Janet's husband for the first time. The sitting was over.

Janet was not impressed. Dorothy was barely out the door before Janet said, "I love these people telling me that Marcus is helping me. The last two years of his life he was virtually in a coma from the beatings the robbers gave him when they broke into our house in Buffalo. He couldn't even help himself."

I asked whether the culprit had been caught.

"Caught!" Janet's voice rose shrilly. "The police captured him, and the judge let him off. He wept over him, saying he was of a minority that had never known social justice. He had never even had toilet training. And so he was free to rob and kill because he lacked toilet training. Would you believe it?"

I had seen too many judges weep over young criminals to question what she was saying.

"If there is life after death," I said, "the spirit would not reflect Marcus's condition at the time of death, but in his prime, as I understand it."

"Would he be young and sassy?"

"Ageless, I would gather. He chooses his own condition and there is no time or space, as we understand it, on the other side. Or so they say."

Her eyes squinted into mine. "The reading wasn't too bad, though a little general, except for that Marcus business. I can't buy that."

In the face of this attitude, I saw no reason for contacting

Maria Moreno. "She is convinced spirits are her sole source."

Janet shrugged. "What difference where it's from, so long as it's accurate?"

But the next day, as if in response to a summons, Maria unexpectedly appeared.

"I have come," she announced, "to do a reading for the novelist, Taylor Caldwell."

"Have you read her books?" I asked, too immune to surprise by now to comment on her dramatic appearance.

She shook her head. "I have heard her name. The spirits say she writes of Jesus. Tell me nothing. Clarita and Pepe, they know what is necessary, as do the doctors."

Janet eyed the short, dark figure curiously. "Thank you," said she, "for cutting short your holiday."

Maria pointed a determined finger at the author.

"You are in great trouble."

Janet's eyes fairly bulged. "You're telling me!"

For the second time in twenty-four hours, Janet sat with a medium, this time separated by the width of a coffee table.

Maria waved her arms around her head a few times, windmill style, as if she were physically conjuring up the spirits. Then, turning her eyes heavenward, she soon announced, "I see Bill, two Bills, they have something to tell you."

I looked inquiringly at Janet Caldwell. Her lips formed an enigmatical smile.

"I had two early husbands named Bill. But they never had anything to say while I was married to them. So I don't know why I should listen now."

The two Bills apparently drifted off, as another misty

figure moved into Maria Moreno's screen.

"There is a man who says you should go ahead and do what you want, and not listen to publishers or agents. He tells you to go by your own intuition, which you did all the time when he was here.

"You have to do this book karmically. For in one incarnation, you were against the Christians, but later became a convert at the time of Nero, and worked as a scribe."

I was struck by Maria's tuning into a project that the novelist and I had quietly planned together—a story of Jesus, titled, *I, Judas*—opposed by some for reasons best known to themselves.

"This book will succeed as no other you have done. It will draw on the knowledge both you and Jess Stearn gained from being together during the Christian era. It will be a wonderful portrait of Jesus and the people who followed and fought him."

I had not anticipated anything like this. But Janet gave me a sly smile. "Did you put her up to this?"

Maria, thankfully, was deeply absorbed. Nevertheless, she seemed to reply. "The masters want you to do this book because of the good it will do." She paused, apparently groping, then said, "Thank you," as if speaking to her guides. "They say that certain people want complete control over you for their advantage."

I was struck by Maria's unaccustomed vocabulary, and typically, as I was learning, she responded to the unspoken thought. "The masters are speaking through me, using my vocal chords," she explained.

She had more news for the author. "There is a man who wants to marry you, but is already married. They don't want you to do it. He is after your money. Keep the situation as it is."

Janet smiled uncertainly. "I really don't think he's interested in my money." Her voice held a rasping edge. "Isn't there anything about me but my money that would attract anybody?"

"I have never seen you look better," I quickly responded, and indeed I hadn't. The author looked and acted years younger than her age, and her agile mind was never more alert, her biting tongue never wittier or saltier.

"There is one man who wants to have sex with you," Maria went on unconcernedly, "but you should put him off, as he has ulterior motives."

"I suppose he's after my money, too," she snapped. "I'll have you know I'm still a woman."

Maria, groaning, had put her hands to her head. "Oh, it hurts me, it hurts me," she cried.

Janet followed her closely. "That's what Marcus did after the hoodlums beat him up." She sighed. "How horrible they should get away with it."

Maria shook herself out of this mood. "The one who did it will pay for it yet. It's his karma in this life."

"Pay for it—not a chance," said Janet bitterly. "The judge said he hadn't been toilet trained, and that had to be considered in handling the poor man. They never consider victims like my husband. He was toilet trained. I just get so tired of the bleeding hearts trying to appease their little consciences to compensate for their secret prejudices."

"He will pay for it," Maria repeated, "and soon. There is one man who wants you to know that. He also says to remember him when you tell a certain publisher where to get off. They need you more than you need them. He

195

wants you to remember that."

"He sounds like somebody I knew very well once. Who, may I ask, can this fount of knowledge be?"

Maria's lids were closed, and she was breathing rhythmically, a mark of her deep trance state. She almost breathed the answer. "Marcus, it is Marcus who is speaking to you. He wants you to know that he will always be with you."

Janet was in no mood for sentiment. "If he knows so much, why can't he tell me what's going to happen to all those books I optioned off to the movies, and they never made?"

"This was a great disappointment to you both, but you will soon have good news about this."

"Hollywood took seven books and they're all in mothballs," she said with a wry face.

"Cheer up," I said, "Maria sees an end to the drought."

Janet's underlip shot out in a typical gesture. "We'll see," she said truculently.

On this happy note the sitting ended. Janet graciously took the medium's hand.

"You were certainly right about a number of things."

Maria tapped herself expressively. "Not me, the masters. I know nothing."

"Anyway," said Janet, "you did a good job, even if you were off on Marcus's assailant. They say you can't get away with murder. But they didn't know about the judges we have on the bench these days."

Taylor Caldwell flew back to Buffalo, to finish up a novel preparatory to working with me on *I, Judas*. But two weeks later, I received a telephone call asking me to fly to Buffalo to salvage our project. Certain advisers were exerting unusual pressures, even to accusing her of disloyalty, to abort a book she had her heart set on doing.

On arriving in Buffalo, I reminded her of what Maria Moreno had said. "Follow your own intuition."

She nodded her agreement, and that problem was resolved.

The next day, at breakfast, she pushed a Buffalo newspaper under my nose. It didn't seem an unusual story in this day and age—a man had been shot down on a Buffalo street, and taken to the hospital in critical condition.

I glanced through the story quickly, then looked questioningly at my hostess.

"That man," she said, "clubbed Marcus to death."

I reread the article, trying to recall what Maria Moreno had said.

Janet refreshed my memory. "She said that he would suffer for what he did to Marcus, and very soon."

I couldn't resist. "And do you recall her source?"

A startled look transformed her features. "Why, it was Marcus, wasn't it?"

Like so many others, Taylor Caldwell struggled against the belief that death must be the end. Occasionally, a flash of remembrance struck her, but she put this down to racial memory or the Jungian collective unconscious. When I reminded her of the inexplicable flow of historical detail from her well of consciousness, she lightly dismissed this as imagination. And she shrugged when I mentioned her regressed recollections of actual people and events. At times, there seemed no explanation for our own close relationship, except as some ongoing chapter from the misty past. Her army of readers was eagerly awaiting the promised masterpiece of Jesus, and she had chosen to collaborate. "We work well together," she explained. And yet she had become world-famous as a novelist who marched to her own drum. She normally spurned editorial criticism, but in *Search for the Soul* and *The Romance of Atlantis* yielded graciously to whatever changes I proposed.

Maria Moreno had mentioned a previous relationship accounting for this present closeness, but Taylor Caldwell laughed with amusement. "You don't really believe that, do you?"

I wasn't sure what I did believe. I would be impressed by the information flowing out of the medium, thinking she might indeed be in touch with those who had crossed over, and then common sense asserted itself.

While questioning spiritism, the novelist accepted the psychic, because she was psychic herself. She had publicly predicted such tragic events as the assassinations of President John F. Kennedy and Martin Luther King. "I accept clairvoyance and telepathy," said she, "because they work. But nothing has ever haunted me except my mistakes."

I played the devil's advocate. "But think how Maria Moreno's guides tuned into your problems and projects."

"There was nothing that couldn't be explained by the psychic. She could have been clairvoyant, tuning into the past, present and future, as psychics do without guides. Or she might have dredged it out of me telepathically. I knew the various situations she touched upon. And I certainly knew my late husband's name."

Still, she had a desire to believe. With the biblical three score and ten behind her, she was searching, like so many, for an explanation of life as well as death. "Napoleon once said it was just as remarkable to have been born once as twice."

There was an orderly rhythm in the universe, the

measured movement of the planets, the change of seasons, the tides of the sea. It was endless, timeless, without beginning or end, and were we not all part of it?

"Of course," she said, "and so are the insects."

Our paths parted and I saw her next a month later, after the Christmas holidays, when we met in New York to talk over *I, Judas.* She mentioned facetiously that she had not yet made her sale to the movies. I said, "Give it time."

As we sat in her suite, overlooking Central Park, I was struck by her preoccupied air. She smoked one cigarette after another, chain-fashion, sipping at her coffee, and gazing out abstractedly at the snow-clad trees.

"I must tell you something," she said finally. "I couldn't help thinking of what the mediums had said about Marcus back in California, and I suppose I was looking for reassurance. At any rate, during Christmas week, when I was feeling particularly sorry for myself, I happened to look up at a group of five jade pictures on the wall of my bedroom. Focusing on a framed peacock that Marcus had been especially fond of, I said in a loud voice: "Marcus, if there is a hereafter, give me a sign."

At that, almost startling her out of her wits, the picture fell to the floor with a thud.

"Nothing like this had ever occurred before," she stressed.

It was my turn to be skeptical. "Pictures are forever falling."

She shook her head. "I examined the picture hook carefully. It had not been pulled out of the wall or bent in any way."

"Are you sure the picture wire did not snap?"

She watched the smoke drift lazily toward the ceiling. "There was only one way," she said. "It had to be lifted up and pulled from the wall by an outside agency. There was no other way."

10

The Healing Spirits

D R. JUSSEK was properly skeptical about psychic healers. Even so, he could conceive of magnetic energy radiating from certain individuals and having a beneficial effect on others. It was all within the realm of possibility, particularly when, as in the case of healer Douglas Johnson, there was a noticeable emanation of heat, bringing blood to the troubled areas. But how did one conceive of spirits, inconceivable in themselves, performing healings from the stratosphere on actual bodies?

Yet, Jussek with the true curiosity of the scientist, was willing to put Maria Moreno's spirits to the test, especially as he himself needed help and felt he had nothing to lose. He had been bothered with a bad knee, hardly able to walk, and colleagues had advised surgery to repair damaged cartilage. He had the layman's dread of the knife, and was impressed by reports from Maria's clients, claiming relief from headaches, tension, rheumatism, and sundry ailments, possibily psychogenic in origin.

The medium's credentials were pragmatic. She had correctly diagnosed artist Kathleen Bleser, of Hermosa Beach, as having Ménière's disease, an imbalance of the inner ear; and she had advised dancer Ann Miller, every indication to the contrary, of ripening cataracts.

Maria's diagnosis of Jussek had corresponded with the medicos, pinpointing tissue damage on the inside of the knee joint. The doctor, an exercise enthusiast, had given up jogging, yoga, even simple calisthenics, because of the pain.

With surgery the only other recourse, he was not self-conscious about asking for a psychic treatment.

"As an acupuncturist," he smiled in retrospect, "I had seen apparent miracles, without knowing precisely why people were helped. It was enough that it worked, and it is my feeling that medicine would be the better for it if more doctors were open to what helped their patients, however eccentric or bizarre the treatment."

And so, Dr. Jallikete, with Dr. Dermetz in attendance, gave Dr. Jussek an intramuscular injection. While the spirit therapy was taking place, Jussek suppressed a smile of amusement, anticipating the reactions of medical colleagues. At least, he told himself, it was painless, and inexpensive, for Maria Moreno had no fee for the sick or the disabled.

"It would be a sacrilege of my gift," said she. Feeling she was but an instrument of God, the medium had a healthy, if impersonal, respect for her own powers.

"I don't know what I say," she pointed out, "but I see them get better."

Many doctors came to her, and she saw nothing unusual in this.

"They are people, too," said she, "and they don't take good care of themselves, not even taking their own advice. They work too hard, smoke too much, and eat badly."

Maria had formed an attachment for the acupuncturist.

"He is a good man," said she, "and must be helped, so he can help other people."

The session with Jussek took but a few minutes, and there was no doubt in Maria Moreno's mind of the outcome.

"You will be walking as good as new," she promised. "The doctors say so."

Again, the doctor was hard-pressed to suppress a smile, as he reflected on the malpractice risks involved in such unorthodox surgical procedures.

"In a week," said Maria Moreno, "the tissue will be completely healed. But you will feel stronger tomorrow."

The following day, as he climbed out of bed, the doctor tested his knee gingerly. There was no familiar twinge of pain. He took a few steps tentatively. Still no pain. On the street, near his home, he broke into a run, but quickly stopped when it bothered him. He remembered her injunction not to jog or subject the knee to stress for six or seven days.

"It just felt so good," he said, "that I felt capable of any exertion."

But he now heeded the advice of Doctors Jallikete and Dermetz, whoever and wherever they were, if only in the mind of the marvelous Mexican medium.

Gradually the pain and the swelling lessened. After one week the symptoms had subsided completely.

"I put on my jogging clothes, and started to leg it around the park near my home. I ran for three miles, without stopping, and before the week was over I was doing my usual five miles. Whatever Maria Moreno did had worked."

As luck would have it, my own knee, jammed against

203

the floorboard of a car rammed from behind, had been similarly hurt. I had been hobbling about for weeks, curtailing my own exercise routine. Doctor friends suggested I had broken the capsule of the knee joint, and proposed orthopedic care. I had already made an appointment with a reputable therapist, when Dr. Jussek's remarkable cure suggested this relatively easy and inexpensive treatment.

Maria pressed the inside of my knee, at the precise point of the injury. Much like grandmother, when I was a child, she said soothingly, "The doctors will fix."

Quickly slipping into trance, she summoned Doctors Jallikete, Dermetz and—new to me—Dr. Dondich.

She readily explained, "All the doctors in the universe are available to the Masters."

"And who is this Master?"

"Master Rampa," said she, employing a familiar name. "With so many lives, he has perfect understanding of the universe."

In my case an injection was not necessary.

"They will manipulate the joint, so that the knee will relax."

"I had been thinking of an osteopath," I said.

She shook her head vigorously. "That would only strain it."

"Why," I asked, "is the spirit manipulation different?"

"Because it uses the force of energy, not of pressure or movement, which could be hurtful."

I was enjoined to put a glass of water next to my bed at night, and drink from it.

Call it imagination, but the next morning, for the first time in weeks, my knee was free of pain. I walked on the beach, did some floor exercises, and even jogged a bit. But a few days later, I carelessly missed a step, and came down hard on my leg, feeling a throb of pain. I seemed to be back where I had been.

Maria was sympathetic. "The doctors will make it well." Slipping into trance, she wheeled her arms around her head in familiar windmill fashion.

Doctors Jallikete and Dermetz rallied to the cause, and another manipulation was performed.

"It is already healing underneath," said Maria. "You only pulled the tendon a little. Think of it as being perfectly well. You will be better in a week."

For the first time, she had involved my own mind in the healing processes. Later, with my knee fully restored, I mentioned this to Dr. Jussek.

"I can only speculate how she does it," he said, "but it seems obvious that the method varies. Sometimes it's one doctor, with spirit surgery, another time it's manipulation, or diet and exercise, or, as in your case, applying your own mental powers to the healing. The masters apparently know you went through a mind-control course and wrote *The Power of Alpha Thinking*."

We seemed no nearer an explanation. But Jussek theorized: "Conceivably, there are vibrations that we have not yet isolated, and one of these could be a healing vibration, with an atmospheric force touched off by an unidentified energy process."

"One unknown touches off another unknown, to yield a known result?"

Jussek shrugged. "It's not that esoteric, when you consider that X-rays, radio waves and television beams all produce visible results through an invisible, imperfectly understood process."

He was concerned with cases that had not yielded to traditional therapy. Maria had agreed to do whatever she could to help a terminal leukemia victim, of middle years, and a young soccer player, whose lower-back condition kept him from earning a livelihood.

The leukemia patient was an engineer of fifty-five years. His name was simply Bill. He had been afflicted for two years, and was in the last stages of the disease. He seemed withdrawn and cold, but it could have been only a mask for the fear that clutched at his heart. He had never been to a psychic before, and obviously didn't know what to expect. Nevertheless, he didn't mind anybody sitting in, as long as he was anonymous. He had been on chemotherapy, and it periodically reduced a typical rash of 100,000 cells per cubic millimeter of blood to a normal range of five to ten thousand. But with time, the treatment's effects diminished and cell damage to vital organs, including the liver, increased. He was willing to try anything, meanwhile adhering to conventional treatment.

Maria had been given no information. She sat in a small room, opposite the engineer, and quickly went into trance.

"The masters," she said, "are making all doctors available for this case. They will examine him first, and see what is wrong."

She held up her head as if listening. "He had X-rays, you say, Doctor?"

Eyes closed, she turned back to Bill, who was staring at the wall behind her.

"Is this true?" she asked, checking on her invisible doctor.

Bill nodded mechanically.

"On the face?"

His head bobbed again. "For face cancer," he agreed laconically.

She shook her head a few times. "The doctors say you have a condition of the blood, beginning in the marrow of the bones where the blood forms." She paused for a moment. "Thank you, Doctor. It is Dr. Jallikete. He is here with Dr. Dermetz and Dr. Karnacke."

I stole a look at Bill. His head was in his hands, and his eyes closed.

"The doctors," she went on, "say you have leukemia. Is that not right?"

His head came up slowly. He glanced for a moment at Jussek, then nodded.

"Yes, I have leukemia."

"The doctors say years ago you had long treatment with penicillin and other antibiotics. This affected the vascular system, causing inflammation of the blood vessels, and affected the output of the marrow."

"I did have prolonged treatment with penicillin," he acknowledged.

The examination continued: "The doctors say you had an operation on the prostate, and for a hernia."

"That is right." He shifted in his chair uneasily.

Without opening her eyes, Maria said, "Don't move. The doctors are working in that area."

He became rigidly still.

She now got up and stood behind the engineer. "You have leg pains?"

Jussek was listening intently. "That's symptomatic of the illness."

"And a problem with the liver?"

He hesitated. "Indirectly."

ors say to eat raw beets, boiled and taken
nned foods. Once a week the doctors will
ic energy to the astral body."

___dea what the astral body was, and how it
presumably functioned.

"It is the ectoplasm, that leaves the body, identical to
it in form, during sleep or the subconscious state," she
explained.

"What good does it do to treat the astral body when the
actual body is lying there ill at the point of death?"

"When the astral body returns," said Maria, "it draws
the energy it has gained back to the physical body."

What was all this astral business?

"The astral body," she elaborated, "is the vehicle of the
soul, and separates man from the animals. It is God in
man, and it remains after death, a link to the hereafter."

This was certainly explicit, if not provable.

The session ended shortly thereafter. Perhaps it was the
power of suggestion, but in a few days Bill reported that
he felt better than he had for weeks.

"The most amazing experience I ever had," he said.
"She seemed to know everything that had ever happened
to me."

She had mentioned in passing how concerned his wife
—and his mistress—were, and this, ironically, had impressed him even more than the diagnosis of leukemia
linked to the loss of bone marrow function.

"How did she know," said this epitome of middle-class
respectability, "that I had a girlfriend?"

Dr. Jussek was not optimistic. "The patient has the
more serious type of blood cancer, myelocytic leukemia,
which gets progressively worse and is normally terminal

"In time," Jussek whispered, "leukemia damages the liver."

"The doctors want a transfusion. Do you know your type of blood?"

He nodded.

"Type O, is that not right?"

He blinked a bit, remaining silent.

"Answer her," Jussek prodded.

He nodded affirmation.

The transfusion was singular, to say the least.

Maria explained: "The doctors say that one side of the body is negative, the other positive. They must exchange the positive and the negative, so that the blood cells will change. Dr. Joachim (still another doctor) is looking over the way they change these cells experimentally in Houston. He is there, and he will see how they use blood plasma to help make these changes. He will take the energy from the left side and put it on the right side, to polarize the system."

It was a little too much for me. The patient, Bill, seemed deep in thought. Only Dr. Jussek didn't seem at sea.

"Houston," he said, "is a leader in experiments dealing with leukemia. It is astonishing that she should get anything like this."

The doctors had additional plans for the ailing man.

Maria raised her hands, and announced, "They are raising his astral body into the atmosphere, one hundred; one hundred and fifty; two hundred feet. They are taking cosmic energy and putting this energy in the astral body."

There was a diet regimen, curiously mundane after this trip into space.

in three or four years. He may be just experiencing the ups and downs characteristic of this cancer."

Sure enough, improvement was short-lived, and the fatigue, depression and bodily distress soon returned.

"The mind can do wonders," the doctor pointed out. "Impressed by Maria, he may have been susceptible to positive suggestion."

I couldn't see how this could have been a factor when prestigious doctors hadn't been. But I wondered whether we might not have stumbled on a valuable nugget of information.

"Is there any possible connection between prolonged use of antibiotics and leukemia?" I asked.

"We know," said Jussek, "that antibiotics, including penicillin, may kill blood cells, but there have been no studies that I know of to show their effect on cell production."

There seemed to be a recent unexplained rise in cases of leukemia affecting young people in apparent good health. I recalled the shocking case of Ernie Davis, football's Heisman Trophy winner, dead at twenty-three. It had seemed such a tragic paradox.

"I can't say for sure," added Jussek, "whether there's any connection between the use of antibiotics and the breakdown of the vascular system, but it would be worth looking into. Leukemia has become the number three killer in the country, after heart disease and somatic cancer, without anybody understanding why."

Significantly perhaps, the use of antibiotics, including penicillin, had become prevalent after World War II.

Another physician friend, the distinguished surgeon, Dr. Robert T. Crowley, of New York City and Palmdale,

California, had observed a depressed function of the bone marrow after protracted use of antibiotics.

"There is often an adverse effect on the circulatory system," said he.

In autogenic mind control, self-hypnosis, the healing qualities of the subconscious mind were apparent. Evidently, Maria had attained this frequency in reading for Bill, touching off an energy process that later dwindled for lack of stimulation.

"Could it be possible," I asked Jussek, "that an energy displacement, beginning the self-healing process, may be initially strong enough to cure twisted knees, but must be reinforced for more complicated disorders?"

The same possibility had occurred to him. But it was only theory, of course.

He was impressed by Maria's apparent insight into the Chinese doctrine of yin and yang, the body functioning normally only when there is a balance between positive and negative factors.

"How would this simple, uneducated woman know that the right is positive, the left side negative? When she suggested taking the blood marrow out of the positive side and transferring it to the negative, I could only marvel where this information was coming from."

"Do you believe in her doctors?" I asked.

The doctor in him shrugged. "She has something. I'm just not sure what it is."

But he produced still another case.

Eric Thiele, a professional soccer player, tended goal for the Los Angeles team, until disabled by a disk condition in the lower back. In constant pain, he had tried various therapies before turning to acupuncture. He was a

211

slim young man with tousled blond hair, and an engaging personality, but his blue eyes were clouded by fear.

"I'm only twenty-six," he said, "and soccer is not only my living but my life."

He arrived with actress Rosemary Cord on his arm.

"May she sit in?" he inquired.

Maria smiled. "The doctors don't mind."

As before, Dr. Jussek assured us that Maria had asked no information, and been given none.

Eric and his girlfriend had never been to a medium before, and didn't know what to expect. They were in for a surprise.

"You know a Rosemary, is that not right?" said Maria.

Eric blinked, then nodded.

"There is a strong love between you?"

The two exchanged tender glances. "Very much so."

As she did so often, Clarita now summoned Maria's corps of doctors. Maria's eyes were closed, and her face impassive.

"The doctors," she announced, "have come from the other side to help you. It is your back, not right? You first put it out when you were a little boy, and lifted another boy up from the floor."

Eric shook his head uncertainly. "Could be, every kid does something like that."

Maria seemed distracted, as if listening to more than one voice.

"Yes, Doctor," and then in an aside to Rosemary, "You have a neighbor, Anne, who was just in an auto accident. She was driving a yellow car."

Rosemary's eyes widened. "It happened yesterday. She was in her cream Volkswagen."

"She is in a coma, in intensive care in the hospital. Her husband is anxious for her life. His name is Jack, not true?"

Rosemary and Eric again traded glances.

"The doctors will help her. She will feel better tomorrow. In twenty-four hours, she will open her eyes."

"I hope so," said Rosemary, "the doctors are not optimistic."

"It will be all right, Dr. Dermetz is at her bedside."

But there was no doctor shortage. Dr. Jallikete, and a Dr. Fritts, stayed on to treat Eric. He waited expectantly.

"You feel pain on the right side of the back." She shook her head ominously. "It is so sensitive the doctors say I must not touch you. The problem is in the disk. You've had heat lamps, ice packs, needles. The doctors say the problem was aggravated because you play football [soccer in Latin-America and Europe] and keep leaping up and down, jarring the lower back."

Eric looked startled. "Yes, as a goalie I have to jump around a lot to block shots."

"There are calcium deposits, because of the injury, and the pressure causes a problem with disk."

Eric's face grew more solemn than before.

"The doctors say they are going to help you. Acupuncture is good, but the needles must be injected into the instep of the foot. This affects the muscles in the back."

It was Jussek's turn to be startled. "How did she ever know that?" he whispered. "That's a specific for the lumbar area, because of the nerve connections with the instep. We even inject B-12 into this area for sacroiliac problems."

I wondered why the doctor hadn't applied this particular technique before.

"I tested him, and he didn't seem sensitive in this area."

Maria continued. "They say you should follow a vegetarian diet, purifying your system, and make a tea out of green parsley."

Meanwhile, her doctors would inject (imaginary) the lower right spine to relax the disk.

"It will not be simple because it has been wrong for so long."

Eric's face grew even longer.

"But don't worry, they will help you. Hot water, like whirlpool baths, will be good. Sit in them for a while. And don't forget the parsley tea."

"I won't let him," promised Rosemary, as the session ended.

Like Bill, Eric, felt an immediate response.

"It is remarkable," Rosemary reported the next day, "but he feels no pain for the first time in a long time."

Again, it could have been the force of suggestion.

"Perhaps," said she, "but I've been telling him right along that he had nothing wrong with him, and that only exasperated him."

As with Bill, Eric seemed to relapse after a while. But with the acupuncture to the instep, his back did seem to become more mobile. He had been helped, but felt no confidence about resuming play.

Meanwhile, Rosemary marveled at the magnitude of Maria's mediumship.

"When she told me about Annie's accident, I thought she might have picked it up from my mind. But she mentioned that the collision had occurred with a car driven by a dark-skinned man. And not until later did I learn the driver was a black man."

Annie responded, as Maria had forecast.

"At the very hour Maria had predicted," Rosemary recalled, "Annie opened her eyes and said hello."

Weeks later, I heard from Eric again. He wanted another reading.

"But why," I said, "if it didn't help that much?"

"I'm much better," he said, "and I've been back practicing for a week."

"That's great," I said, "what's doing it?"

"The whirlpool baths, I've been sitting in a warm Jacuzzi for two weeks, and it's making all the difference."

I thought back. "It seems to me she had recommended something like that."

"I think so," he said.

"And the parsley tea?"

He shook his head. "I forgot that."

Maria, as usual, was ready to contribute. She remembered Eric, but not what she had told him. However, she soon tuned in to his back problem. And went a little further as well.

"Your legs are bothering you," said she.

He nodded. "I've been running around, and it's an effort."

"It won't hurt you. But use hot water to relax the muscles."

"That's what's been helping me."

"So the legs ache," she repeated. "So rub some heat on the legs."

Eric looked up helplessly. "How do you rub heat on?"

"It is a fluid," she said, "just rub it in."

I came to the rescue. "There's a preparation named Heet, which is recommended for muscular aches and pains."

"I'll get it," Eric promised.

Maria reflected a moment. "The doctor says there is pressure on the disk." This was an elaboration of an earlier diagnosis. "He says you have a pinched nerve, and it causes pressure in the sacral area. Follow?"

Eric nodded, obviously encouraged that he did not have a ruptured disk.

"Continue with the whirlpool baths," she went on, "and take gelatin, it will help with the healing."

"What's this gelatin?"

She spelled it out slowly. "Take it in different flavors, so it will taste all right."

Eric still couldn't understand, having apparently never heard of gelatin in his Italian homeland.

"Ask for Knox gelatin," said Maria. "Everybody will know what that is, and take it every day."

He busily wrote it down on a pad. "And while you're at it," I put in, "have Rosemary make the parsley tea."

"She has been giving me parsley."

I shrugged. "If you don't do it Maria's way, you can't complain."

Two days later, Eric was on a regimen of gelatin and parsley tea, along with a vegetarian diet, and Heet.

As before, Maria emphasized the naturalness of the healing process. "It is all part of the law of the universe, but the sick person must completely relax before the healing vibration can enter his consciousness." It was as simple as the sunshine or the rain, a manifestation of energy on a corrective level, and in this world of ours, there was nothing but energy. "Some universal laws control sound and light, permit airplanes to fly and man to land on the moon. Others allow the radio and television. They all are governed by vibrations of electrical energy. In the same way, there are laws we have not discovered yet—the laws of energy that permit materializ? substances from the atmosphere, as Jesus did w. fishes and loaves of bread. There are also energies atmosphere that can be harnessed in the proper frequencies to cause healings. These are not miracles, these are but the laws of nature that science does not yet understand. Not understanding how it is done, they do not believe, even when they see the results."

In studying Maria's corps of doctors, I had overlooked the obvious.

"If they are doing all this healing," said a senator client, "then they are helping from another dimension of space, time and experience."

They were themselves manifestations of survival!

"Whatever is happening certainly isn't originating on this plane." Dr. Jallikete had come to him in spirit. "My sinuses were so bad before that the ear, nose and throat specialists kept me in a dark room twenty-four hours at a time to ease the pain."

"And with Dr. Jallikete?"

"I felt an instant end to the pain."

There was no trickery, nor anything else that could plausibly explain her results. "Maria says that since no medium is there, the spirits introduce cosmic energy into a glass of water while the patient sleeps. And when he drinks the water in the morning, it has an immediate purifying effect."

Senator Richard Dolwig had been a moving force in the California legislature for twenty-four years. He had been head of the influential Government Efficiency Committee and an intimate of governors. He looked ten years younger than his sixty-seven years. Looking into that rugged face, it was hard to conceive that he had recently suffered a stroke, heart surgery and struggled with high blood pressure, hypoglycemia, varicose veins, chronic indigestion and an infectious mouth disease.

Because of additional pressures, brought on by heavy litigation, his doctors on this plane offered him little chance of survival. "There's not much prospect of his even getting to court," the earthbound physician told Dolwig's wife.

But even with the odds against him, the Senator looked better than ever.

"It's all this painless surgery I'm getting," he smiled. "Maria sends her doctors in to me during the night while I'm alseep and in the morning whatever organ they worked on is repaired.

Spirit Doctor Peter Karnacke treated an enlarged heart. "One evening when I was particularly low on energy he mentally replaced my heart valve and the next morning I felt like a new person."

"Just like that," I said. "Who is this Peter Karnacke?"

He laughed. "Oh, one of Maria Moreno's menagerie. It wasn't a real operation, you know."

He turned to his attractive wife, Beth. "Tell him about your experiences, my dear." She had been listening closely, nodding from time to time. "I had surgery and Dr. Jallikete helped or I might not have got through it." Suffering severe abdominal pains, she had consulted a urologist. He had found nothing wrong, but the pain persisted.

"Go back to the gynecologist," advised Maria, "and tell him you have a growth." Again, Beth was put through an intensive examination. This time a sizable growth was found. "They called it an octopus fibroid because of the way it was entangled around the tissue."

It was imperative that the surgery be performed at

once, but Beth had picked up a bad cold, and asked for a postponement. The surgeon said any delay would be hazardous, and she reluctantly agreed, even though the cold had worked itself into her lungs.

Maria, consulted anew, announced hopefully that Dr. Karnacke would sit in on surgery and assure its success. Beth was brought into her hospital room preparatory to surgery, and was sitting on her bed fretfully crying when the entire room was filled with a radiant light and a heavy scent of roses filled the air. She sat up, heartened, taking this as a hopeful sign. Meanwhile, at the hour of surgery, Maria had gone into trance elsewhere, summoning her doctors.

"During surgery," Beth recalled, "the nurses woke me for a routine spinal tap." At this time, sedated, she saw an impressively tall, blond man in white robes gazing at her with a reassuring smile. He was so close she could have reached out and touched him. "He had a complexion," she said, "of the purest porcelain."

The operation proceeded under anesthesia, and when it was over, her first question concerned not the surgery but the blond figure who had given her such a sense of security.

"Who is the handsome blond doctor?" she asked.

One of the younger doctors replied, "Oh, that was Stoner, he stayed out in the hall."

"This doctor was in the room."

The physician shook his head. "It couldn't be." He ticked off five names. "That's the whole crew."

Two days later, the same blond doctor, a vision in hospital garb, called on her. "He just floated into the room and said all would be well. I was not to worry." It occurred to me that the blonde could very well be a hallucination induced by the sedation.

Beth tossed her head. "I got the definite impression he was making sure that everybody at the hospital did their job. And he helped me over that terrible cold. It left me overnight."

He had leaned over her bed and said with a comforting smile, "All will be well. Your cold will leave you and you will heal rapidly." She sank back on her pillows and felt a wonderful sense of total relaxation. She went into a deep sleep. When she awakened, she felt a new vitality.

As we continued our discussion, it became obvious that the sittings for the senator and his wife appeared to be inordinately concerned with illness.

"She invariably brings in the consultants who respond to the greatest need," the senator explained, "and we've had quite a siege of illness."

But some friends from the past, including a former Chief Justice of the U.S. Supreme Court, had also appeared. Maria had somberly quoted Earl Warren, a Dolwig friend when he was governor of California. "There is a scandal building up around you, but you will weather the storm."

Beth, too, had some modest communication with those who had passed on. Elizabeth, her mother, had come through this time.

"Someone in spirit is asking for Baby," Maria said.

"That's surely my mother," said Beth. "She called me Baby to the last day of her life."

Beth had naturally been concerned about her husband's legal problems.

"Don't worry," the spirit said.

Her mother usually told her what she wanted to hear, so she pressed her further.

"Are you sure, mother?"

She could almost see her mother rear back and laugh. "No, Baby, I'm not sure."

Beth got a good laugh out of this. "It was so characteristic of mother that it really made me think we had contact. She was always putting me on."

11

Edgar Cayce Makes A Call

IN THE PALACE AT MONACO, Princess Grace was playing the Ouija board with actor Eddie Albert. Some inconsequential information came through as their hands raced over the board, and then, involuntarily, their fingers spelled out a vaguely familiar name—Edgar Cayce.

The two looked questioningly across the board, and knowing that the sage of Virginia Beach had been dead some ten years at this time, the spring of 1956, they ventured half-humorously.

"Let's see what the prophet has to offer."

For the next few minutes, their fingers skimmed wildly over the board.

"Cayce," or what purported to be Cayce, said the Princess, "predicted that in October of that year, 1956, England and France would be joined in a war embracing three continents, but the United States would not be involved."

The prediction was not taken seriously.

"None of us," recalled the Princess, "could conceive of a conflict in which England and France would be going it alone in a three-continent war without their traditional ally."

In October, of that year, as predicted, England and France joined forces in an invasion of Egypt, sweeping in from both Europe and Asia for their African landing.

Neither of the actors, Eddie Albert nor the former Grace Kelly, were notably psychic, narrowing the possibility that the information was a clairvoyant dramatization of their subconscious minds.

When I mentioned the incident to Hugh Lynn Cayce, whose life was spent spreading his father's work, he smiled indulgently.

"Edgar Cayce always comes through," he said, "whenever somebody has read or talked about Cayce before the reading."

But the elder Cayce kept making his presence felt.

Ten years later, in 1966, having decided to do a book on Cayce, I discussed the project briefly with my editor, Lee Barker. Several hours later, the phone rang. It was 1 A.M.

I could make out the familiar throaty voice of the medium Bathsheba, who had gleaned some fleeting fame by predicting Chicago Mayor Cermak's assassination years before.

"Edgar Cayce just came to me," she said. "He says your book will be a great success. Call it *The Sleeping Prophet*, he says, and deal with his health readings, reincarnation and his prophecies. It will be an instant bestseller. He will help you, and it will go easier than any book you have done."

I murmured a polite "Thank you," and hung up, beyond surprise at this point.

Writing the book, I summoned the image of Edgar

Cayce whenever stuck, and finished in rapid order. *The Sleeping Prophet* seemed a good title in any case, and it promptly pushed to the head of the bestseller lists.

Edgar Cayce functioned without a guide and his son did not accept spirits.

"Whenever a medium reads for me," he said, with an amused smile, "my father invariably turns up. But he never seems to have anything important to say."

Yet Edgar Cayce and his son believed in reincarnation, and the father gave many readings about past lives in India, Egypt, Persia, Tibet and similarly glamorous places.

"Reincarnation," Hugh Lynn explained, "is evidential in present lives, the habits, dispositions, and karma people carry over from one life to the next. But when a medium says Edgar Cayce is coming through, you don't have anything to go by."

In Santa Barbara a medium, having just met Hugh Lynn, proclaimed Edgar Cayce's presence in the room. He said the father was well pleased that we had joined forces in a motion picture of his life. Since the project had been discussed earlier in the medium's presence, there was certainly nothing exciting about this playback.

"I would have been surprised," said Hugh Lynn, "if he hadn't appeared."

"Would it impress you," I asked, "if your father came through a medium who had no idea who you were?"

"I would still expect him to say something. There should be a significant reason for a spirit appearance."

"Just appearing," I said, "establishes life after death."

"But what proof is there in an appearance? The dead must have some reason for appearing. Something must occur to support the concept that life is a continuous cycle."

"I know somebody who seems to evoke the dead in purposeful fashion."

He shrugged uncertainly.

"I'll make the appointment without identifying you in any way."

He still seemed uninterested.

"She has a number of guides in the field of medicine," I prodded, "and has helped many sick people."

Hugh Lynn had been hospitalized recently with an apparent urinary indisposition, marked by extreme pain. There had been no definite diagnosis, and the prognosis was uncertain.

"If you can do it easily," said he, suddenly interested.

I made the appointment by phone as he stood by.

"I would like to bring somebody over this afternoon," I said, not mentioning any name.

Maria Moreno cheerfully responded, "Tell me nothing, it is better that way."

When we arrived at her modest apartment, the sound of Chopin floated pleasantly to our ears. The radio or record player, I thought. But it was Maria's fourteen-year-old grandson, Leslie. He was drumming away at the piano with all the expertise of a concert pianist.

"He was taught by Chopin," Maria explained casually.

"Chopin?" I exclaimed.

"Oh, in another lifetime," she laughed. "I gave Leslie a reading, and Ferdinand Chopin said how pleased he was."

I shot a quick glance at Hugh Lynn. He seemed perfectly relaxed with Chopin.

"But you generally don't remember what you say," I pointed out.

"It was on tape." She gave Hugh Lynn an inquiring

look. "You brought a recording machine?"

The machine was promptly turned on and in a few moments, she was in trance. "Dr. Jallikete, Dr. Dermetz, Dr. Karnacke, they are all here," she announced.

I caught a look of amusement on Hugh Lynn's face.

"Gertrude is here, too," she said, "and she blesses you. She is pleased with what you are doing."

Hugh Lynn didn't bat an eyelash.

"Gertrude is my mother's name," he said.

Gertrude had very little else to say, and I groaned inwardly, surmising what must be going through Hugh Lynn's head.

As Maria slid into a deeper trance, Hugh Lynn sat guarded and watchful, not at all impressed by the mention of a name that any Edgar Cayce fan would know.

And then, suddenly, the whole tenor of things changed. Abruptly, with a grunt of pain, Maria reached forward, and clutched at Hugh Lynn's groin. "You have an inflammation in this area."

Hugh Lynn tried his best not to look embarrassed.

"Dr. Jallikete," she said at last, "is conducting an examination."

Hugh Lynn asked with exaggerated casualness, "Can you tell me more about the inflammation?"

She pursed her lips.

"The doctor asks about your right kidney, does that bother you?"

She twirled around and dug her fingers into the small of his back. "This is where the pain is?"

"Your fingers are right on it," he said gingerly.

"You have had X-rays?"

Hugh Lynn nodded.

"They didn't show a spot there? Your doctors didn't

tell you there was nothing growing inside?"

"They don't know what it is."

There was a note of reassurance in Maria's voice. "Dr. Jallikete says you are a very healthy person. You are a man that does not have a great deal of illness, but"—she touched the region of the kidney once again—"but you do have something there."

"Yes," smiled Hugh Lynn, "I do have something."

"But it is not serious, don't let them tell you it is serious."

"It is painful."

Hugh Lynn had been sufficiently ill to postpone an earlier trip to California, but I had assumed that he was fully recovered or he would not have made the long flight from Virginia Beach.

"I didn't realize you were in that much pain," I said.

"I try to live with it, but it would help to know what it was."

Hugh Lynn's doctors had suggested various treatments, including radiation apparently, for Maria soon stressed: "Stay away from radiation, and don't let them open you up. It is not necessary. There is only a little spot and it is benign. You don't require any exploratory surgery. Your doctors tell you different things."

Hugh Lynn looked at her questioningly.

"Now my doctors will tell you what they can do. The trouble is in the pancreas, in the adrenal glands. Drink a lot of water, and eat beets [a good old reliable, apparently]. Don't buy them in a jar, but cook fresh, and make a salad with it. Don't throw away the peelings. But wash them off and make a juice of them with water. Take them without vinegar."

From Hugh Lynn's poker face, I had no inkling of

Maria's accuracy, and was put off by a reserve, more reflective of test conditions than a wish for help.

"Why," I thought, "does he close himself off from a helpful vibration?"

But I was apparently doing Hugh Lynn an injustice.

Maria seemed intrigued by Hugh Lynn's right kidney, locating the focal point of the pain once more.

Hugh Lynn winced the least bit as her fingers continued probing the area.

"That is where I would like help," he said mildly.

"Don't worry. The Japanese doctor is smiling at you. He will make it all right."

She looked up to the ceiling, concentrating.

"All right," she said finally, removing her hands. "You are now all right. The Japanese doctor has cured you with an astral injection."

There was an injunction, which I found amusing, since it paralleled the advice of Edgar Cayce.

"Stay away from carbonated drinks. You drink Pepsi Cola and Coca Cola?"

"Not now, but I used to."

She shook her head. "Everything carbonated is not good for you."

In his health readings, Edgar Cayce recommended Coca Cola as a kidney purifier, but mixed with plain water, never carbonated.

Hugh Lynn obviously didn't always follow his father. But Edgar Cayce himself had eaten pork and chain-smoked, both outlawed by his readings.

The sitting had apparently turned into a health reading, similar to some given by Edgar Cayce. And the dead were conspicuous by their absence. But not for long. With the diagnosis and treatment completed, Maria again assumed her birdlike listening posture.

"Eileen," she cried suddenly. "She is in the room. She says way back she was a medium and went into a different type of trance. She appears now to bless her dear friend who is here." She turned to Hugh Lynn. "She loves you and all of your family."

She had not mentioned the medium's last name. But I had thought immediately of Irish-born Eileen Garrett, who had at one time been close to Edgar Cayce.

Hugh Lynn gave her an inquiring look.

"Who is this Eileen?" I asked.

"I see a lot of shamrocks," she said, mentioning the emblematic flower of Ireland.

"I know an Eileen," said Hugh Lynn. "Can you get a last name on that?"

Maria frowned, and motioned as if to summon help. "Did she have problems with her hearing?"

"Yes," murmured Hugh Lynn.

Maria's face suddenly cleared. "She was plump, heavy, and Irish. Garrett, Garrett, that is her name. She has a sense of humor. She is teasing me. Don't ask so many questions, she says." Maria broke into a chuckle as if appreciating a good joke. "She wanted her life made into the movies, but it is not being done."

This seemed to lead naturally into the Cayce movie Hugh Lynn and I were involved with, to be filmed from a book I had written.

Her eyes fastened on Hugh Lynn.

"The doctor will protect you because you must live a longer life to do what has to be done here. He told me you want to go into the movies, but you must be careful of the results. There have been delays, but this is the proper time. There is somebody very important to this movie."

She groped about for the name. "Eddie, Ed, Edgar?" She shook her head. "The energy is not strong enough. Maybe later."

For a moment I thought she had latched on to the elder Cayce, psychologically, or in spirit. Hugh Lynn obviously thought as much.

"Do you have a last name for this person?" he asked.

She appeared not to hear him, but went on with her impressions.

"This motion picture has a more important goal than just to make money. It will open up people to an understanding of life after death. This is your mission. You must put your mind to it."

Hugh Lynn leaned forward. "Who is telling you this?"

She seemed to be cogitating. "Ed, Eddie, Edgar." A sweet smile softened her face, and her voice rose almost in exaltation. "This man has glasses, and is tall." She paused. "It is Edgar Cayce. He is speaking about the motion picture to his son." For a moment I thought she was about to plant a kiss on Hugh Lynn Cayce's cherubic countenance.

"And you," said she, holding his hands instead, "are his son."

Her voice was ecstatic. "Wonderful, wonderful," she cried, unable to get over the visitation.

If this was indeed Edgar Cayce, then it was an Edgar Cayce who wanted it understood that he had other credentials. He mentioned his secretary of many years, Gladys Davis, stated that her health was generally good, touched on a problem with her leg, but of a minor nature. He made a passing reference to an old friend, Harold J. Reilly, the physiotherapist who was a well-known exponent of Cayce's physical therapies. Further, he took cognizance that Reilly, of Oak Ridge, New Jersey, had recently published a book on these treatments. "There has been a long-distance call to New Jersey about these books," said he. And indeed there had, for the book had become a bestseller and Reilly's publishers were after him to join in their promotions.

In his celestial awareness, he even seemed to enjoy the presence of Eileen Garrett. "Bless you, dear friend," he said, using an expression he often employed in his lifetime. He seemed to know she had called.

But the motion picture was uppermost in Hugh Lynn's thoughts. He was in no mood for digression, nor did he acknowledge my own rather smug smile at the mention of his father's name. With a single-mindedness familiar to his associates, he inquired:

"Isn't Edgar Cayce interested in what we will show about him?"

"Very interested," Maria replied. "But first, you must be sure who will be in charge of the movie. Otherwise, somebody [presumably Edgar Cayce] will not like it over there. Let the right people manage for you, and everything will be right."

In his zeal to present his father's work properly, Hugh Lynn limited the areas the film-makers could explore, and they had resisted this move, precipitating a stalemate. He felt he could not be too careful. Though I was slated to adapt the screen play, he considered all the possibilities. "Who is going to write it?" he asked.

Maria said in surprise, "You don't have a special person now?"

I answered for Hugh Lynn. "I'm planning on it, but who does Edgar Cayce think should write it?"

"It has to be a person who knows how to handle the

psychic. If you use people that do the other kind of movies, they won't understand and this would disgust you."

Hugh Lynn nodded. "What else?"

"This must be the kind of movie that will open the eyes of the people, so they will know that the mystic's information really comes from God. You need a producer and director who will not make fiction of it. It is very difficult to handle this material, but it will be done and the picture will be a huge success."

Hugh Lynn seemed satisfied. As Maria finished up, he congratulated her on the reading and promised to send her a book that he had written.

I looked at him curiously on the way out. "Well, what did you think of it?"

"Very interesting. I was impressed by the diagnosis. She seemed right on, especially when she located the pain."

"I didn't realize you were that ill."

"I don't know how ill myself. The doctors were so uncertain. That was the thing that had me concerned."

I gave him a sidelong glance. "Do you think Edgar Cayce came through?"

"Whoever it was made sense."

"That isn't what I asked."

"How does one know?"

"You asked what Edgar Cayce thought of the movie."

"Well, she obviously thought her contact was Cayce."

Weeks passed before I saw Hugh Lynn Cayce again, in Virginia Beach. The Cayce movie property had been assigned to a young Hollywood producer with a spiritual side, and Hugh Lynn seemed pleased. "I think we have the right man," he said. I thought of Maria and agreed.

"How is your health?" I asked, "Maria said you had to stay around to help with the picture."

"I meant to bring that up," he said enthusiastically. "I don't know what that woman did, but I've had no pain in the kidney area since the day she touched me."

"She doesn't claim anything. It's her doctors, Dr. Jallikete in this case. You can send him a check."

I had never known Hugh Lynn to praise any psychic but his father. He surprised me now by saying, "I would gladly give that woman a testimonial."

"That's not necessary," I said. "She told me that Cayce wanted you well, and that was good enough for her and Dr. Jallikete. They are on excellent terms with your father."

As a diagnostician, Dr. Jallikete would appear to have few peers and no superiors. And, delightfully, he made house calls.

But all her spirits were equally adept. They excelled at different things for different needs. America's best-known ballad singer, Burl Ives, was still marveling over his sitting, weeks before. "It is hard to believe," said he, "that anybody could tell me what this woman did. It was most amazing."

The minstrel, a massive figure, held out a sinewy finger. "I once had an irritating wart, and her doctor told me it had been removed by a laser beam, and so it had. She said I had been wounded in my left eye, and I shook my head. And then I recalled some forty years before I had been smoking a cigar and riding a motorcycle, when a live cinder flew back into my eye. Nobody knew this but me and I hadn't remembered it. Years later, an eye doctor noticed the scar, but since it didn't affect my vision, he suggested I leave it alone."

234

He drew a hand across his ample midsection. "I'd lost a hundred pounds dieting, and it had left a girdle of loose skin constantly irritated whenever I moved. I had a plastic surgeon remove this excess skin in a very painful operation. She not only tuned into the surgery, but the pain I had experienced."

Pepe, the financial adviser, had examined the singer's career, in the same way Dr. Jallikete had gone over his body.

"Pepe kept picking up the name Franklin, and said that I would do something featuring this name. Maria had no way of knowing that I had been quietly involved in a bicentennial musical documentary on Benjamin Franklin."

The production had not yet materialized, but Pepe said it would. And on the basis of what the hunchback said, Burl Ives was reasonably sure that he would go on the road with it. "He seemed to have more information than I did."

Burl's father, Frank, had come through. But aside from expressing pleasure at his son's success, he had not offered much. Burl's attractive wife, Dorothy, an interior decorator, had been thrilled by the manifestation of two persons through Maria's Clarita.

"My sister, Mary Lou, and her husband, Eddie, came through at a time when I was still feeling badly over their loss." Eddie had died of diverticulitis a year before, and Dorothy's sister had followed shortly thereafter. It had been a bitter blow for Dorothy.

She had little doubt about the authenticity of the communication. "Maria said that Eddie had literally exploded, and that was what the doctors had said. He had just burst open." There was a pleasanter side to their appearance as well. "They wanted us to know they were happier than ever, blissfully together."

"Maria pointed out that they were soul mates, and soul mates are together for eternity."

For a moment, Burl and Dorothy Ives felt themselves on the verge of solving the mysteries of an infinite life. There was suddenly a purpose and a continuity that gave existence a meaningful design. Life wasn't just a process of sleeping, eating, drinking, working and play. "Everything is alive," said Burl Ives. "And it is all vibrations and cosmic energy, and we are all part of it, even though we may not understand how it works!"

In their gratitude, they had given Maria Moreno a check, and left with a buoyant step. They had not got to their car before Maria's daughter, Romyna, came flying after them.

"You made a mistake," she cried, "my mother said no more than ten dollars."

They looked at the check. It was for a hundred dollars.

"We made no mistake," said Dorothy Ives. "That was nothing for a glimpse beyond the stars."

12

Valentino Drops In

M ARIA MORENO truly lived within herself, in a world
peopled by her guides and the people they came
to help. Hollywood stars and their movies meant little
or nothing to her. This was a transparent, narcissistic
colony that she only felt sorry for. It was no accident that
she hadn't heard of Mae West, nor that there were only
two actors whose names she knew—countryman Cantin-
flas, whose actual name, Mario Moreno, was almost like
hers, and Rudolph Valentino. She had never seen any of
Valentino's pictures; he was an historical figure to her.
"I was a child when he died." But the name somehow
lingered in her intelligence, as it had for millions who
had never read a line about him. There was something
intangible that seemed to keep his fame alive, while other
silent stars of equal fame, such as Douglas Fairbanks and
Tom Mix, faded with the years.

Even now there was a Valentino revival. His life was
being filmed for a new generation, and posters of his motion pictures were collectors' items. Aspiring young actors
flocked to his old films, hung his pictures, and devoured
what little information there was about him. "He comes

through so vitally," said actress Rosemary Cord, "that it is hard to believe he is dead."

And, indeed, she wasn't quite sure that he was. For, with other young people living in a Hollywood development known as Valentino's Villas, she had a variety of experiences which led her to believe that the spirit of the departed Valentino lived on.

Unlike Maria, Rosemary was well versed in Valentino lore.

"Valentino had no horror of dying. His seances during his lifetime convinced him of life after death. With his wife Natacha Rambova, he experienced many visitations from the other side, with the help of spirit guides." There were several of these, Rosemary knew their names—Meselope, Black Feather, White Cloud and Jenny. The seances were held in his Hollywood home overlooking Valentino's Villas, at his celebrated Falcon Lair near Beverly Hills, and in the French chateau of Natacha's stepfather, cosmetic tycoon Richard Hudnut.

From her living room window, Rosemary pointed to the heights overlooking the Villas. "The house he built there for Natacha was known as the Temple of Love."

We had been chatting in a small, high-ceiling room, which looked out on a court with flowers and trees. Rosemary Cord had been speaking quietly of the curious happenings in the stuccoed Villas, a short distance from the Hollywood Bowl. Having learned in her research of Valentino's seances, she had collected her own little coterie of friends for sessions with the Ouija board. The results had been startling, and mystifying. While not clear-cut in character, they were sufficiently tantalizing to spur her on. "I am sure," said she, "that Valentino is trying to tell us something."

238

I looked at her uncertainly. "That would mean that he had to be here."

"Oh, yes," said she, casually, "Rudolph Valentino has visited my home several times." Others had noticed his presence as well. "Gates squeaked open, with nobody there; footsteps sounded without visible cause, shadows without substance fell on walls, there was a rustling of bodies, and people were pinned down in bed by an invisible force."

Anybody would have been skeptical.

"Are you sure," I said, "that it isn't all imagination?" With 1976 the fiftieth anniversary of the screen lover's death, I anticipated his apparition would be popping up in female bedrooms all over the land.

Rosemary shook her head good-naturedly. "My boyfriend, who is an unbeliever, also saw him, as did several of my neighbors. There was no question of his presence."

The boyfriend, Eric Thiele, the soccer player, had ridiculed Rosemary's own experience, until he had his own. It had shaken him to a point where he no longer wanted to talk about it.

"He had been lying down," Rosemary said, "when he suddenly awoke with the immediate consciousness of his body being numb and cold."

He got up to get a blanket, and he was startled by the figure of a dark young man standing by the fireplace in a relaxed pose. There was a faint smile on his lips. He was strangely familiar. And then the marveling athlete recalled where he had seen him before. His face was that in the poster hanging downstairs in the living room, portraying a costumed Valentino in *The Sainted Devil*.

The figure stared at him silently.

Visibly shaken, the young athlete was speechless for

several moments, then remarked with an awkward flippancy born of his discomfiture: "You couldn't loan me some money, could you?"

At this apparent sign of materialism, the apparition abruptly dematerialized.

I had considered Rosemary covertly as she told this story, and found nothing odd in her manner. She was obviously not a nut.

"How," I asked, "did you happen to have the Valentino poster?"

"It was given to me just before I left New York City a year ago for Los Angeles."

"Perhaps your awareness of Valentino made you susceptible to suggestion."

"Even so, how would my suggestibility influence my boyfriend? He doesn't believe even now. He has gradually convinced himself it was all a dream."

"But why should Valentino make his presence known to you and the others?"

"Valentino lived in Whitley Heights on the hill overlooking our home, and frequently walked and rode horseback over this ground."

"If he chose any place for his return, I would have thought it would be his famous Falcon Lair."

Rosemary laughed lightly. "Is there any reason that he couldn't appear in any number of places of special interest to him?"

"If he goes to all that trouble, there should be a good reason for it."

"Perhaps he wanted the truth known about his death."

"There was really nothing mysterious about that, except what unknowledgeable people made of it."

She gave me a dubious look. "How can you be so sure,

when he seemed on the verge of getting better and then mysteriously collapsed?"

"He died of peritonitis, from a burst appendix. It was in all the newspapers."

"Don't you find it odd that a man in his position, with the world literally at his feet, should neglect his health to the point of endangering his life?"

"Not when you realize that he had a death wish stemming from his broken marriage with Natacha Rambova."

She didn't seem impressed. "According to him, that's not the way he died at all."

Eager fingers, including her own, had spelled out the Valentino message on the Ouija board with no impulsion on their own part. It said he had died of foul play.

"Slow poisoning," Rosemary elaborated, "it went on for months."

To be sure, Valentino had complained of abdominal pains for some time. But even so, why would anybody poison this innocuous man who was the greatest lover the screen has ever known.

"He said it was a neighbor, who was jealous of him." It still didn't make sense.

"Why," she suggested, "don't you walk around, feel the vibrations, and talk to a few others who have sensed his presence?"

I looked around curiously. From the poster likeness decorating a wall near a large fireplace, the silent screen star looked out as big as life. A sombrero was rakishly perched on his dark head, and he was clad in a colorful costume. But what caught my attention were his eyes. They seemed liquid and alive, touched with the gleam of a faintly ironic smile. The stark sex appeal, the electric magnetism, were evident even in this vintage poster.

241

"He comes right out at you, doesn't he?" I said.

Rosemary nodded, without saying anything.

She introduced me to a tall, lissom blonde of thirty or so, Ellen Levin, and to a second young beauty named Debbie. They were neighbors, living in nearby duplexes and, like Rosemary, were convinced Valentino was in communication with them.

Ellen seemed just a little sheepish about her experience. "But it was as real as anything I have ever experienced," she maintained. "I had not even been thinking of him. His name meant nothing to me, except for the legend. I had never even seen one of his pictures. Nor had I seen the poster"—she indicated the likeness on the wall with an airy wave of the hand—"for I hadn't met Rosemary yet."

"In other words, yours was an independent experience?"

"Exactly, and there were three of them. The first was about a year ago. I had but recently moved into the Villas. I had gone to bed, and was trying to sleep. Suddenly, without being conscious of any sound or movement, I became aware of a body weighing me down."

In spite of myself, I was startled, and looked at her closely. She was an attractive young lady, with no apparent need for sexual sublimation.

Nevertheless, I asked, "Were you living alone at the time?"

She smiled. "It was nothing like that. I don't have a thing for ghosts and I wasn't at all frustrated. I have normal appetites and means of expression."

"Did you cry out?"

"I remember what my mother once said about not making any resistance if I was surprised by an intruder.

So I didn't move for the longest time, lying still on my stomach and hoping he would go away."

"How long did this continue?"

"Oh, for a few minutes."

"If he was on top of you, and you were lying face down, how were you able to see him?"

"After a while, curiosity got the better of me, and I turned my head. I couldn't quite make out all the features, but the hair was dark and sleek and heavily pomaded, rising in the front, and there was a smile on the lips."

There was no menace in the figure, and she was no longer conscious of the weight. She nervously jumped out of bed and stood up, and the figure disappeared. She was so wrought up by the experience that she couldn't get back to sleep.

She was not a kook, and she made no great bid to be believed. It was a matter of indifference to her. She was merely reporting an incident, in the same way she would have described a trip to the zoo.

"What made you think it was Valentino?" I asked.

She shrugged her slim shoulders. "I didn't at first. But when Rosemary's boyfriend mentioned his visitation I put the two together."

"You saw the poster in Rosemary's living room?"

"Yes, but there was only a general similarity, chiefly with the hair style. I hadn't seen the full face in the dark."

Several weeks later, spirit paid her bedroom another visit. This time she felt a human leg against hers. She was cooler now, accepting the intrusion as another visit from spirit. As she sat up in bed, the spirit again vanished.

I was understandably curious.

"How did you know it was a human leg?"

"It felt like a human leg."

Again she had a hard time getting back to sleep. She felt somebody trying to tell her something, what she didn't begin to know.

"I wasn't imagining it," she said firmly, "and I'm not a frustrated female."

The next time, a friend was in the house, napping on a couch. She herself had been in a light sleep, and had awakened to the sound of a chanting voice across the room. She got up to investigate, and the sound, totally indistinguishable, increased in volume as she drew closer to the fireplace.

There was nothing there, but the chanting persisted. She shook her friend by the shoulder. "Wake up," she cried, "somebody's in the room."

He groaned and turned over. "Go back to sleep," he grumbled, "and forget your spirits."

As he spoke the chanting stopped.

I really didn't know what to make of it. I could have written off the entire group as looney, but unless it was all a pointless hoax, something had to be going on for these diverse people to get fundamentally the same message.

I mentioned the situation to Dr. Jussek after Eric, bothered with a bad back, had become his patient.

"Perhaps," I said, "Maria Moreno might tune in if she gave a reading in Valentino's Villas."

Ever the scientist, Jussek cautioned, "Just don't tell her what it's for."

By this time, Rosemary Cord and her boyfriend had moved out, and a friend, Susan Antone, had taken their apartment.

When I mentioned Maria to Rosemary, she was understandably acquiescent. "She doesn't know anything about Valentino, I trust?"

Rosemary was quite knowledgeable about the screen idol, having researched him thoroughly after the Ouija board experiences, looking for the culprit, I presume, who might have done him in. She rattled off the names of his more celebrated movies: *The Four Horsemen of the Apocalypse, The Sheik, Blood and Sand, The Eagle, Son of the Sheik, The Sainted Devil,* and *Monsieur Beaucaire.* "He really lived his parts," said she, "acting like a sheik even with his friends while filming the role."

He had danced his way to fame with the tango, and his heavily pomaded, sleek, black hair, dark good looks and elegant attire had given the word sheik the symbolic meaning it still has today. He died at the peak of his career, at thirty-one, and so perhaps it was only natural, having never been anything but young, that he should still appeal to the young.

It was a young group we joined in Rosemary's old apartment: Rosemary, with her boyfriend; Ellen, hostess Susan Antone, neighbors Kim Gardner and his wife Paula, and Jennifer Barker, an aspiring artist. They sat around casually, but still with an air of expectancy. Maria, enjoying young people, looked around with a benevolent smile. "I do nothing myself," she explained. "It is all through my guides, Clarita, Pepe the Hunchback, and the spirit doctors. I do not know what I say, and I remember nothing."

She shook herself vigorously a few times, then closed her eyes, and shuddered. "I feel a hand on my shoulder," she cried.

Everybody in the room exchanged meaningful glances,

and I, for one, was getting ready for Rudolph Valentino's imminent entry. But with an obvious effort, Maria threw herself into the role of Clarita, warding off whatever it was that had been obtruding on her.

"There is a wounded spirit in the room," Clarita said finally, and we all leaned forward expectantly. "She"—at the pronoun I fell back—"is very troubled, and wants everybody to know that she is sorry for what she did." I had no idea who she was talking about. "She is a singer, from Texas, anybody know who that is?"

Only Susan looked up brightly. "I come from Port Arthur, Texas, and I knew a singer from there."

"She says she was on drugs and took an overdose." She frowned and began to spell out a now familiar name. "J-A-N-I-S J-O-P-L-I-N." Maria's head turned questingly. "Why do I get this name?" It was the second time, as I recalled, that the restless spirit of Janis Joplin had manifested itself.

Susan Antone, a brown-eyed girl with sensitive features, seemed to have received a jolt. "She was from my hometown, she was born there."

"She was very young?"

"In her twenties."

"It happened not far from here, yes?"

"She lived in an apartment only two blocks away, and died there."

"She is still earthbound," said Maria, "she was disturbed by the way she died. She was driven to it."

Susan nodded thoughtfully. "She may not have known what she was doing."

Hoping for Valentino, we had drawn the equally ill-starred Janis Joplin, grounded like the screen star, at the height of a meteoric career. Perhaps that was the message, of the bird who flew too high, too fast, only to reach an exalted atmosphere in which it could not survive.

But Janis Joplin, if it was she, had a message of hope, and encouragement.

"She says she has been reborn in spirit. She has developed her faculties, and is leaving the old life behind. She is looking forward to coming back soon, and profiting by her mistakes. She will keep away from drugs and the people who use them. They are the dead, not knowing there is no advancement in their use."

If this was indeed Janis Joplin, the message was twofold: the continuity of life and the disaster of drugs. She was once listened to avidly by her peers. Perhaps they would still listen.

Maria's spirits now zoomed in on Susan Antone.

"Who is Tita?" she abruptly asked.

"That was what I called my grandmother. It's Arabic, and I am of Arabic ancestry."

"Tita sends her blessings."

"Thank her," Susan said softly.

"You have been through a lot, from a broken heart."

Susan's eyes moistened. She was unable to speak.

"Tita is blessing you."

There was still another message for Susan, and this was only proper, since it was her home, graciously opened to strangers.

"Mollie is here, you know a Mollie?"

Susan gulped hard. "Yes," in an uncertain voice.

"She says she hopes you got the ring."

Tears again came to Susan's eyes. "Mollie was a very dear friend, and I had given her a ring to wear. She was only twenty-five when she was killed in an auto accident in Texas. Her husband returned the ring to me."

"She is happy now, she is rejoined with her baby."

Susan's eyes widened incredulously. "Mollie's baby died in an auto accident, before her mother did, when she was about a year old."

We had now heard from Tita, Janis Joplin, and Mollie, but aside from the mysterious arm there was no suggestion of anybody else, certainly not of Valentino. The sitting concluded with incidental messages for most of the young people there. And, as usual, the audience was impressed.

"You liked the reading?" said Maria, as I drove her home.

"It was all right."

She wagged her head. "You know, JessStearn, there was a ghost in that house, but I didn't want to frighten anybody."

I could hardly restrain a laugh. How droll!

"How did you know there was a ghost?"

"I saw his arm, up to the elbow, black satin sleeves, very elegant, and a sapphire, very expensive, on the finger." This arm had touched her, leaving her chilled.

Was this Valentino she was talking about, and if so how had the clothing and ring materialized?

She laughed. "If the spirit can manifest an arm, how much easier to materialize a jewel or a piece of clothing?"

I didn't know what to say.

"Something wrong?" she asked, giving me a sidelong glance.

"You tuned off what you were supposed to tune in."

It was the first time I had given her any kind of a clue.

"I did not want to take the energy from the people. The ghost was drawing energy, which is why I was cold."

She sensed my disappointment, and put her hand on my arm. "We can do it again sometime, the spirits come back when they have something to say."

The next morning, bright and early, the telephone rang. It was Maria Moreno. "I couldn't sleep all night. I have a terrible headache. The ghost was angry. He kept showing me his black sleeve."

"What was he angry about?"

"Because I turned him away."

"Have you any idea who it was?"

"How would I know when I ignored him?"

She wanted to make amends. "I must read tonight or I will not rest. He is disturbed with me."

Since Susan was fascinated with Maria, the sitting was quickly arranged. It was to be a closer session, with fewer people, and no smoking.

"Does smoking bother the spirits?" a smoker asked.

"It bothers Maria," I replied, "it clouds her channel."

The group again included Rosemary, her boyfriend, Ellen, Jennifer Barker, at twenty the historian of the lot, and of course a thrilled Susan Antone.

Rosemary drew me aside. "Have you told her about Valentino?"

"I haven't even hinted at his name."

Maria soon composed herself, as we formed a small semicircle about her, two or three of the girls lounging back on a king-size bed. "Please be comfortable," Maria enjoined, "for the energy is very important tonight."

I groaned inwardly, knowing how these sittings totally depleted me.

Maria explained, unusual for her, why she had suggested the sitting. "Last night I saw this arm, and knew it belonged to somebody very charming, darkly handsome, very Spanish or Latin."

I was rather bemused by this description. Valentino was thoroughly Latin, his mother French and his father Italian. And, intriguingly, in *Blood and Sand* he played the Spanish matador, Juan Gallardo, with whom he claimed a spiritual communication, enabling him practically to live the role of the bullfighter.

Maria had no trouble holding our interest.

"What is the difference between a ghost and a spirit?" somebody asked.

"Both are manifested by energy. But the ghost is a more mischievous reflection of the spirit, often playing tricks on people. The spirit is more concerned with philosophy and the improvement of the soul."

A ghost was also earthbound, not involved in astral flights as the soul spirit was. "The guides," said she, "have the ability to contact the spirit from this planet."

This seemed to suggest that the spirit was not in the room.

"He is at a distance," she agreed, "but he projects here, like a television program screened from one coast to another, and so we see the impact, through his manifesting the energy at his command."

"Then how, if not here, could he touch your arm?"

"It was an ectoplasmic materialization, invisible to the ordinary eye, a manifestation from afar of his powerful energy."

As yet Maria had not gone into trance, continuing with her explanation. "I had the feeling last night that somebody who knew this house was trying to make contact." She looked up. "And some of you also had this feeling, not right?"

There was a chorus of nods. Maria, satisfied, now closed

her eyes, and flailed her arms, presumably whipping up enough energy to manifest her guides. One could have heard a ghost drop in the silence.

Breathing a little heavier than usual, she spoke now in an unfamiliar accent. "Simon Atala is here," she announced. "He is Arabic, and knows about Arabic things. Simon tells me about this handsome man, who wore Arabian costumes, long flowing robes, and an Arabian turban." She stumbled momentarily over *burnoose*, a long flowing robe with a hood, typically Arabic, worn by Valentino in *The Sheik*. "I hear the music playing a song about a sheik." I remembered vaguely that the picture had launched the musical hit, *The Sheik of Araby*. But I wondered why, if it was Valentino, he was manifesting his screen personality.

"He was a gentle soul normally," observed Rosemary Cord, "but he lived his parts twenty-four hours a day. He became the despotic sheik during the filming of *The Sheik*, imperiously ordering people around like a real sheik."

Simon Atala quickly established himself as a superior guide. "Simon says a big tree was just cut down in the front, not right?"

"That is so," said Susan.

"And somebody drowned in the swimming pool, and it was covered up."

"That happened long ago," said Jennifer Barker.

"He tells me of a gas leak in Ellen's apartment."

"I just reported it," said she.

Maria had not yet come up with the Valentino name, but the clues kept mounting up. Just as I wondered how long she would be off on this tangent she clutched at her stomach, and began moaning softly.

"The man of the arm tells me he had these pains in the stomach, something terrible."

She paused, on the brink of another disclosure. "He did not commit suicide, as some say. He just exploded inside, then died suddenly." At least, she had accounted for his inexplicable relapse after he seemed on the road to recovery. " 'I wasn't sorry to go,' he says. He was sick for two weeks." Valentino had been in the hospital for only a few days, but a week before had resisted efforts to get him to a hospital. " 'I was very lucky,' he says, 'but life was too short. I would have liked to have done more.' "

He was indeed a young man, said she, born before the turn of the century in Italy. Jennifer Barker had observed that Rudy was born in 1895, on May 6, and died in August, 1926. He had been in this country only thirteen years.

Maria got intriguingly warmer. Eyes closed, she turned to Rosemary's boyfriend, Eric. "You saw a shadow of a man about thirty or so."

Eric nodded mutely, his jaw hanging down a trifle. He had resolved to stay out of the discussion, as he felt that seeing a ghost hardly suited his image.

But Maria moved on quickly. "The medium feels like ice," said she, with a tiny shiver. "The arm is touching me again. It is an idol." She paused dramatically. "It is Rudolph Valentino." She spoke almost casually, without the same sense of excitement that had marked her revelation of mystic Edgar Cayce. And then she mentioned a name I had never heard before, and spelled it out: "G-U-G-L-I-E-L-M-I. . . . It is he."

Actually, this was his father's surname. The young Italian immigrant had taken the name Valentino for his American debut, unceremoniously discarding the Rodolfo

Guglielmi on his baptismal papers and passport. And so Maria had finally named her man of the arm. And in his trail there were others, the dead who had a significant role in his life. "Mae Murray is here," said Maria, naming the blonde star who had given Valentino his first bit part, and who tried to console him after Natacha Rambova walked out. "She is a charming lady. She died very old, and had a bad fall before her death." She had died only a short while before, in her eighties.

And with her was Vilma Banky, the Hungarian beauty who had starred in Valentino's last picture, *The Son of the Sheik*. She had also tried to relieve his loneliness. Actor Adolph Menjou also made an appearance. I had not even realized the two were acquainted, but Rosemary Cord mentioned that Menjou was featured in *The Sheik*.

Maria had never seen a movie with either Valentino or the mustached Menjou. But now she was tuning into this stellar performer, one of the few stars to bridge the gap from the silent screen to talkies. "He looked more like an Oriental, not so?"

I laughed inwardly. Menjou did have a Japanese cast to his features, when you thought about it.

In the midst of all this, Maria had begun to chuckle herself. "This idol had great magnetism and sex appeal, but he says he was not the great Latin lover the world thought he was. He loved more for companionship. He remembers the lady with the black veil, and the black dress. She loved him in a secret way, but there was nothing between them."

Rosemary had boned up on the mystery woman. "She used to visit Hollywood Cemetery on the anniversary of his death, and put flowers on his grave."

Many claimed the title "Lady in Black," but Rosemary

identified her as Marian Benda. She had been Valentino's last date, accompanying him to the Park Avenue party where he was stricken with the abdominal spasms that hospitalized him. She was also dead now, as were Murray, Banky and Menjou. Significantly, there had been no visit from Pola Negri, the Polish star who had hoped to marry the Sheik. She was still alive.

It was quite an assemblage, but it added little to the Valentino image. Maria, unconcerned, seemed to be sniffing about. "The house he built was destroyed, he mentions it now. He misses his horses."

Valentino's palatial home, overlooking Valentino's Villas, had been condemned for the Hollywood Freeway, and then leveled. "He had built it for Natacha, in 1922, the year they were married," said Rosemary, "buying the surrounding land for privacy, and to maintain his horses." He had moved in 1924, the year construction began on the Villas. They were finished in 1926, shortly after he died. "He was quite a rider," said Rosemary, "so he used the stables regularly."

So far the communication had been conducted solely through the Arabian guide, Simon Atala. He seemed to be an authentic Arab. "Not only is it an Arabic name," observed Susan Antone, "but she pronounces it with a perfect Arabic accent"

In life, Valentino had been close to mediums, and perhaps this was why he was now so accessible. He was a believer. He had used various mediums to contact his spirit guides, and governed his life by their advice. When his career was at a stalemate, Black Feather had predicted, correctly, an end to studio contractural difficulties and a rocketing career, facilitated by a new business manager, and marriage to Natacha, unsure then of her own heart.

254

Even their falling out had been presaged. But this Valentino wouldn't accept, because it ran counter to his own conviction that Natacha was his soul mate for all time.

In the room now, there was a close affinity to the dead star. One could almost sense it in the attitudes of the young people intrigued not only by the screen personality but by a tragic young figure who had boldly ventured into the metaphysical world, long before this had become fashionable. For they, too, were fascinated by the possibility of a world beyond and by the concept of reincarnation. And in their interest they gave off a psychic energy almost akin to an electric force.

Rosemary Cord was very much aware of this energy. "On this wave of energy," she whispered, "it is quite possible that Valentino's spirit guides would manifest themselves."

And sure enough, though Maria could not have heard us, the reason for Valentino's manifestation was soon related by her to this desire to let people know that death was only the beginning.

"He is busy trying to develop himself, so he can come back as a teacher, to bring people closer to God. He was trying to understand God before his death, and for this reason was interested in psychic phenomena. He had a guide on this side, an Indian spirit (Black Feather), and he tried to communicate through him to show there is life after death. He will continue to communicate with the help of these guides."

The group had been listening intently, showing a lively personal interest in anything touching on Valentino's life.

With a wrinkled brow, Susan Antone waved an arm toward her friends, some now reclining in their fatigue, their energy sapped as the session wore on.

"Does Rudy like us?" she asked.

"Oh yes. He wants you to know that man creates energy with his thoughts. Because you remembered him, hanging his posters, caring for his memory, you have made it possible for him to manifest in this house."

A light dawned in Susan's eyes. "I brought a poster of him from Texas, not even knowing there was a Valentino's Villas."

"And I," said Rosemary, "brought one from New York, not knowing I would take this apartment."

"And I," said Jennifer Barker, "have been asking questions about him all over the place, not knowing exactly why."

Maria Moreno's eyes were still closed. "By showing all this interest, you produce ectoplasm-like energy, which makes it possible for him to respond."

"What form does that response take?"

"It varies," said Maria, just as the lamp on a night table suddenly went on.

We all looked toward the lamp, startled. Nobody had gone near it. Was this the energy Maria had been talking about? As we exchanged wondering glances, Eric casually reached over, and turned off the lamp. But the mystery remained. Why had that lamp gone on at that moment?

"Man creates waves of energy with the soul body," said Maria, "and this he is trying to show you."

Ellen, with the most ghoulish experience, had been the quietest until now.

"There have been no more bodies," said she, "but I keep hearing the hissing sound of steam, and I can find no cause for it."

"He is trying to speak to you with a direct voice—

without the medium—but he is not able to pull enough energy together, so you get only the sound he has energy for."

Looking around the room, I could see that the energy of the group was noticeably flagging. Two or three had sprawled out on the big bed, and others were nodding drowsily in their chairs. I was barely able to sit up myself, and it was not yet midnight.

But tired as they were, they were not prepared to call it a night.

"Does Rudy have a message for us?" asked Susan.

"He tells you to use your creative energies, these are your soul energies."

"Will he come back?"

"As long as people remember him, that gives him the energy to manifest himself."

"Why does he act up like he does?"

"In real life, he says he always lived his roles. When he made *The Sheik*, he ordered the lesser people around. And when he played the bullfighter, he went stomping around like one. And so in spirit, he can't contain himself. He must play the ghost as well."

Just like an actor.

Since the spirits seemed so omniscient, we asked about the world, in general.

"Can he tell us what will happen?"

Simon Atala had been replaced by Clarita, as the conversation turned from the personal to the mundane.

"There will be devastating earthquakes, and volcanoes. Great commotions in Japan and South America, with bloody rioting. And in the Andes, there will be sheets of ice, like glaciers. There will be a collision in the atmosphere. It will be a period of great unrest."

It seemed to me that there were already great commotions in Asia, Africa, the Middle East, and South America.

"And how will this affect us?" asked Susan.

Maria drew a deep breath. "He wants me to tell you that you will all be protected. Good night."

There was a chorus of tired voices. "Good night, Rudy, good night, sweet prince."

13

Rudy Tells All

MARIA WAS OVERJOYED at identifying the spirit of Valentino's Villas. "Valentino's arm touched me," said she, her eyes agleam like any bobby-soxer's.

"You got his real name, Guglielmi, and spelled it out correctly," I said.

She was as pleased as a child with a new doll.

"I did that? How nice."

"But you didn't get the way he died. You just said his stomach exploded. So it is still a mystery."

"Maybe he doesn't want it known," she said.

In a few days, I had tracked down all pertinent information about the silent screen idol. Rather than be buried in his native Italy, he had asked that Hollywood, where he had achieved success, be his final resting place.

He had died with Natacha's name on his lips.

"Please raise the shade," he said. "I want to see the sunlight." But the shade was already up, and the room flooded with sunlight.

She had never been out of his thoughts. His whole life had been dictated by her likes and dislikes. Natacha had not enjoyed the house on Whitley Heights, so he had acquired another, the Falcon Lair, named for a picture that flopped. She didn't like one studio, so he switched to another. She frowned over a script, and he wouldn't do the picture. As the French say, she was under his skin.

The marriage lasted only three years, but separation seemed an eternity. In this tragic interlude for Rudy he still felt Natacha would come back, having left, as he thought, because he had knuckled under to demands that she no longer oversee his pictures. But their differences appeared to run deeper. Many thought she was just too cold for the Latin lover. He needed a voluptuous Pola Negri, a sex symbol like himself. But for Rudy there was only Natacha. He consulted George Dareos, the famous psychic, still alive and well in his nineties, in San Bernardino, California. And Dareos dashed all his hopes, telling him they would never be reunited, not on this sphere, at least. "But she is my soul mate," he cried, unable to accept the inevitable.

He desperately missed their seances, with Meselope, Black Feather, Jenny and the rest. But he had retained his interest in the metaphysical until death and presumably beyond.

Maria had provocatively latched onto Valentino's continuing interest in the metaphysical.

"You pointed out," I said, "that Valentino was still working with his guides."

"It must be," said she, "if he is still communicating."

And so he seemed to be, right from the beginning. Shortly after Rudy's death, Natacha had reported several revealing messages from the husband she spurned. But I found it odd that the wife who refused to communicate when he needed her so badly should now communicate when it was too late.

Maria shook her head. "It is never too late."

I regarded with some misgivings the commu.
from Rudy that Natacha had so vividly describe(
report, *Rudy: An Intimate Portrait.*

The actor discussed his transition, spiritual development, and celestial meetings with such outstanding
teachers as Helena P. Blavatsky, founder of the Theosophi-
cal Society, naturalists John Burroughs and Luther Bur-
bank, opera star Enrico Caruso, and producer Charles
Frohman. He was not as lonely as he had been, nor did
he resent the wife who had rejected him.

But even Natacha had felt her report would be skeptically received. "From those who are not ready to believe, I ask only that they at least reverence or respect the
spirit in which [the messages] were given—the spirit of
love and service."

Maria nodded her head wisely. "Many years ago there
was much skepticism, but people are ready to believe
today because psychic phenomena has been proven."

She was familiar with the automatic writing Natacha
claimed to be receiving. "In trance, I write plays this way,
using words I don't ordinarily know. It is all a surprise
when I look at it later, for I remember nothing while I
am putting it down. Some outside force is moving my
hand over the paper."

And so, too, Natacha asserted that Rudy's message
merely flowed through her, transcribed by her mechanically, without the slightest knowledge of what was being
written until she read it back later. Mediums were helpful, but Natacha, as Rudy had said so often, could handle
the messages herself. She was that psychic.

Natacha's report was fascinating, whatever its source.
It was replete with the fears, hopes, and memories of a

dying man with the eloquence of a writer of poetry.

"While I was very ill, but before it was known for certain that I was to pass over, I suddenly saw Jenny [the spirit guide]. I was so surprised that I think I called out her name. It was only for a moment that I saw her. She stood before me in a glow of rose-colored light. She looked at me and smiled, just as she used to in her earth-days when she knew I needed encouragement and held out her arms.

"Her smile seemed to voice the idea, 'Do not worry,' but I did not hear her speak. The vision was over in a second. But I knew then, Natacha, that I was to go. Deep inside I felt my earthly days to be over. It frightened me. I did not want to go. I had a strange sensation of sinking out of everything. The world seemed dearer and brighter than ever it had before. I thought of my work and how I loved it. I thought of my home, of my things, and my pets. Rapidly one thought after another rushed in a tumult through my brain. The thought of cars, travel, yachts, clothes and money. All these material things seemed doubly valuable to me now.

"The feeling that suddenly these things were about to be swept away from me, or I away from them, appalled me. My body seemed deadly heavy and at the same time something within me felt very light, as if I was about to be lifted. Time began to seem very important. Some-thing unknown seemed looming up before me. There was a dreadful sense of immensity all around me which startled my very soul. I began to think of hundreds of things I had intended to do—important things, trivial things. Even letters that I had intended to write swept across my consciousness. But the fleeting though intensely clear vision of Jenny had in some way pushed the power to accomplish these desires far, far from me. Her strange, beautiful smile, her outstretched arms, and the unearthly light around her haunted me."

He remembered now their moving him into surgery. "At this time there was a rumbling sound around me and a jolting sensation as of a moving vehicle. I am not sure, but it seemed to me that I heard George Ullman's voice. Dear George Ullman [his business manager and close friend]. The thoughts of people crowded into my mind. Faces of those I had seen but a few days before, and the faces of people I had known long ago in the past. I thought of my fellow workers, of people who relied on me for help, people of all sorts that ran after me for one thing or another. Many, many memories of my father and mother. Childhood. Italy. School. My first journey to America. My first papers of citizenship. This rush of thoughts drowned my pain. The most ridiculous experiences even, yet all so vivid, surged through my memory. Follies, pleasures, griefs; everything I had ever done seemed to come from somewhere and arise to the surface. It made me dizzy. I lost consciousness.

"When I came to, the operation had been performed. Everybody smiled encouragingly at me. I had to keep quiet, although I felt as if I had so much to say—so much. But all through these last days, although at times I felt stronger, a weight of dread lay on my heart. I felt that if I could only get up and begin doing many things I had neglected I might lose this dread. Of course they would not let me get up. Your message was near and comforted me. I had a remarkable feeling that I might soon see you, that at any moment you might walk into the room.

"I had difficulty in breathing and knew that all was drawing to an end. I was dreadfully frightened. It was too sudden for me to understand it. I don't believe I was actually afraid to die, Natacha. It was the unknown before me. You know how I was always made uneasy by suspense—anything unknown. I tell you, Natacha, that I began to know then that I was changing. I could feel it taking place in my body and mind. Something seemed to be dropping away. There was at times a straining sensation, as if some part of my being were tearing itself loose."

Like Doctor Jussek's friend, Vera de Fernando, he seemed to be experiencing a gradual exodus of the spirit.

"I thought of what would happen to my body afterwards—funeral, cremation, the ground. This gave me a sense of horror. Then the priest came. He seemed like a light in the dark. I turned to him with all my fear, my horror, my uncertainty. My childhood again emerged. Dim cathedral aisles swam before my eyes.

"The last sacraments!

"After the simple ceremony was over, I felt already away from the earth. My mental attitude was changed. The Church, like a strong friendly hand, was holding me. I would not be alone. Fear left me. Faces about me grew dim. Silence. Darkness. Unconsciousness.

"I do not know how long this lasted. Just as if awakening from a long deep sleep. I opened my eyes, experiencing at the same moment a feeling as of being rapidly drawn upward, then wonderful bluish light, then Black Feather [a spirit guide], Jenny, and Gabriella, my mother.

"I was dead.

"I was alive.

"This, Natacha, is the remembrance of my passing."

As I read aloud, I looked over at Maria, and saw her

tears. "It is beautiful," she said, "how can you doubt it? She must have loved him to express it so clearly."

For a while after death, the actor was wholly earthbound. He wandered up and down Broadway, not able to gain anybody's attention, frustrated, unwanted, unloved. He tried to contact Natacha, still obsessed with the wife who stayed in France, as life had slipped away from him in a New York hospital. He held only love for her.

"Rushing back and forth from New York to you [Natacha], right after my passing as I did in some unaccountable, subconscious way, and finding the means of reaching you through George—this channel, medium, or whatever you may call him—must have brought me to the particular attention of his teacher, Helena Petrovna Blavatsky." This was a reference to the Russian-born occultist, who had been a prime force in the metaphysical field before her death in 1891. She was to expedite his spiritual development. But meanwhile he faced a period of adjustment, from his own funeral, which he watched with mixed feelings, to his distressed realization that he was no longer involved in human affairs.

"It was during the time they were taking my body to the West. I was just beginning to feel the loosening of the public's thoughts which had been centered upon me. But as newspaper notoriety began to die down and my remains were being piloted to their earthly resting place, I began to feel more alone. The moment the flattering effect of the public's attention was removed, I realized how separated from all these people I was, so far as sight and sound were concerned. They believed me dead and gone, and so of course to them, dead indeed I was. As you well know, Natacha, I have always been easily touched by praise and flattery. The struggles I had gone through, and the obstacles I had overcome, made the pleasure of public attention all the greater.

"But now there was no one to praise me. I began to feel bitter that I had been cut off in the very height of my activity. I'm afraid I valued myself pretty highly, for I could not see how things could go on without me. There was no one to talk to about it. I wandered up and down Broadway. It seemed just as real to me then as ever it had before. But no one took any notice of me, I could hardly comprehend that they could not see me. I grew tired of dodging out of the way of the hurrying people who seemed determined to run into me. Once I jolted against a woman who had headed straight into me and she shuddered and grasped her companion's arm, saying, 'My, what a cold wind struck me.'"

Maria Moreno had been listening quietly, but at this she gasped. "You see what I say when his arm touch me. I feel a cold chill, like he says. He took the energy."

I visualized Valentino's ghost rolling down the street of dreams every entertainer had hoped to conquer.

"Why," I asked, "couldn't they see him?"

"Because they're on a different vibration. You can't get a television program on the radio set."

"So how could he see them?"

"Because in death he is in a higher dimension. That is how in trance I am able to feel his arm and see the sapphire ring."

Valentino actually wore an expensive sapphire ring, so she had somehow got that correctly.

She motioned for me to continue. "I think he is going to tell us something about life after death."

Rudy was shocked to find himself unable to communicate. "I rushed up to a group of actors standing on the

266

corner of Forty-seventh Street and Broadway, near the Palace Theater. I seized one of the men by the arm and shouted, 'I am Rudolph Valentino,' but he paid no attention and went on laughing and talking.

"I felt so helpless and useless, and yes I felt dead. At that moment I did not believe in God, for how could God, who let me succeed in my earth-life, be so unjust as to let me fail now?

"The injustice of it drove me nearly frantic. Here I was perfectly strong and well, only having stepped out of my physical body, not dead, but full of force and life, and standing right on the corner I had stood on hundreds of times before, and yet not a soul could understand that I was there. Natacha, I do not believe I ever have loved people or yearned for their companionship so much as that moment. And then it dawned on me what was wrong. These people did not mean to be cruel. But they had never been told the truth. Here I was, dead to the world, and all because the churches had inbred in people's consciousness the false idea that spirits cannot reach back through the veil. My own Church, the Roman Catholic, understood these facts. The priest who gave me the last sacraments, he knew it would give my soul a peaceful passing. But what sacrament could continue to give you peace when you frantically banged on the doors of peoples' consciousness and yet not a single door would open?"

Maria Moreno had been drinking this in avidly. "It's not right to blame the churches," said she. "It is for people to learn for themselves that the other side exists, then like the young people at the Villas, they are in touch with the spirits."

But Rudy was vehement on this score.

"There will never be real peace and happiness on the earth until the truth of life-everlasting is made clear to the people. The churches have not been able to wipe out crime and injustice. But the truths of life and life's continuance will wipe them out. For people will then understand why they were led to do wrong. They will see how useless it is to fool themselves and other people. For spirit sees all."

Both Maria and I disagreed.

"The churches," I pointed out, "stress that Christ died to prove that death is the beginning."

She nodded. "But they don't tell us that the spirit and soul live on, and communicate. Why shouldn't this be if life is continuous?"

Just as he was despairing, Valentino's spirit found help on the other side. "I thought of you, Natacha, and of the cablegrams you had sent me while I lay so ill, and, suddenly, with this cheering thought, someone touched me on the arm.

"I turned and looked. A heavily built woman with very kind eyes was standing beside me. The vehemency of her language nearly bowled me over. 'Hellfire and damnation,' she said, 'so this is how the churches have knocked the wind out of you. Come, there's nothing the matter with the dear old churches except that they're bat blind. What you need is a friend. I'll be it—I'm H.P.B.—Madam Blavatsky.'

"Natacha, I didn't know what to say I was so surprised. And the initials H.P.B. meant nothing to me. I did not remember ever having heard them before. But this strange being only laughed, and said, 'Come.' I lost consciousness for how long I don't know, but suddenly I awoke and found myself standing in the big stone hall of

Uncle Dick's chateau (Richard Hudnut). It was night and the big chandelier on the stairs was lit. H.P.B. stood on the top of the stairs and beckoned.

"I went up where so often I had gone in my earth life. She led me into Muzzie's room [Natacha's mother] and there I saw you and Muzzie sitting. George [the medium] was sleeping, as I thought, in a big easy chair. 'He is in trance,' said H.P.B., 'now you will be able to speak to your loved one.'

"That, Natacha dearest, is how I first came to communicate with you."

At this, I came to a stop. "You notice that Natacha comes off as the dearest of all."

Maria smiled. "But she was, in his eyes, if not yours."

The relationship with Blavatsky had blossomed.

"H.P.B. talked to me about reincarnation and theosophy. She laughed and said she would enjoy seeing certain theosophists turn up their noses at the idea of her bothering with the ghost of a dead motion picture actor. But she added, 'If theosophy does not teach love and assistance to every living thing in creation, what in thundering blazes does it teach?' This sounded pretty sensible to me and I said so. But of course I do not know much about theosophy or theosophists. When I asked H.P.B. what theosophy meant, she said, 'Theosophy is life and how to live it.' That silenced me pretty thoroughly, for it seemed like a rather large order."

The session ended abruptly. "The force is weakening. I must leave. Coming again soon. Good night."

I found Maria nodding.

"So why did the force weaken?" I asked.

"The medium, this George, he only had so much energy, like my Clarita, or Pepe. There were no young people to draw from like the other night."

Rudy's relationship with Blavatsky flowered in heaven, and he developed rapidly under her guidance. "There are so many things to learn that it is pretty confusing at times. I have to let go, it seems, of the old way of looking at things. In the earthworld, we look only at the outward appearance of people and things and events. We can't help that because we only see the outside. But here we see the outside and the inside as well. It is really very interesting, for the inside lying within the outer shell is always more bright and more active than the outside. It makes me think of the hidden fires of old Vesuvius. In this way, when I now look at earth-people, I see through the body and surface personality and look right at the real self inside. Sometimes this is duller even than the body. Again it is much more brilliant and beautiful.

"It is strange but since I am in this new plane of life, I do not feel hurried or rushed anymore. I used to always feel when I wanted to do anything that I had to hurry up, that there might not be time enough. But here it is different. Here, I seem to know somehow that there will be time enough and that all I need to do is to go steadily ahead."

If nothing else, we were certainly gaining insight into Valentino's personality, as reflected by the woman he loved. And as Dickens' Sydney Carton had said when facing execution, it was a far better place he went to.

"I have such a wonderful sense of freedom now, and no fear. I feel as if I could accomplish anything if I could just know how to go about it. People on the earth feel that way too, but there they always have the sense of great obstacles to be overcome. Here, I do not feel those obstacles. I know I only have to be shown the way

270

and then start out to accomplish it. I am sure I will be able to do good work in a while. If I learned to be a good actor when on earth, why can't I be a good helper after I learn?

"I do not walk up and down Broadway anymore. There is no use in it. Nobody knows I am there. And it is too dull for me to be happy there."

I looked up to find Maria beaming. "You see, he is advancing, no more Broadway."

"He is getting smarter, he doesn't want to be mugged in Fun City."

The spirit that Natacha materialized kept edging away from the old life. "I sometimes find myself in theatres where my pictures are still being shown. But somehow they do not seem as real to me as they used to. I do not feel so stirred when an audience is moved by my acting or the acting of others. Something about the earth is growing fainter."

Blavatsky had made things much more interesting. "I began to love this strange woman. Suddenly, as I looked at her I saw that she became double—turned into two personalities—and appeared in two bodies at the same time. One stood a little behind the other. The one I had seen first was young looking and very beautiful, so beautiful as to be awe-inspiring. The other was a huge, bulky form, dressed in a shawl and red petticoat, with a scarf over the head, showing her hair which looked rather crinkly. But the eyes were the same in both—brilliant, piercing and yet very kind.

"The beautiful, slender young figure turned and pointed to the bulky aged one, and said, 'That is the H.P.B. that the earth-people remember. But I am the H.P.B. of now.'

"Then behind the bulky form appeared many forms

271

—a long line—one behind another, and yet all seeming to dovetail or merge with each other in an unexplainable way. H.P.B. laughed, and again spoke, 'Those are my former selves. A damned lot of trouble they have made me too. But now they are all chained together and come and go as I order them. Like this.'

"She waved her right arm in a sweeping gesture and instantly all these forms were swept out of sight. The one that had stood right back of the bulky form had been a man, dark-skinned like a Hindu. Turning in a kind of flash on me, she said, 'That was the shell of the body of the man through which my spirit expressed itself before I came to earth as the Old Lady.'

"After seeing her former selves appear and disappear in this fascinating manner, I was anxious to see my own former selves and asked her how to do it. But I was nearly knocked over by the gale of words she launched at me, calling me stupid and fool. But she wound up saying, 'Poor ignorant darling, can a baby run and leap before it has learned to creep and walk?' "

He trusted Natacha's intelligence. "There do not seem to be the right kind of words to tell these things with understanding. But I am doing the best I can and trust to your own keen insight. You used to get thoughts quickly. I hope you do now."

Natacha's understanding was better than mine.

"Shouldn't the universe be a very crowded place with all those incarnations stacked up in rows?"

Maria was clearly amused. "It is all in the thought form, it takes up no room or space, but requires only the right vibration to manifest itself."

"But how can she be young and beautiful and fat and not so beautiful at the same time?"

"She is powerful enough to control the creative energy, and everything is made of this living force." She pointed to the chair she was sitting on, the glass window, a passing car. "They are all made of living cells, each used in a way to shape what the manufacturer wanted. And with the thought, this cosmic energy can be projected by the superior entity into the desired form."

I found it difficult to fit this thought into my own frame of reference. It was hard to accept what the finite mind couldn't understand.

With each new appearance, Rudy seemed to offer more in the way of spiritual insight. Subjectively, Natacha may have projected this herself. But like the people of Valentino's Villas, she was certain the force was outside her. How else could Rudy reveal how he had spiritually straddled two worlds?

"Because I knew something about life after death before I came over, it has not taken me so long to find myself. That is, to acclimate myself to these new conditions. My automatic writings that you enjoyed so much, Natacha, taught us a great deal. You remember the writings given from the spirits of Jenny, Meselope, Black Feather, Oscar and many others.

"We did not always pay as much attention to them as we should have. It was easy just to find them interesting. It is difficult to put real help and advice into our daily lives, isn't it? But since I have come over, the memory of these writings has served to put me into closer touch with life as it really is, and not the false aspect so often given out by people who know little or nothing about it. And my natural powers of observation have helped me to progress quicker than if I were slower in that respect."

It all read easily, like any other conversation. What

was there about automatic writing that established it as direct communication from beyond?

Maria explained:

"The pen just glides over the paper, without the writer thinking about what is being written or consciously directing his hand. I am writing a novel that way myself now. It just flows from my spirit guides."

I couldn't restrain a smile. "How I wish I could write that way, instead of trying to think things out and hit the typewriter keys a million times or so."

"You will with development," she assured me.

"But how do we know it isn't a fake, or the product of that person's own hysteria or suggestibility?"

"Study what is given, and then judge, with faith in the other life. Without some desire to learn of the other side, there is no point to read on."

And so I continued, quoting Natacha, quoting Rudy:

"I find that our powers in the body are about the same, but heightened to a considerable degree when we are freed from it. I am the same old Rudy you knew before, only now I am a Rudy heightened in perceptive faculty. And I seem to feel emotions more keenly too. Spirits tell me that it is because I am still in my astral desire body. They tell me that this body, enmeshed in the earth-body, is what we experience sensations through. The earth-body itself does not feel, being only a material covering or shell for the astral body which does feel. I am so glad to be able to tell you this, so that when you have any sort of a pain, you will know it is not in your earth-body, but in your astral body. Spirits have shown me how easily this astral body can be vitalized by the currents of vitality. They say these vitalizing currents are the life emanations of God. When the astral body is cut off from this supply, it cries out in pain, which is really a warning for you to try to bring it into contact again with the currents of healing. When this is done the cause of pain is of course removed and the pain ceases. Then H.P.B. has shown me how this astral body often withdraws itself from the physical body. This happens to people who are in deep sleep."

There was an explanation, too, of how the messages may have been planted in Natacha's subconscious mind. "At night I have seen your astral body emerge from the physical, and I have then been able to get very close to your consciousness and to talk to you. You have sometimes remembered this vaguely upon awakening and thought it to be only a dream. But it was no dream. It was the living reality."

I looked up to find Maria eyeing me with an approving smile.

"You see, he knows that the astral body is the vehicle of the soul, and that it receives the healing vibration."

I recalled how she had raised the vibration of Bill, the engineer, to attempt a healing of his leukemia. "You worked on the astral body in trance," I said.

"And the person got well?"

"For a while he seemed better."

"It has to be repeated, just like any other treatment, for the needed energy."

There was more about the astral body, a phenomenon I had never witnessed or experienced. "When George [the guide] goes into a trance, his astral body comes out. In the earth-life when this happens, the astral body is connected to the physical body by a shining kind of cord which seems to be attached to the head. I do not yet understand just how this is, but this is what I have myself seen.

"Spirits have told me that when an anesthetic is given, the astral body emerges, and that is why there is no longer any sensation left in the physical body. This is all so interesting to me. When people on earth are able to heal others by putting their hands on them, it is because they are simply allowing the vital currents to flow through them into the devitalized body or part."

As I thought about it, this was what I had so often observed. I had seen Maria Moreno do as much with Hugh Lynn Cayce and others, and Douglas Johnson radiated a current of heat that appeared to revitalize the sick and infirm. As for anesthesia, it frequently induced a heady state of mind, in which some reported out-of-body experiences.

"It all makes sense," said Maria Moreno. "This is really from the other world, JessStearn."

In the new world of Rudolph Valentino, the spirit people could review their actions on earth and grow out of their mistakes.

"There is a way," I read on, "of showing them picture-like flashes of their own past actions. This is the nearest thing to a motion picture that I have seen here. But it is not really that. It is all done by thought-process. H.P.B. says it is the instructive incidents in a soul's past brought forward and out of the astralight. This is all done in the hope that people will realize their mistakes and start to change their attitudes of thought. If they do desire to change, work is at once given to them. They are given what they are most adapted to. In that way they lose sight of self in seeing others being helped, and so begin to build the thought-substance that will form their homes (thought-homes).

"If they do not desire to change, but hang to their old ideas stubbornly, they are turned out to wander alone. No one feels at all sorry for them. This surprised me very much at first. But how can you feel sorry for them when all they have to do is to change their minds to begin to earn all they desire? I am told they do not wander around very long. The supreme indifference by which they are met soon brings them to their senses."

There was a hard practicality in this spirit world of Rudy's. "At first, I began to think it was wrong to try to get rich in the earth-life. But H.P.B. tells me this is not so. She says it is right for people to be rich if they do good with their riches. She says they have at some time earned the right to possess those riches and that they are being tested. What they possess in the future seems to depend on what use they make of what they possess in the present."

Natacha, from her millionaire parents' chateau, was enjoined to pass on this gospel for the rich. "Learn these truths now, Natacha dear, and teach them to your friends. Do not wait till the time of your coming over here."

Rudy had been very profligate in his time, squandering a million dollars a year, at a time when fifty dollars a week was considered sufficient for a family of five. He had spent five thousand dollars for a dog, an Irish wolfhound, providing him with a veterinary for the long train ride from the East to California. And he had always been a soft touch. But he was learning. "H.P.B. says it is not true generosity to give recklessly. Thought and common sense must be used always. Only the really needy should be reached. And not too much help should be given at once. This would make weak people weaker. The best help, she says, is the kind that helps people to help themselves. In that way they grow strong and more reliant."

Rudy had some explanation of the unusual magnetism which had assured his success, and yet made life a constant trial as he was virtually picked to pieces by throngs of idolizing women. "I would like to become a guide. But friends of my profession whom I have met here tell me I had better stick to the theatre. It turns out that the unusual magnetism I possessed when appearing on the screen was due to the fact that I have been an actor in previous lives."

It was also due, I suspected, to a slim, athletic build, sensuous lips and melting eyes, and, above all, the image of a screen lover who overwhelmed the women he loved with an ardor that left them limp.

I recalled Maria's reading at the Villas. "I thought he was aiming to come back as a teacher."

Maria gave me an almost pitying glance. "How could he be anything but a teacher, when he has learned so much."

His new world was like the silent screen. "No words are actually spoken, as upon the earth. The ideas are all expressed in thought. And as ideas are universal, all earth-plane languages merge into one in this afterlife. So all the spectators, no matter what their language on earth may have been, understand fluently the thought-language of the drama."

Maria had surprised me with a smile on my lips. "Yes, JessStearn?"

"This may be why they call it heaven. It's so perfect."

She looked thoughtful. "This Natacha was really the soul mate. She wants to be joined with him on the other side. And this provides the energy for the communication."

"Too bad," I observed, "that she didn't want to be joined on this side."

"They will work it out one day," said Maria, "it is their karma."

Meanwhile, they were to bring understanding to an unbelieving world. And, truly, there were some kernels of wisdom in the pot-pourri being served up by Natacha's nimble fingers. Only recently, I had read medical reports concerning the benefits of musical therapy. And here, fifty years ago, Rudy was saying:

"Guardian spirits of certain souls in the earth-world often use music to quell storms and to avert disasters when it does not interfere with karmic laws. You know there are stories and legends of sailors mysteriously becalmed. These stories are all founded on psychic facts. Certain healings are also affected by it. Florence Nightingale, the well-remembered nurse of your world, told me this. She says that very often patients lying near to death's door hear, as in a dream, glorious voices, or ethereal music, and are soon after restored to health and earth-life. And how often, she says, does the departing soul hear this wondrous music of the spheres as it leaves the body and is received beyond the veil?"

He had lost none of his earthy enthusiasm.

"Oh, Natacha, cara mia, that veil is not far away, nor is it so thick as earth-people like to believe. Buona notte, for the present. I will come again soon. I feel so happy, so fortunate to be able to reach you again, and you, carissima, know why."

In life, Rudy had a furious temper, challenging critics to mortal combat, and once stalking into the city room of the *Chicago Tribune* to punch a critic in the nose. But all this had changed.

"It seems so strange to me now, as I look back on my earth-life, how blind to realities we are while there. We are always standing right on the verge of truths and yet in our blindness pass them by. If only our inner vision was more developed. There would then be no misunderstandings, ridiculous and foolish as they always are when looked back upon, such as yours and mine were. Had we that keener vision, we would see that such petty difficulties are only like winter frost on a window pane. Frost that would melt at the first warm breath of a word of love. But, no, we do not wait to even try to see. We act at once, impetuously and without reason. Our anger—muddy-red, and blinding and bewildering—suffuses our faculties, clogs our perceptive channels, and altogether drags us downward. H.P.B. has explained this so well to me, because at first I was quite confused as I looked back upon our differences and our parting.

"Now it is all much clearer to me. She says that when this red cloud of anger surges over us, it attracts, through appearing in our aura, the attention of destructive entities, both human and elemental. This muddy color is to them an invitation to advance. They swarm about us, and through the vibration of our anger, slip into the depths of our consciousness. Their delight in destruction, and their intense desire to drag down other souls to their own level, is so great that our anger is intensified. We finally, when we give in to anger repeatedly, fall under their dominion entirely These entities do not let go easily.

"You and I were both headstrong and prone to rapid anger, and H.P.B. has shown me how we both attracted destructive forces that ended our earth-plane union disastrously. But now we know that that was only frost upon the windows of our soul. The unclouded vision of my spirit has melted that now."

As Rudy now explained the phenomenon of spirit communication, Maria Moreno appeared to hang on every word.

"This place where I am living is the Astral Plane. But that term is very expansive. When we used to get automatic messages about it, I always thought it was a realm of rather low spirits. Now I find that while it does take in those misguided spirits, always very close to the earth, still it embraces many progressed souls as well. It seems to be, as far as I can make out, a place of progression, where many problems are worked out. It is a place where souls are awakened to realities. It is in a sense the purgatory of the Roman Catholics. I used to worry a good deal over purgatory. Well, here I am in it, and I do not find it anything other than interesting. Of course, if I were stubborn and clinging to old desires and prejudices, jealousies and quarrels, I should most likely find it a pretty lonely place. These are the lonely ones here, the discouraged ones, and the evil ones too, but help, when sought, is ever present.

"It is strange how people in the earth-world like to say that communications are possible, but only from the ignorant, evil or misguided spirits. Being the nearest to earth does not in any way make them the nearest to humanity at large. In fact, the guides tell me that it separates them more completely. They are near only to people who attract them and who are somewhere in their natures of like caliber. But there are exceptions. Under certain conditions these souls are allowed to communicate for purposes of gaining deliverance for themselves. At other times to serve as illustrations to certain lessons that guides are giving."

This, of course, turned up the reason for Valentino manifesting himself at the Villas. It was obvious to Maria. "Not only to show the hereafter, but to encourage this group, who are so much like him, in their research into psychic phenomena."

There was still another reason. "Why am I striving to communicate to you? Because I love you. And I love the people of the earth. If my new learning, that I am gaining every minute, hour and day, every atom of time, is of profit to you, it may be of profit to others."

˜Now came Rudy's blueprint for a seance. He described not only how he was able to reach Natacha, but Rosemary, Ellen, Eric and Susan as well.

"Being now in the life of the spirit, I am vibrating at a much more rapid rate than when in a physical body. I could come to you, directly, and speak all day, and yet you would not hear me. Your vibration is so much slower. And you can sense things in your own vibration." And that was why he couldn't make himself known that frustrating day on Broadway.

"But mediums are vastly different. Thank God for the power that lets such peculiar physical organisms exist. They are so constituted as to possess variable rates of vibration. When a medium is to be used, he (or she) is put in working order by special guides who have made a study of this."

Maria's head was bobbing up and down in vigorous assent. "He is right. Clarita, Pepe, and the doctors, they all help me."

As somebody who had researched the psychic for

twenty-five years, I had thought there was very little new psychically. And yet here was Rudy explaining the medium's modus operandi in detail.

"Now I will tell you exactly how I communicate with you, Natacha. You decide to have a seance. You and Muzzie [her mother], Aunt Tessie [Mrs. Theresa Werner] and Uncle Dick [stepfather Richard Hudnut], you are all seated in your chairs in a circle. George [Wehner] is in his easy chair—we call it the Receiving Station. George [the medium] relaxes, and making his mind a blank, leaves the body. His mother takes charge of his soul in its astral body and takes care of the astral cord, for it is the connecting link between spirit and matter. His mother is the best one to do this service as she is nearest to him in vibrational key. In a way, it is fortunate for George's psychic work that his mother has passed to the life of spirit.

"White Cloud [a guide] takes charge of the sleeping physical body, which is limp and empty now. The body is vibrating much more rapidly than in normal activity. The blood is drawn magnetically inward around the nerve centers and spinal cord and brain. The body is now giving out certain musical sounds, if you could but hear them. Sometimes there is not enough magnetism in the medium's body to accomplish the entrance of a spirit, so a surplus is drawn from the sitters. Other guides do that. When enough magnetism is obtained, we, by means of it, are one at a time drawn into the physical organism of the medium, animate it—often clumsily at first—and speak to you as best we can.

"At first I could not learn to enter the body very well and could only get in a word or two. That was because I was told to focus my mind upon lowering my vibrations to the rate of the medium's. This is done through sound. The sound I spoke of, coming from the medium's body, is the pitch we have to key our vibration to. We sing in our mind the same tone, as it were. But I found this extremely hard to do. When I started to speak to you, I would forget to keep the vibration-note in mind and immediately up would go my vibration and I would find myself out of George's body. Then White Cloud would help me to be drawn in again by the attraction of the magnetic current. I could hear you all saying, 'Oh, don't go, Rudy, come back and talk to us.' It takes practice to be able to enter a body, stay there and to speak clearly and fluently to our loved ones. That is why with many mediums the messages are sometimes trifling and incoherent. But George's vibration is unusually steady at most times, and that is why we can control him so long at a time and speak so clearly through him."

Maria Moreno's distinguishing feature was her use of names, and she nodded again as Rudy explained: "Now about names, Natacha dear. You, and others, have remarked how often spirits are able to give their names clearly through George's mediumship. And when you went to other mediums you got very few names. The reason for this, I find, has to do with sound also. Our given name is the name that belongs to us inherently. At any rate, the name that identifies us, whether it was a baptismal name or a name assumed, is the part of the full name that represents us. Now it seems that this name, in some way, as yet unexplained to me, is a power—a vibrational power. And whenever it is thought of or called into being, it sounds its individual keynote.

"So when, during communication, we are keeping our mind on the vibration-rate-tone, in order to stay in the

284

body and attempt to give our name to you, the keynote of the name sounds. This, confusing with the vibration-rate-tone, upsets our concentration and sometimes dislodges us entirely from the body, or causes us to mumble or to give the name indistinctly. It is hard to hold two sounds in the mind simultaneously. Try it and see. And the moment you let go of the medium's vibration-rate-tone, which keys you to him, up bobs your own vibration and you have to let go of the control. With a medium like George, whose vibration is so generally steady, it is much easier to hold the tone, as his tone is not so constantly wobbling up and down as in the case of many."

Natacha could only agree, for Rudy's assumed name, Valentino, apparently had a stronger vibration than Guglielmi. And in her own case, born Winifred Shaughnessey, she had taken the name Natacha Rambova, which seemed to exert strong vibrations.

Maria had no argument with this, but she was beginning to wonder about the long sessions. "He must have a better reason for all this communication."

And so he had.

"Life on earth would be vastly different, I am sure, if people only knew the actual conditions they were going to face sooner or later through death. That is why I am anxious to tell these facts as I discover them. It is interesting to me to see how people here, people who are at all awakened, seem bent only upon trying to unfold their latent spiritual qualities. You see, we have all left behind the things of earth: our business, professions, money, property and all our worldly pursuits. We find ourselves absolutely shut away from all this, that is, from continuing with it in the same old way. We discover ourselves standing ready to begin an entirely new life, and with what seems, at first, an apparently blank future before us. Unless we know something of this future state before we pass over, this literally new birth comes as a very great shock."

Rudy was especially concerned for the slumbering film community.

"Dear, gay old Hollywood, the scene of my struggles and triumphs, what a place it is of undeveloped souls. There are wonderful souls there. There are broken souls there. And there are many souls that might be great were they not being suffocated by the intense materialism of that artificial life. With the knowledge I now have of life, gained by my clearer perceptions, and the help of my teachers, I would not care to return to the life of Hollywood. Life there is superficial and a sham, and such conditions are not lasting. I always did love the outdoors and Nature, and that, I think, is what sustained me through it all. People do not realize its importance in their lives. It is important because it is so closely linked to us, to the physical body, and at the same time with our inner character. Earth-bodies are composed of the elements of earth, the same currents of force flow through them, and all the beauty that the earth can produce is reflected in our inner character."

And so with this philosophical gem Valentino bade his goodbye to Natacha—and to us.

Maria seemed a creature bemused. "How beautiful," she sighed. "Such a beautiful man. It is good that he still communicates with the people here."

I had no idea whether Rudy had actually come through to Natacha. But there was no gainsaying the insider's report on the functioning of mediums and guides. And certainly nobody could argue with Rudy's new philosophy. Faith could conquer mountains, and life was ever-lasting, but Jesus had said it all long before, and few had listened. Why should they listen now to an actor?

"Because," said Maria, "the times are different and people are searching."

Down through the years, Valentino's spirit seemed to have roamed old haunts. Millicent Rogers, the Standard Oil heiress, moved out of his Falcon Lair after one night. The ghosts were too much for her.

Five years after his death, the American Psychical Research Society endeavored to communicate with the actor. His medium, George Wehner, was the channel, and actress Ruth Roland, a dear friend, participated.

Miss Roland asked: "Does a person on this earth need to be psychic in order to communicate with a person who has died and does such a communication have to pass through a medium?"

Rudy presumably answered: "I would say that anyone in the earth, who desired to communicate with one who had passed over, would have to be psychic to get a communication. And what was that about a medium?"

"Does such a communication have to pass through a medium?"

"It would not because the person getting the communication would be his own medium. He would be psychic. Psychic means sensitive. Such a person would have to be psychic enough to feel the vibrations."

Forty-five years before the incidents at Valentino's Villas, Miss Roland had asked: "Have you ever returned to haunt your house in Hollywood?"

"Yes. I have returned, to walk around the place and live again the old days in memory. It is the same as when you sit in a chair and think over past days. When we (the spirits) think of a place, we are there immediately. In living the old days over again, I have gone to that house and wandered through the rooms, thinking of the old happiness and sorrows. Sometimes people have heard me walk around and have felt my presence."

Maria Moreno had listened, intrigued, and again she nodded her agreement. "He is still walking through the house, and over the stable grounds, projecting his energy from a distance."

"And will he ever stop?" I asked. "Is he doomed to patrol Valentino's Villas for the rest of eternity?"

Maria Moreno's face was wreathed in a radiant smile. "I meditated, and visualized my guides. They told me that when people accept his message, and believe in psychic phenomena and the other side, he will have no more reason to return."

14

Of Spirits and Reincarnation

NOTHING COULD DISMAY Maria Moreno. Unlike Graham Greene, her faith in her God never flagged or faltered. She had indispositions herself, and like the healer Kathryn Kuhlman gave of herself so unstintingly that she often lacked the energy to send out healing vibrations for her own body and mind. One evening, after a busy day, she was so fatigued she could hardly sit up. Yet, just as that day in the cemetery, in meditation, a spirit had impinged on her, to warn of a crisis close to someone she loved. She immediately called her daughter Romyna in Hollywood, and told her to summon a doctor.

"You must have a stomach operation right away," said she.

It was too late for her spirit doctors, so she had been told, and Maria's spirit guides were inclined to let qualified earthlings do the work when it was at all possible. The next day, Romyna went into the hospital, and had a gall bladder on the verge of bursting removed. Another twenty-four hours, and it could very well have been fatal.

Why had Maria's warning not come earlier?

She threw up her arms. "The physician cannot help his family unless they consult him."

She did not regard herself as a healer, or even a psychic. As a medium, as the word suggested, she was an instrument, a go-between, and that was enough for her. "Is it not better that God should speak through me than I should speak for myself?"

She was constantly surprised when some implausible event occurred, and she had forecast it. But it saddened her that she could predict a catastrophe, and still not help anybody. With actress Rosemary Cord, I had heard her announce that Central America would be rocked by a devastating earthquake in two or three weeks. This was in January of 1976, and the following month, a series of quakes in Guatemala took twenty thousand lives and left a million people homeless. As the terrible news sifted in from the broken land, she cried all that day. And yet she never questioned the wisdom of the Lord.

"Understand his laws, and then you know that death is not cruel, but necessary so there can be a complete rebirth."

Her powers were a never-ending source of wonder, and somebody was forever calling to say that some prediction had materialized.

"I woke up one morning," said Rosemary Cord, "and heard over the radio that a new asteroid was in orbit, and might collide with the earth."

Only a few days before, Maria had mentioned this fragmentary planet, calling a collision inevitable.

"We will know when it happens," she had said.

Rosemary's boyfriend, Eric Thiele, had steadily improved. "I am sure his back will be completely well," said Rosemary, "if he continues to do as she told him."

When last I saw him he was practicing with his soccer team regularly.

While celebrated for her predictions, Maria herself was unpredictable, and that may be one of the strongest arguments for her spirit world. There was nothing calculated about any of her readings. Completely spontaneous, they just flowed out of her clear channel. She saw not only what the sitter wanted to know, but far beyond that. Without introducing her, I had accompanied the well-known patron of the arts, Mrs. John Conte, of Los Angeles and Palm Springs, to Maria Moreno's. I had no idea what Mrs. Conte's interest was, aside from her preoccupation with a major investment, the NBC television station she and her husband owned and operated in Palm Springs.

She was a practical lady with little interest in spirits or psychic phenomena, except for what help might be gained through it.

As a lover of music and a supporter of philharmonic orchestras from Philadelphia to Los Angeles, she was immediately enthralled by the piano playing of Maria's gifted grandson Leslie. "Why, the boy's playing Chopin," she exclaimed. And, indeed he was, rendering the most difficult of compositions like a virtuoso, after only two years of practicing.

Even as she sat down opposite Maria, I could see her straining to catch the music from the other room.

"He plays well."

Maria beamed proudly. "He is inspired."

Mrs. Conte may have caught an off note. "He has talent, but he should have superior instruction."

Maria shrugged. "He is applying for a scholarship."

Mrs. Conte turned her head, listening. "I will recommend him for a scholarship."

Maria thanked her, saying, "But it is not necessary."

"I would like to do it."

Maria closed her eyes, ending the conversation. She was in trance within a few moments, breathing with an even rhythm. She said nothing for a while, and then as the music subsided, she started to speak more slowly than usual.

"There is a great artist in the room. He was connected with a symphony orchestra, and he was a man of great fire. His name is Arturo Toscanini."

At this mention of the late conductor of the New York Philharmonic Orchestra, Mrs. Conte gave me a sly smile. "What would you expect with the boy playing the piano in the other room?"

Maria was in too deep a trance to overhear.

"The great Toscanini has a message for his friend and colleague, also a great conductor. He is worried about his heart condition, and feels that he should rest." She paused. "They are spelling out the name for me now: O-R-M-A-N-D-Y."

"Why, that must be Eugene Ormandy, the leader of the Philadelphia orchestra," cried Mrs. Conte. "I lived in Philadelphia for years, and knew him there."

There was no question now of Mrs. Conte's interest. "Ormandy had been working too hard, and I told him from time to time that he should ease up on his schedule. There is nobody of his stature in the music world today. He is virtually irreplaceable."

"He will be all right," said Maria, "if he cuts down on his activities. They tell me that."

"But why," said the practical Mrs. Conte, "should Maestro Toscanini be interested?"

"They were great friends, and admired each other. And Mr. Ormandy, who was the younger, would listen whenever Toscanini told him something."

Mrs. Conte smiled. "Everybody listened when Toscanini talked."

"Tell Mr. Ormandy then," said Maria, "that is why Toscanini came here today."

This now out of the way, she waited for the message she had come for. It wasn't long arriving.

"By the end of the year, Pepe says, your situation will turn around."

"And how will it happen?" asked Mrs. Conte.

The television station had not been mentioned, but both seemed to know what the subject was.

"It will happen by itself, you won't have to do anything about it."

Mrs. Conte whispered in an aside. "That seems very unlikely. Nothing gets done without somebody doing it."

After the reading, she stood by the piano for a few minutes, entranced, still marveling at the boy's playing. "You are sure he has only been playing for two years?"

"Yes," said Maria, "but it is easily explained."

"And how is that?"

"He had been playing for a year, without instruction, only his mother teaching him to read music, when he looked up one evening, while he was playing Chopin's *Revolutionary Etude*, and saw an image of the composer in the hall. He blinked, not believing he was seeing right. But then the composer smiled, and he seemed to be telling him he was pleased at his playing. The next day, he began to play like a virtuoso, fast and precise, with great articulation, like a master, like a Chopin."

Mrs. Conte had smiled uncertainly. "I will certainly

have to help him with that scholarship now. Chopin might be displeased with me if I didn't."

For my part, I didn't understand how Chopin's appearance, even in person, could have helped Leslie play.

"But you don't understand," said Maria. "I did a reading for Leslie, and they told me later what I said."

She waved her arms, and her face was wreathed in a big smile.

"In a previous life, Leslie was a disciple of Ferdinand Chopin, and he learned his piano from him."

There could be no arguing with a teacher of this stature.

As we left, Mrs. Conte chuckled to herself. "The whole family is in the spirit business," said she.

I next saw Mrs. Conte after the first of the year.

"You know," she said, "things have turned around. Several people have approached us with offers for the television station, but we're not interested."

"That's what Maria Moreno told you."

"That's right," she said, with a start. "She did mention it would be resolved at this time in my own mind."

"How is the scholarship coming?" I asked.

She smiled. "It's in the works. How can I go against Chopin?"

Maria's gift appeared limited only by her desire to help those who needed direction. She was not impressed by the rich wanting to be richer, or by the young wanting to know who their next lover would be. "I only have so much time, and I would like to devote it to serious-minded people who want to improve themselves, not just indulge themselves and their weaknesses."

She had not relished the path police officer Dave Tillotson had taken, and this feeling may have affected her subconscious mind. As Jussek pointed out, she had divided loyalties. "She wanted to help Tillotson the man, but didn't want to be an agency of vengeance. It may very well have influenced her reading." She had not solved the Tillotson murder. But she had stressed the clues that could have led to the killers, if the sweeping investigative powers of the state had been brought to play. But like Edgar Cayce, who eventually balked at punishing people, she stopped just short of an incriminating revelation.

"In her subconscious mind," observed Jussek, "there was an obvious block against joining in a vendetta. But she did say enough to serve the mandates of justice. She mentioned not only the first names of the killers, but described what institutions they had been in, where they lived, and what had happened to them since. She even described the shopkeepers who knew the killers, and why the slaying had taken place."

But this was not her greatest contribution in this sad case. I had observed a gradual softening in Tillotson's mood, and a dawning realization that perhaps the best interests of justice would be served by a retributive God. I had been intrigued, as were the others, when he seemed finally to accept the presence of his mother.

"That was really most impressive," said Jussek, "for it showed Maria's gift as a compelling force for good."

Maria's spirits flowed through her with impressive messages. But the message of survival was clearly the most important communication, not only of a celestial nature but earthly as well. For it was keyed to an eventual return to the scene of former triumphs and disasters, providing the opportunity to atone for past transgressions and profit by earlier achievements. "Whatever we are comes out of somewhere," commented the Rev. Douglas Johnson, and Maria Moreno heartily agreed. "And we must go somewhere," she added. "Why else did Christ say we died to be born again?"

Without reincarnation, her spiritualism was meaningless. "It is a question of evolving spiritually, so that man can eventually learn the meaning of life, to find peace and end wars, to live side by side happily and enjoy the fruits of living. Progress is not mechanical; without love, we only make bigger machines of destruction."

All this was said consciously, but it had come to Maria from her own readings, taped and then played back for her. "If it comes through my subconscious," she said, "then I know it to be true."

If Maria didn't believe in reincarnation, then she believed in nothing. "The people must work out their karma, and by their choices they determine how they shall start their next life."

The churches did not accept this Eastern concept, but for Christ and the Apostles, there was no questioning that everlasting life and the rebirth of the spirit were synonymous. She took pleasure in opening to Matthew 16:13, and quoting Jesus asking his disciples:

"Whom do men say that I the Son of Man am?

"And they said, some say that thou art John the Baptist; some, Elias, and others, Jeremias, or one of the [ancient] prophets."

Maria saw only what was written. "In talking about Jesus being Elijah or Jeremiah, they had to be talking about reincarnation, as these prophets had died long before."

She laughed at Taylor Caldwell's disavowal of reincarnation. "She really believes," said she, "or she wouldn't be doing the book on Jesus with you. She remembers the lives you had together in Jesus' time, when both were scribes. It's something she has to do to prepare for the next life."

I did not feel the novelist was compulsively driven.

Maria disagreed. "She cannot help herself, any more than you can."

I was not as sure of this as of her prophecies. From a world cruise on the S.S. *Rotterdam*, Taylor Caldwell had elatedly cabled: "Just sold movie rights to Universal Pictures for *Captains and Kings*. Rejoice with me."

Another of Maria Moreno's predictions had abruptly materialized.

Jussek's hypnosis had advanced some background for the medium's powers, tracing her reincarnations as a psychic, and her relationships to the various guides employed in establishing cause for survival. We had a fuzzy picture of her in the Middle Ages, and as a roving gypsy, but clearly she was in a growth pattern and had not yet achieved her present status.

"And that," Jussek pointed out, "is what reincarnation is all about, constant growth, self-realization of one's purpose in life, until the individual is a fit companion of God."

"But why," asked an iconoclast, "does God need petty, grasping, not overly intelligent man?"

Maria Moreno, as usual, had an answer. "Like the human father, God gains fulfillment from the success of his children, and finds pleasure in their attaining the goal of perfection he has set for them."

Maria Moreno had pictured an elaborate network of planes and dimensions where the dead prepared themselves for their return. There was apparently some remembrance on the part of the returned, sublimated in attitudes and aptitudes not readily explainable by heredity or environment. Grandson Leslie must surely have been a musician in a previous life. "How else," said Maria, "could he play the piano without a lesson? Deep down, he remembered."

The great Mozart at three had composed music which the pianist Joseph Hofmann could play at this tender age. From what misty past did this prodigal talent emerge? It was indeed a meaningful world if the lessons of the past and the skills so carefully nourished could be developed for posterity's enrichment. Were all the joys and sorrows of mortal man for naught?

It was revealing at times to test the reincarnation pattern against the backdrop of related human activity. For most of his life, the American singer and actor, Burl Ives, had cherished the dream of being a Freemason. He had left Illinois, and gone on to fame and fortune, never finding time for the study required of aspiring Masons. Only recently had he decided to heed the call of a lifetime and become a Mason. It was the first thing he had ever joined. "You might almost call me a professional nonjoiner." And there was nothing that had brought him greater satisfaction. It was almost as if he had been a Mason all his life. He felt completely at home with the sacred rites and secret meanings of Masonry, and with other Masons.

When he consulted Maria Moreno, he was primarily concerned with his career, hoping for new challenges. He was delighted by the prospect of doing Rex Stout's gargantuan Nero Wolfe as a psychic sleuth, as Maria indicated. However, he was even more intrigued when

Maria mentioned his wife Dorothy would soon pick up a book and there see a picture of the man whose reincarnation he was. It seemed absurd on the surface. But Maria had even described this figure. "He was a military man in the Civil War, and a great leader of men. He was very learned, but self-educated."

Dorothy and Burl Ives were surprised that there should be a physical resemblance between two different incarnations of the same spirit. But Maria had an explanation. "Normally, people don't look like the person they were. But when the thought patterns are similar, and the personalities are much alike, then the features too become similar. After a certain age people begin to look like they think."

Husbands and wives, closely knit over the years, often resembled one another in their latter years.

Shortly thereafter, Dorothy Ives visited a friend in Hollywood and was shown a book on Masonry, *The Morals and Dogma of the Ancient and Accepted Scottish Rite of Freemasonry*. It was by Albert Pike, a prominent figure in American Masonry in the nineteenth century, Sovereign Grand Commander of the Ancient and Accepted Scottish Rite of Freemasonry of the Southern Jurisdiction.

As she thumbed the pages, Dorothy Ives's eyes suddenly stopped. For there, looking back at her, was a perfect likeness of her husband. There were the same strong features, the massive shoulders, the great sinewy hands, the patient, introspective expression. But the caption under the picture spelled out Albert Pike. Pike, who died in 1891, had been a general in the Civil War, a jurist, poet, and transcendentalist, believing in reincarnation.

The book was out of print, and the owner refused to let it go. But a few days later, an unsolicited book on the occult, *The Phoenix*, arrived from the Philosophical Research Society of Los Angeles. In it was a full-page picture of Albert Pike. It was virtually impossible to distinguish between Pike's picture and a recent photograph of the singer-actor.

I matched the two pictures myself, side by side, and would have sworn they were of the same man. But there were equally startling resemblances between strangers. It certainly didn't establish reincarnation.

"We might not have thought very much about it," Dorothy agreed, "if Maria hadn't so accurately predicted our coming across the picture, linking it at the same time to reincarnation."

Pike was from Arkansas, and many of Burl Ives's folk songs were reminiscent of that section. Moreover, anybody knowing the singer would agree that he fit Pike's description: "A giant in body, in brain, in heart and in soul. So majestic in appearance that whenever he moved on highway or byway, every passer-by turned to gaze upon him and admire him. Six feet, two inches, with the proportions of a Hercules and the grace of an Apollo."

A big man, Burl Ives had a lithe grace and pantherlike power. Beyond the physical, their interests were similar. Masonry, the occult, poetry, American folklore. However, as a neophyte, Burl was loathe to claim any relationship to the Plato of Freemasonry. "Let us just say that this is what Maria Moreno saw, and that it eventuated as she saw it, without any conclusive evidence."

Still, both he and Dorothy were intrigued at a Masonic benefit in San Francisco when his backup singing group mentioned how much they liked the picture of him on the auditorium wall. He explained it was a far more famous Mason than he—Albert Pike.

Maria had not been wrong about Dorothy or Burl Ives in any verifiable detail. On one occasion, Maria had pulled in a message from a Laura. "She is a good friend of yours," she told Dorothy Ives. "She is telling you that she just passed over, and you were in her thoughts."

"I don't know any Laura," said Dorothy Ives, ransacking her memory.

But Maria persisted. "She has an unusually deep voice, almost like a man's."

Guiltily almost, Dorothy had to confess she could recall no Laura. But a month later she was filled with contrition. "I must have had a memory lapse. For I later learned that a very dear friend who lived in the San Fernando Valley had passed away suddenly. She had died exactly two days before I saw Maria. Her name was Laura, and she was famous among friends for her husky voice."

With everything, I had been mystified most by the lingering scent of carnations in Paula Petrie's home, and the M stenciled on the bathroom mirror. How did some invisible spirit, writing with an invisible pen, etch a highly visible initial on a mirror? Could not some prankster, knowing about Paula's preoccupation, have stolen in unnoticed and had his fun in this way? It would not be the first practical joke on the gullible.

Jussek did not agree. "First of all, there were two witnesses, Mrs. Petrie and her friend. And, second, speaking of manifestations, would you say the hand you saw in Mae West's apartment was a hoax?"

I could still plainly see the davenport, picking out the position of everybody in the room—Mae West, Paul Novak, Maria, Jussek and myself. There was not a chance of anybody faking that hand. But even with others reporting it, I still wouldn't have accepted it had I not seen it myself. Never before had I ever spotted any physical phenomenon. And I accepted it only because I credited my own senses.

"No," I told Jussek, "I saw that hand just as you did."

Jussek thought a moment. "In the Bible Christ made wine out of water, and five loaves into food for the five thousand. Believing in Christ, we must believe in his miracles, a miracle being only that which we don't understand. Obviously, Christ used the energy in the atmosphere to bring about this molecular miracle. And learning from their masters, the spirits may use energy forms to produce the necessary vibrations to materialize whatever they desire—the scent of flowers, clothing, an arm, a jeweled finger, or a hand."

By this time I wasn't sure what I did believe. It varied day to day. I would be impressed by the material flowing out of Maria, convinced she was indeed in touch with those who had crossed over, and then common sense would assert itself. How could we presume to solve the riddle of the universe, the mystery of life itself, that had eluded the intellectual giants of the past? Or perhaps that was the problem, the intellect, that narrow, arid, imitative, self-limiting conscious mind, closing off the boundless horizons of an endless continuum in the smug assumption the world was cast in our image.

In the void between knowledge and wisdom, there had to be some faith. Not everybody could sit with a Maria Moreno, marveling at what came through, but there were enough to pass on the word. For, as Jussek had said, she made one believe in God. And believing in the designer, one could see the design. Hearkening to a distant voice, while still on this sphere, Rudolph Valentino may have summed it up best:

> *"The serenade of a thousand years ago,*
> *The song of a hushed lip,*
> *Lives forever in the glass of today,*
> *Wherein we see the reflection of it*
> *If we but brush away*
> *The cobwebs of a doubting faith."*

Epilogue

By Eugene Jussek, M.D.

To a medical man the changes from life to death are familiar states and are to be dealt with. For most of us, death appears to be final. Beholding the sudden emptiness in the face of a person who has just passed on, one is confronted with the old question: What happened to the life-essence of this being?

With all of our technological progress we have not yet found the answer to this. We are almost succeeding in building a human body and a human brain, but we cannot supply it with the essence that gives it life.

Some religions deal with the concept of resurrection of the spirit and the flesh (according to one's merit—either to heaven or to hell).

Carl Jung, famous Swiss psychiatrist, in delving into the dream state, maintained that part of our psyche continues beyond physical death and that this part is not subject to the laws of space and time.

Bhagavan Krishna taught that the embodied soul is continuously conscious not only of all stages of present life, but also of attaining another body after death.

Paramahansa Yogananda, well-known teacher from

India and disciple of Krishna, urges the adoption of certain disciplines (yoga) to develop higher awareness during which state one may come to realize the (scientific) truth of reincarnation. The well-known Swiss physician and nutritionalist, Bircher-Benner, published patient cases of *déja-vu* (spontaneous invasions of glimpses into past as well as future happenings).

Sensitives are able, while in an altered state of consciousness, to tune in to past, present and future lives and occurrences. This is particularly true under certain conditions, such as hypnosis (state of altered consciousness).

Thus hypnosis seems to be a channel through which to witness the survival of the soul. Many cases of such soul survival have been researched extensively by professional men as well as by lay hypnotists.

On several occasions I was able to witness this regression phenomenon in my medical practice (in patients who were being hypnotically regressed into childhood for symptom removal). These thoughts find support in complete shock states where the cerebral cortex, the seat of consciousness, ceases to function. In spite of a total loss of consciousness, vivid dream experiences and other forms of perception were reported.

The late Dr. P. Niehans told me of two patients who after technically being dead were revived, one by his father, chief surgeon in Bern, Switzerland, by heart massage, one many years later by Dr. Niehans himself by artificial respiration. Both told the identical story: I was walking down a dark tunnel, cheerfully and without any difficulty in breathing. At the tunnel's end I saw a bright light. Then someone seized me by the nape of the neck and I woke up. He concluded that story by saying: "Why then should we fear death? Dying may indeed by difficult, but death is easy."

I myself agree, that consciousness does not depend on the existence of bodily tissues, and that death does not end consciousness. I derived this knowledge from my studies of yoga philosophies and the experience gained in meditation and its related stages.

I am certain that it will be possible for all people to develop a higher state of awareness whereby the continuity of consciousness will be experienced to an extent where death will lose its fearful grip. It will be regarded merely as a necessary part of an evolutionary process.

Having been privileged to witness many of the occurrences presented in this book, I came to admire the sensitive and objective mind of the writer reporting them.

And in Maria Moreno we have a remarkable channel to the other side. She is the most amazing psychic I have ever witnessed. She not only made me think of the infinitude of the universe, but gave me cause to wonder whether she had been chosen by God to give humanity an encouraging glimpse into the continuity of life. With her unique powers she was able to implement what the great humanist Jung could only speculate about when he said: "The question of immortality is so urgent, so immediate and also so ineradicable, that we must make an effort to form some sort of opinion about it."

About the Author

One of the most respected writers and journalists in America, Jess Stearn is the author of over 20 books on psychic phenomena, including *Edgar Cayce: The Sleeping Prophet, Yoga, Youth, and Reincarnation, The Search for a Soul, The Power of Alpha Thinking,* and his recent bestseller, *Soulmates.* He is currently working on a new book on Edgar Cayce's reincarnational companions through time.

BOOKS BY JESS STEARN

Soulmates
Elvis: His Spiritual Journey
I, Judas
A Matter of Immortality
The Romance of Atlantis (WITH TAYLOR CALDWELL)
*The Power of Alpha-thinking: Miracle of
the Mind*
A Prophet in His Own Country
*Dr. Thompson's New Way for You to Cure Your
Aching Back*
The Search for a Soul
The Miracle Workers
Time for Astrology
The Reporter
Adventures into the Psychic
The Seekers
The Search for the Girl with Blue Eyes
Edgar Cayce the Sleeping Prophet
Yoga, Youth, and Reincarnation
Grapevine
Door to the Future
Sixth Man
Wasted Years
Sisters of the Night